Millard F. Eiland

Contemporary
Public
Communication

Contemporary Public Communication: Applications

Molefi K. Asante
Jerry K. Frye

State University of New York at Buffalo

PN
4121
A725

Harper & Row, Publishers
New York   Hagerstown   San Francisco   London

Chapter opening photo credits: Chapter 1, p. 2, J. Berndt, Stock, Boston; Chapter 2, p. 18, Ellis Herwig, Stock, Boston; Chapter 3, p. 44, Roger Lubin, Jeroboam; Chapter 4, p. 54, Peeter Vilms, Jeroboam; Chapter 5, p. 76, Henry Monroe, DPI; Chapter 6, p. 90, Graves, Jeroboam; Chapter 7, p. 110, Roger Lubin, Jeroboam; Chapter 8, p. 128, Christopher Morrow, Stock, Boston; Chapter 9, p. 144, Joseph Kovacs, Stock, Boston; Chapter 10, p. 166, Nicholas Sapieha, Stock, Boston; Chapter 11, p. 182, Dave Bellak, Jeroboam; Chapter 12, p. 204, Ellis Herwig, Stock, Boston.

Sponsoring Editor: Larry Sifford
Project Editor: Richard T. Viggiano
Designer: Andrea C. Goodman
Production Supervisor: Kewal K. Sharma
Photo Researcher: Myra Schachne
Compositor: American Book–Stratford Press, Inc.
Printer and Binder: Halliday Lithograph Corporation
Art Studio: Vantage Art Inc.

Contemporary Public Communication: Applications

Library of Congress Cataloging in Publication Data
Asante, Molefi Kete, 1942–
    Contemporary public communication, applications.

    Includes bibliographical references and index.
    1. Public speaking.   I. Frye, Jerry Kay, 1941–
joint author. II. Title.
PN4121.A725   808.5   76–41374
ISBN 0–06–046321–X

Contents

10

Presentation of Public Communication   166

11

Collective Communication   182

12 The Miracle of Communication   204

13 Selected Speeches   210

Preface

This book contains a straightforward presentation of public communication. By design we have concentrated on an approach that emphasizes substance as integral to method. Our fundamental assumption is that technique alone does not and cannot make commendable communicators for contemporary societies.

We extend and clarify our assumption by providing students with a text that seeks to fully educate. A book on public communication should not be a sophistic manual, nor should it be a "how-to" book without a philosophical base. Those using CONTEMPORARY PUBLIC COMMUNICATION: APPLICATIONS will find innovative concepts, recent research findings, multiracial and multinational illustrations and references, and an emphasis on communication for effective human interaction. Thus, our philosophical inclination is admittedly humanistic; our theoretical orientation is eclectic.

Our purpose is to write a textbook for contemporary society that includes a rethinking of the *why* as well as the *how* of public communication. The maxim "if you don't have anything to say, keep your mouth shut" may well be restated: "If what you say publicly is meaningless to society, keep your mouth shut." We are not crusaders; in fact, it is our view that the contemporary public speaker and student of public communication have been in the vanguard seeking an approach to public communication that reflects ethical considerations. We have searched the literature, made observations of public speakers, and recorded here what constitutes commendability in the contemporary communicator.

The emergence of texts emphasizing interpersonal communication brought about a deemphasis on public speaking and the rationale of discourse. We do not disparage interpersonal communication, but we have been concerned with the lack of critical thinking, the absence of clarity, and the inability to articulate and defend ideas publicly among contemporary students. Many of our students have requested a volume that would capture the pluralistic and international dimensions of contemporary societies while providing the significant principles of commendable public talk.

Believing that a textbook should educate completely, we have provided names of authors, experiences, concepts, and examples with which students may not be familiar in a glossary after the last chapter. Concepts, such as "rhetorical situation," are explained in the text, and footnotes are included. In no case do we add concepts or names without a purpose. Our view of a humanistic, pluralistic approach to public communication has been carried through in our own writing.

Successful public communication should be based on good models. Throughout the book you will find references to some effective public presentations, and in Chapter 13 we have included sample speeches from historical and contemporary sources.

Students who follow suggestions in this book should be able to communicate effectively and appropriately in many different situations. Our ideas are practical for classroom or all speaking situations. Whenever an occasion calls for reasonable approaches to exigencies, the assumptions upon which this volume is based are valid.

Writing is a painful task. Our colleagues and students who have seen our suffering and vicariously experienced it with us have been our best critics. We extend apreciation to them for their judgment and wisdom. We thank our typists, Marilyn Coughlin, Lateefah Heusen, Dorothy Horst, and Anne Fink, without whom this book would not have been presented to Richard Viggiano in any readable fashion.

Molefi K. Asante
Jerry K. Frye

Contemporary Public Communication

1 Contemporary Communication

WHAT YOU CAN EXPECT:

Chapter 1 establishes our focus for communication. It outlines our basic belief that human communication should be substantive and meaningful. To this end we touch upon axiological principles that help to set the initial tone.

The direction of this chapter is clearly humanistic and contemporary. We see public discourse as a productive art, organizing society and aiding in the creation of new social orders.

Chapter Outline

The Public Perspective in Communication

The single most significant characteristic of the human race is the ability to communicate. This statement implies more than mere expressiveness; it suggests that information can be transmitted between human beings in ways that are understandable. Every time a communicator attempts to influence another person, even if it is no more than getting the other's attention through the mass media, the process becomes public. In this book we are primarily concerned with the public perspective in contemporary communication inasmuch as it is that perspective which concerns how we send and receive messages within the context of large publics. Thus, whenever you discuss the future of American democracy with your classmates, express your views on premarital sex to a public assembly, appear on television discussing Carlos Castaneda's newest book, or deliver a public discourse on bionics, you are engaging in a communicative process that is public. In our view, *when other people are involved in the communicative event, either as message originators or receivers, the public perspective is operative.* While most of our conversations probably occur in dyads or small groups rather than large groups, these dyads and small groups become public when information is shared through the mass media. They must therefore be viewed from a public communication perspective because information is transmitted from one person to others. As students in public communication, you will want to become as proficient in dyads and groups as in public discourse. In order to become skillful in public discourse a student must be open to all learning experiences. Thus, we intend to provide you with interesting, challenging, and intercultural examples and information. The contemporary communicator should be able to effectively and competently communicate in a number of settings. Our concern is that you are able to function in a society where public communication formats can change as rapidly as the latest technological advance in mass communication. Because of these advances in technology, most communication will always have to be viewed with a public perspective in mind. Thus, communication operates and occurs within interrelated public contexts that include both the communicator and his or her audience.

The Personal Perspective in Communication

Throughout the history of public communication, from the days of Corax and Tisias in the fifth century B.C. to contemporary times, the communicator has had to attend to his and her own strengths, weaknesses, frames of mind, resources, and skills. Communicators who are applauded for their abilities in persuasion and eloquence (in the sense of propriety and judgment) spend a considerable amount of time thinking and organizing their communications. The awareness that one must take personal stock of one's logical arguments, value appeals, and propositional assertions in a public discourse is the beginning of wisdom in public communication. This is what Daniel Webster understood when asked how he could respond to Robert Y. Hayne with such brilliancy during the Senate debate. He replied that he had spent forty years preparing the speech. We do not mean to discourage you if you plan to present speeches during your class. Few communicators ever achieved Webster's prominence as a speaker even after fifty years thinking about what they were going to say. However, we believe that learning to recognize your personal powers and talents will enable you to combine experiences to produce much better speeches than you might imagine possible. This is what we mean by personal perspective in communication. When a person is able to bring personal experiences to bear on a discourse, the result is similar to that brought about by the introduction of personal experiences into conversations. These personal experiences may be personal observations, readings, evaluations, and involvements. What we read and observe becomes as much a part of us as what we are involved in; it is all a participatory dimension of our lives. Sharing our experiences can frequently cause others to see how they can perfect their communication by following our pattern. Benjamin Franklin's dictum, "Speak not but what may benefit others or yourself," can surely be used with value.

The Functions of Public Communication

What, then, are the functions of the one trait that most distinguishes man from other animals? There are five basic functions of public communication.

1. To provide an opportunity for opposing ideas to be discussed in the open arena.
2. To promote causes, ideas, sentiments, and thoughts.
3. To allow for public condemnation of evil or public praise of good.
4. To pose options, possible or impossible, to interest groups.
5. To present information.

It has long been considered a chief function of public communication to allow speakers of opposing views to present their ideas before the judgment of audiences. Throughout the rhetorical tradition there have been *forensic* speakers who demonstrated the highest form of the art of discourse. Clarence Darrow's defense of Loeb and Leopold ranks with the most powerful discourses ever given on the nature of crime and punishment. The use of systematic reasoning based upon the attitudes, beliefs, and values of audiences is a chief requisite for effectively presenting ideas in the public communication arena.

The function of discourse to promote causes, ideas, sentiments, and thoughts may come under the purview of the *deliberate* speech. It has also been called broadly the *legislative* speech because of two reasons: (1) it is closely identified with legislators; (2) it is usually concerned with getting something done by modifying law, mores, or behavior. The great deliberative discourses, such as Henry Clay's "Compromise of 1850" and Frederick Douglass' "Fourth of July," are memorable.

Perhaps in modern times no communicator used public communication as an instrument of blame and praise as effectively as Martin Luther King, Jr. He was a master of the occasional address in which the speaker used the occasion to condemn or to praise. In his speech "Honoring Dr. DuBois," King said of the famous intellectual:

> Above all, he did not content himself with hurling invectives for emotional release and then to retire into smug passive satisfaction. History had taught him it is not enough for people to be angry—The supreme task is to organize and unite people so that their anger becomes a transforming force. It was never possible to know where the scholar DuBois ended and the organizer DuBois began. The two qualities were a single unified force.[1]

When communication functions to praise or to blame, it isolates and separates symbols so that the cognitive response of the audience is to the picture created by the communicator. Martin Luther King's portrayal of William Edward Burghardt DuBois serves to illustrate how a communicator may use praise to sustain or create an image.

Posing an option is a function that surfaced in public communication during the 1960s and early 1970s. Although this function had been inherent within the communicative situation, it did not blossom until numerous black and student protest leaders decided that the public discourse could be used to pose a threat. It was different in that it did not seek to present opposing sides and let

[1] Arthur L. Smith and Stephen Robb, eds., *The Voice of Black Rhetoric: Selections* (Boston: Allyn & Bacon, 1971), p. 210.

the audience decide, nor did it seek to promote an idea as such, nor to merely praise or blame, but to threaten as a discourse tactic.

A public communication can also function to present information, such as when a person declares himself or herself as a presidential candidate; when information is presented on the number of crimes committed annually within a given community; or when a communicator gives instructions on how to build a house. The informative communication is usually intended to give knowledge or produce understanding. Information may be presented as a *description,* a *narrative,* or an *exposition.* For example:

Description
The Internal Operation of the United Nations
Sickle Cell Anemia
The Black Holes in the Universe

Narrative
One Day in the Life of an Astronaut
The Rise and Fall of Penn Central
An Account of the Vietnamese Evacuation

Exposition
How Basketball is Played
The Nature of Human Redemption
How the soviet Politburo works

Homeostatic Considerations

A public communication may be considered an attempt to get one's house in order; that is, it is a person's adjustment to the present and potential disorder created either by prior communications or other events. When someone presents a discourse that arouses concern, agitates an issue, poses a threat, or takes a side, then the stage is set for some other communication to reestablish what had been *homeostasis.* In a real sense, our house may be said to be out of order if we expect certain items of furniture to be placed in given positions and discover they are not. Similarly, when our symbolic contexts are unorganized or disorganized by whatever cause, we experience this "house not in order" quality. What most of us seek to do in such instances is to straighten things out. Our most effective means of getting our symbolic contexts tidied up is to introduce communications. These communications may cause further disequilibrium or they may produce a homeostasis within the context.

Skillful public communication always seeks to bring about homeostasis even if it is first intended to change the present state of affairs. An agitator for some social or political cause may wish to bring about reform or revolution, but in the end it is homeostasis of the new order that he or she seeks. Lloyd Bitzer has identified a concept similar to this as *rhetorical situation*. He explains that the "rhetorical situation may be defined as a complex of persons, events, objects, and relations presenting an actual or potential exigence which can be completely or partially removed if discourse, introduced into the situation, can so constrain human decision or action as to bring about the significant modification of the exigence."[2]

Bitzer wants to set forth the rhetorical situation as a controlling notion for public communication. Inasmuch as rhetoric is situational, it is the situations that call the discourse into existence. Obviously, public discourse obtains its character from the historical context. Whenever you communicate, you are attempting to alter or to modify reality by your creation. Accordingly, Bitzer sees the rhetorical situation as having three constituents:

1. Exigence: an imperfection marked by urgency, that is, anything that can be modified by rhetoric.
2. Audience: made up of only those persons who are capable of being influenced by discourse and of being mediators of change.
3. Constraints: made up of persons, events, objects, and relations that are parts of the situation because they have power to constrain decision and action needed to modify the exigence.

Our view extends Bitzer's concept by contending that, in public communication, discourse can itself set up *additional* exigencies. The discourse may be the end sought by the situation or the discourse may call into existence other discourses.

However, contemporary communication operates in the public arena and is concerned with substances arising from the occasion and setting. Occasions may represent what has been, what is, or what is proposed to be. The concern, therefore, of public communication is to establish the necessary rational link between or among the several constituents of the situation. Such a task within the public arena indicates choice, and choice implies ethical con-

---

[2] Lloyd Bitzer, "The Rhetorical Situation," *Philosophy and Rhetoric* 1 (January 1968), p. 5.

siderations. Thus, public communication operates within the realm of ethics. It is this dimension of the liberal education that is staked out by the teachers of public communication.

Our interest in writing this book is to reestablish good reasons as the basis of communication. Karl Wallace rightly understood that the substance of discourse was ethical and moral values.[3]

Every communicator is faced with the question: "What ought I to say in this case?" The act of speaking or writing is a direct response to the question. Furthermore, what one writes or speaks indicates the ethical values chosen by the communicator. Giving good reasons becomes the essential task, and audiences judge whether or not the reasons given are acceptable. Wallace presents three broad categories of values: the desirable, the obligatory, and the praiseworthy, and their opposites.[4] From these topics the public communicator is most likely to find the rhetorical topic to be used in presenting ideas.

But all communication is not discourse. Perhaps a greater amount of time is spent in conversation with one other person than in spoken addresses to groups. The regularity with which we discuss, query, make statements, and receive statements suggests that the desirable, obligatory, and the praiseworthy are used in the arena of conversation. Thus, our book seeks to provide a reasoned approach to public communication in a contemporary society that may be used in several genres of communication.

We live in a rapidly changing society and the styles, topics, and ideas of communicative messages are constantly affected by what we are becoming. Culture has never been a static concept, yet at today's pace we use up cultures rapidly. It is almost as if culture has become the victim of our contemporary society. We speak of culture and counterculture, feminist culture, Afro-American culture, children's culture, aged culture, and identify various co-cultures and subcultures within our society. A current expression suggests, after the Indianapolis weather joke: if you want to see a new culture, hang around for a few days.

What are the implications of this dynamic state on public communication? Are we moving closer to absolute identification with our audiences? Or does such a cultural pluralism create a state of confusion and distrust? These are the fundamental issues in con-

---

[3] Karl R. Wallace, "The Substance of Rhetoric: Good Reasons," *Quarterly Journal of Speech*, XLIX (October 1963), p. 239.
 [4] Ibid., p. 244.

temporary society. There appear to be few touchstones in public communication to drive us toward resolution of our basic rhetorical problems. In previous times, perhaps to be spoken of as heroic times, singular figures dominated the public platform and were imprinted in the public mind as touchstones of oratorical excellence. As late as a generation ago, the public discourses of Henry Ward Beecher, Daniel Webster, Frederick Douglass, Henry Clay, and Clarence Darrow inspired students to seek excellence in their public communication.

The poverty of touchstones in purely conversational situations is even graver. Neither the past nor the future appears capable of lifting us out of poor conversation doldrums. Noam Chomsky has helped us to understand how our language is generated; Thomas Kochman has explained the lively art of black street language; and Mark Knapp has described the nonverbal elements of conversation. Scholars have satisfactorily improved the contemporary state of conversations. However, we can look to the structure of the communicative situation for guidance in conversational improvement. In a dyad two people talk with each other. Each speaks in turn if it is what L. Stanley Harms calls an *interchange*. On the other hand, in an *interview* one dominates by asking all questions and in a *tutorial* one dominates by making all statements. Thus, while the interchange is preferable because of equality of opportunity and possibility of sharing knowledge, the conversation easily degenerates into one of the other two forms. Another reason we seem not to have any touchstones in conversation is that some people fail to listen to others. When participants are full of their own ideas, they can easily enter the conversation ill prepared to listen. Each speaks in turn; and while the other is speaking, one marks time until his or her turn comes up again. Lack of listening becomes the principal reason of failure in conversation. It is one of our purposes in this book to provide the public comunicator with enough understanding of the new public communication to find considerable support for improving conversation. Conversational styles are greatly affected by the public communication styles and vice versa.

We all have a stake in more rhetorically educated communicator in the sense that contemporary public communication must concern itself with how well individuals identify the characteristics of rhetorical situations and how well they cope with human problems. A rhetorically educated person is one who has learned not only the principles of human communication in an ethical vacuum, but who has also been taught how to recognize poor arguments, render judgments, classify concepts, formulate good reasons, order words and sentences, and make a critical as well as an analytical statement about public communication.

Communication has given birth to numerous attempts at definition, some legitimate and others illegitimate. Almost all serious writers attempt to define communication so that their readers will have a firm grasp of what the authors have in mind. Our plan is to discuss (1) previous definitions of communication, (2) the definition used in this text, and (3) the limitations of this definition.

Previous Definitions of Communication

Actually, since communication is a term that has an ancient heritage, most people assume it should now have a clear conceptual meaning. Perhaps it should, but it doesn't. Our English word *communication* is derived from the Latin word *communi atus,* which meant something "shared." Of course, the sharing notion suggested by the Latin root word *communicare* serves us well when we think of spin-off terms such as *communal* (as in "communes"—places where several families share a house, land, and generally live together), or *community* (usually meaning a particular social group that varies in size but whose members *share* a specific locality, government, culture, and historical heritage), or *communion* (the religious act of *sharing*, of holding certain beliefs in common, of participating in the association and fellowship of a particular faith), or *communism* (a system of social organization based on state ownership of all property and economic activity and where everything is supposed to be *shared* by the members of that organization). Perhaps you can think of other ways the basic concept of sharing seems appropriately linked to the term *communication*. In general, we might say that to "communicate" simply means to *share* your ideas or your information with others. But this broad, general definition is too inclusive for most scholars. We must be guided by certain limitations. Since there exists no generally or universally accepted definition, writers constantly try to offer their own definitions.

By 1970, there were more than 95 different definitions in the scholarly literature.[5] There are many different perspectives on defi-

[5] Frank E. X. Dance, "The 'Concept' of Communication," *The Journal of Communication* 20 (June 1970), pp. 201–210.

nitions of communication. "Considered as a process, communication can be defined and classified in many ways: as internal or external, verbal or nonverbal, as expressing content or relationships, as being intentional or unintentional, and so on."[6] Although our purpose here is not to be comprehensive, let us look at some of the common elements of all those many definitions. If you actually collected all the available definitions and listed the common elements, you would find most definitions include the following.

1. Communication is the transmission of signals from one person to another. When we communicate, there is an *exchange;* something is given and something is received. That something may be simple information. For example, suppose you meet a stranger who says, "Hello, my name is John. What's your name?" You probably reply by stating your name. Thus, communication has taken place. You have *exchanged* your names. The other person knows your name and you now know his name. You have *shared* your names. But wait, how did this happen? To answer this question, we must discuss some additional common elements.

2. Communication involves the conscious use of symbols directed toward some goal. In the example above you and the other person *intended* to exchange names—you both did so consciously. We also used symbols, in this case *words,* to symbolize our meanings. For example, you both understood the meaning of the word symbol *name.* This exchange of *specific* word symbols was our goal for communicating. You can imagine the confusion when the stranger asked what your name was if you had given the name of your school or the name of something other than what was intended. Most definitions of communication also include a third element: perception.

3. Communication involves the perception of commonly understood symbolic stimuli of language. Again, in our example, imagine the difficulties that would have been involved if a foreign language had been used, one you did not understand. In short, you would not have been able to communicate.

Although we certainly have not discussed all the common elements of definitions offered, those that we have discussed occur frequently enough to merit attention. We also realize that many questions remain about this term *communication;* for instance, here are some questions that trouble those who think about the meanings

---

[6] Larry L. Barker and Robert J. Kibler, eds., *Speech Communication Perspectives and Principles* (Englewood Cliffs, N.J.: Prentice-Hall, 1971), p. 20.

of communication: Does communication *require* at least two people, or can a person communicate with himself? Can one effectively communicate anything more than simple meanings nonverbally? What is the difference between communication and behavior, particularly, between nonverbal communication and nonverbal behavior? Should the definition include unconscious or unintentional exchanges of information? Does the communication process inherently require perception? Can a painting communicate? Does perception always result in a change of our informational store and thus result in communication? Is there a possibility of communicating with inanimate objects? For example, do you believe that the way you dress communicates something? Since the authors live near the Niagara Falls, we often hear people observe the falls and describe their power as awesome or frightening; but can we say that the Niagara Falls communicate their power or beauty? Can one communicate with animals? with plants? What about spiritual communication? Does the body communicate that it hurts, is sick, or is hungry? We could go on, but it seems clear that there are more questions than answers, and to attempt answers here would make this a very different book. Therefore, answers will have to wait for another book, but we hope that such questions have suggested the complexity of the term *communication*. That is the point we are trying to communicate to you.

Public Communication: A Definition

We are now ready to offer our own definition of communication. We realize that it may not be satisfactory to some, but for our purposes in this book we give the following sensory-based perceptual definition: "Public communication is the conscious attempt of humans to change or modify the beliefs, attitudes, values, and behaviors of an audience in the public arena through symbolic manipulation of the senses."

Since we have emphasized the key terms of other definitions, we emphasize the key terms of our own definition.

1. We view *all* communicative attempts as *persuasively* designed to *change* or *modify* beliefs, attitudes, values, and behaviors of others. We realize that there are times that public communication seems something other than persuasive. And we are aware that some writers refer to speeches to entertain, inform, convince, and so on. But

we view all communication as being ultimately persuasive to some degree or another.

2. Our definition focuses primarily on *public* communication, not private, intimate communication. However, the public arena is vast; it includes all symbolic communication: oral, written, printed, electronic, and so on. The differences are quite obvious when one considers the bedroom communication between a husband and wife as compared with a communicator giving a public presentation at the city council.

3. Our definition suggests that persuasion takes place in many forms. It may involve the modification of attitudes, beliefs, values, opinion, or behavior. It may involve merely a change in opinion or it may be an actual behavioral modification; or persuasion may involve a variety of combinations of attitudes, beliefs, values, opinions, and behavior; or unusually powerful instances of persuasion may involve the modification of all these combined.

4. Our definition emphasizes sensory perception. Although this focus seems quite simple, rest assured that a sensory-based perceptual view of communication is more involved than you might think. The focus here is on the five senses (taste, touch, sight, smell, and hearing). Can you think of any form of communication that does not in some way involve at least one of the senses or a combination of them?

5. Our definition concerns *human* communication. Although we recognize that some authors include broad-based definitions of communication, we want to limit our definition to *human* communication.

6. Finally, we emphasize the *conscious, intentional* instances of public communication. We recognize that there are cases of unintended persuasion, but such cases are arbitrarily excluded from the discussion of public communication in contemporary society.

The pervasive nature of communication requires these limitations. Let us review what these limitations are:

1. Public communication: in this book we focus primarily on *public* rather than *private* communication.

2. Conscious, intentional communication: in this book we are concerned with public communication that is *consciously* designed and *intended* to affect other humans rather than communication that coincidentally affects other humans by mere chance.

3. Human communication: in this book we are concerned only with *human* communication rather than communication between

man and animals, animals and animals, man and machines, or machines and machines.

4. Symbolic communication: in this book we are concerned with the use of verbal and nonverbal symbols that are meaningful (i.e., shared) to the various audiences.

5. Manipulation of the senses: in this book we are concerned with the manipulation of human perception in terms of the five senses of touch, taste, smell, sight, and hearing, rather than with extrasensory or parapsychological aspects of communication.

Our book seeks to develop individuals who appreciate the need for communicators to exercise the greatest caution in handling public talk. Public communication should be treated as a sacred trust, not to be violated in government, education, or community activities. The Watergate scandal of the Nixon administration demonstrated the danger of public communicators taking the public's values for granted. What the average man in the street saw as being reasonable, Nixon proponents frequently represented as unreasonable; what the public believed was a valid argument or good reason, the Nixon defenders called inoperative. Public talk cannot be taken lightly; what we say in public usually reflects a great deal on who we are in public.

Humanistic

This book takes a humanistic approach to public communication in an effort to increase the quality of public talk in society. Perhaps with the numerous interpersonal communication books, we will soon begin to correct, if not perfect, our behavior toward each other. We begin, however, from the premises that human behavior can be positively activated by knowledge of values in society. Our procedure is to outline the contemporary forms of communication, pointing toward both skill acquisition and ethical considerations. Communication does not exist apart from human society, and because of this fact our communicative skill is integrally related to the values of society.

In a speech to a group of high school teachers, the intercultural trainer Eileen Newmark remarked that "to be able to perceive our own values and those of the society in which we operate is the first law of communication." Whether it is a law or not, it is basic to our approach insofar as we emphasize ethical considerations.

Communication for public consumption should be based upon

values rooted in the development of the human community. It should state the truth and be calculated for the betterment of society. Communication intended to deceive cannot be commended. The commendability of public communication resides in its support of the tension between tradition and innovation, the wellspring of modern humanism.

Contemporary

A textbook is a symbol. It represents the conceptions and perceptions of the world as viewed by its authors. Our book is such a symbol as it stands for the unequivocal inclusion of the multicultural character of the society in its examples and in its style. What we have done may be open to criticism from purists who do not share our multicultural focus, but we are convinced that too many textbooks are still written with no regard for contemporary patterns. It is one thing to learn from the past; it is another to be lost in the past. Our book is contemporary in yet another sense as we have tried to observe what people *actually do* in public communication situations rather than to develop theories or cite evidence that does not matter in contemporary communication. Society changes, so does the form our communication takes. Thus, there is a certain upbeat in our presentation based not so much on the projection of the novel as on the appreciation of change.

FOR STUDENT APPLICATION

1. Any *definition* should include all aspects of the term, but should exclude everything else; otherwise, definitions are not very useful. Make up your own personalized definition of communication. You may find terms such as *process, share,* and *symbol* useful in writing your own definition.
2. Modern computers are sometimes said to have their own "language." Is it true that if you understand the computer symbols, you can "talk" to the computer and even predict some computer responses? How do computers and this computer age affect your definition of communication?
3. Words themselves contain no meaning. Words stimulate people to interpret word symbols based on their previous experience. Mathematically we could say that meaning is added, subtracted, multiplied,

or divided by people. Think of an example for each of the following: adding meaning; subtracting meaning; multiplying meaning; dividing meaning.

4. The next time you hear a speaker, see if you can determine answers to these questions: What is the speaker's goal? his target audience? What practical result is desired? What *behavioral* response is the speaker attempting to achieve from his audience members?

5. If a person wished to become a teacher or a trial lawyer, communication skills obviously would be expected. Prepare a list of jobs that you feel would demand effective communication skills. Compare your list with other class members.

6. Form three-member groups and ask one member to try to get the other two members to reproduce several geometrical drawings. There are several "rules": (1) Do not use any gestures; (2) do not show them the drawing, state the directions only once; (3) do not allow any questions. What were some of the difficulties involved in this project? What implications do the "rules" have for contemporary public communication?

Readings

BRADLEY, BERT E. *Fundamentals of·Speech Communication: The Credibility of Ideas.* Dubuque, Iowa: Wm. C. Brown, 1974.

MARTIN, HOWARD H., and COLBURN, C. WILLIAM. *Communication and Consensus: An Introduction to Rhetorical Discourse.* New York: Harcourt Brace Jovanovich, 1972.

MILLER, GERALD R., and STEINBERG, MARK. *Between People: A New Analysis of Interpersonal Communication.* Chicago: Science Research Associates, 1975.

MYERS, GAIL E., and MYERS, MICHELE T. *Communicating When We Speak.* New York: McGraw-Hill, 1975.

PACE, R. WAYNE, and BOREN, ROBERT R. *The Human Transaction: Facets, Functions, and Forms of Interpersonal Communication.* Glenview, Illinois: Scott, Foresman, 1973.

PHILLIPS, GERALD M., and METZGER, NANCY J. *Intimate Communication.* Boston: Allyn and Bacon, 1976.

2 Contemporary Forms of Communication

WHAT YOU CAN EXPECT:

Chapter 2 isolates a rather different perspective on communication than what you may have expected. It provides you, however, with guidelines for effectively communicating in contemporary forms.

Our aim in this chapter is to organize material in a way that would be most helpful to you. These common public communication forms are not meant to exhaust all possibilities, but rather to explore how communication is practiced in contemporary societies. We want our exploration to assist you in your own preparation to communicate.

Chapter Outline

Common Public Communication Forms

Modern societies, regardless of their political or economic systems, are highly complex and present the communicator with numerous challenges. In today's society one may be tested by a variety of formats for public speaking. In a typical day an average individual participates in several kinds of communication, ranging from making long, uninterrupted statements to questions and answers. There are newer formats ushered into existence with the predominance of television. Yet mastery of these newer communication formats depends upon the same fundamental principles as mastery of the more traditional forms; that is, a person must possess some information or feeling he or she is willing to share and must seek to express it with propriety. As we shall see throughout this text, propriety is relative to the situation. Practical skills are important for us to acquire if we continue to live in societies where we seek to influence others by our communication. But in addition to our practical skills in presentation, we must begin to formulate ways to evaluate what others do when they employ the various communication formats. The following discussion identifies some of the more common public communication forms.

The meet-the-press format

One common form of public communication may be referred to as meet-the-press format. It is generally employed in a wide variety of specific settings, for instance, in the television shows "Meet the Press," "Issues and Answers," and "Face the Nation," as well as in political news conferences. The meet-the-press format is characterized by a formal situation in which two or more knowledgeable persons in the presence of others ask questions of an expert or authority figure to elicit his most current thinking on an issue or issues. It is a *formal situation* to the extent that (1) persons not identified as questioners of the expert are usually not permitted to ask questions, (2) the expert usually has been briefed over the general area from which the questions are to be drawn, and (3) the presentation is controlled by strict time constraints. Figure 1 illustrates the Meet-the-Press format.

Unlike the traditional interview, the meet-the-press format requires that at least two persons who have some specific knowledge of the subject ask questions of the expert. This allows one person to formulate ideas for questions in which the audiences might be interested during the questioning process. Whereas all questioners will usually have general outlines of questions to be asked, sometimes it is necessary to stray from those outlines in order to follow up on a special topic.

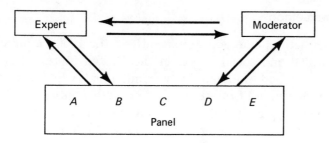

Figure 1 This model shows the control factor of the moderator. The moderator is responsible for introduction, time, and ordering of querists. This is the basic meet-the-press format.

The meet-the-press format is for the benefit of unseen audiences. Participants come together in order to *provide information* to non-participants. Thus, to be valuable the meet-the-press format has to be performed in front of audiences. To a large extent it takes on the characteristics of other television programs by being a performance meant to be judged by those viewing the show.

The meet-the-press format is reserved for experts or authority figures, individuals who by their positions in government, special expertise in science or industry, leadership in social or religious groups, or through notoriety have current information on a particular topic. The expert may have a moderator at his or her side to keep the questions related to a specific topic and to monitor time allotted to each questioner. While you may wonder if *you* will ever be considered an authority or expert, the evidence suggests that many colleges and universities, and several corporations, have students on their panels. Furthermore, you are probably more knowledgeable than your peers right now about something.

Drawing from an old American adage that it is always better to get the statement "right out of the horse's mouth," the meet-the-press format selects individuals who are by virtue of their positions able to give the audience current facts and opinions. A meet-the-press format that simply provides information already available to the audience is boring and tends to make the questioners appear dull. Although it is true that some people talk too much about what they do not know, there are many public figures who do not talk enough about what they do know. Thus, the meet-the-press format is designed to provoke them to talk to the public.

The ask-me method

The ask-me method emerged significantly in the 1960s, a period of intense political and social action in the United States. It is a communicative method initiated by an individual who seeks to respond to a wide range of questions dealing with political, social, or religious issues. Typically, the ask-me initiator makes an opening statement no longer than two or three minutes to the audiences. In order to start the audiences asking questions, the ask-me initiator says something similar to "If you have any questions, ask me," or "I will be happy to field any questions that come to your mind." Saul Alinsky, a leading community organizer of the 1960s, believed that the only way to provide information an audience wants to hear is to allow people to ask questions. You can see how this idea developed during the egalitarian emphasis of the civil rights and student movements. The ask-me initiator refuses to be a speaker because a speaker defines what the audience will hear. However, in a real sense he is a *speaker* whether he is prompted by questions in his own mind or questions from the audience.

Several problems must be avoided when attempting the ask-me method. First, be sure to provide the audience with some information about your special qualifications. There will always be some people in audiences who will not know your specialty. It is for those people as well as a refresher for those who do know you and your topic of interest that the information is given. If you fail to do this, the questions may be less informed than you wish. Secondly, give people time to adjust to the shock of not hearing a speech. This is especially important if they have been led to believe, either by advertisement or by past reputation, that you are going to give a speech. We all know of speakers who ask, "Are there any questions?" and continue as if they had only been making a statement. Well, to an extent it is the opposite extreme when an ask-me initiator says "Ask me" and looks at the listeners as if to say "You stupid people." Give time for people to adjust to the shock by making an additional statement about what you do and the issues surrounding your activities. Thirdly, recognize that although you have succeeded in making the communicative situation informal, there should be some time limit on the occasion. Knowing when you have answered enough questions is the hallmark of a judicious communicator. We all have been in situations where we felt the speaker or some member of the audience had forgotten that a question had been asked and answered earlier. To avoid audience boredom the user of the ask-me method of public discourse must not become repetitious, particularly when the audience has arrived at what we call a *sense of denouement.* The sense of denouement usually comes when a substantial portion of an attentive audience believes that its intellectual needs have been met. When the sense of denouement arrives, people may begin to squirm, become inattentive, and even leave the room. Audiences might be heard mumbling, "Why does he go on and on," or in some black American audiences, "That cat ain't got no cool." People feel that once you have made a point, it is a waste of their time to continue talking.

The dialogue

The dialogue occurs when two public speakers combine their communication skills to address a common topic. Success or failure of this method of public communication is dependent upon (1) the intellectual qualities, (2) discourse arrangement, (3) personal attitudes, and (4) rhetorical aptitudes of the speakers. In a dialogue two speakers act as one and audiences evaluate the discourse in much the same way as they would judge one speaker. Thus, in some respects the creation of a common discourse to be delivered in a dialogue is a more difficult task than a monologue, although the inventional aspects are shared (Figure 2).

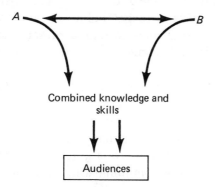

Figure 2 Communicators *A* and *B* produce discourse on same subject to the same audience.

1. What is not obvious about one's intellectual qualities in other discourse situations becomes apparent in a dialogue as a result of the relief the speakers procure for each other. Two persons with an understanding of the topic to be presented—developed from experience, observation, or experiment—will be able to provide the audients with an effective dialogue. However, if one of the participants is obviously better prepared for the discourse than the other, the presentation will appear uneven. To insure that the dialogue will have a favorable impact upon the audients, the speakers must make certain that they have prepared well for the discourse.

2. How the speakers decide to arrange the discourse can have a great bearing on whether or not the message is presented with clarity and propriety. In some cases speakers may choose to alternate on the basis of set periods. When this is done, each speaker has a given time in which to speak on the topic, and once he has finished his allotted minutes, the second speaker begins. Audiences tend to think of this system as being "too mechanical"; the dialogue becomes two separate discourses on the same topic rather than one discourse on the same topic, as it should be. Thus, another arrangement has gained a wide degree of acceptance among practitioners of the dialogue, namely, *interspersalization*. Interspersalization is the process by which the two speakers have verbal interaction with each other as well as with the audience. They prepare their speeches to be presented around certain main points, and when they have selected these key points, any one of the dialogists might begin the discourse. Although they should always make certain that the beginning and ending themes are clear, one of the most embarrassing things that can happen to dialogists is to get before an audience and not know who is to start and who is to end a presentation. Discourse arrangements, therefore, become one of the most important functions for the speakers.

3. Personal attitudes are another important aspect. The fact is that if speakers do not possess an enthusiastic attitude toward the dialogue as a communication format, the audience will not feel strongly about it either. There is an old saying that you cannot make people feel what you do not feel. Unless there is a genuine excitement about the dialogue as a means of communicating information, arousing conviction, or seeking action, it is very dangerous, indeed, to attempt the dialogue. Speakers who have attempted the dialogue with little preparation and almost no enthusiasm have failed to get

favorable reaction from hearers. In some cases the listeners are blunt, "Those speakers didn't give a damn about their audience," or "They didn't know what they were doing; it was a farce." Such comments are not atypical when speakers are nonchalant about the dialogue. Because it involves the audience in more mental activity (concentration on two rather than on one speaker) making connections between thoughts, ideas, and speakers, remembering who said what to whom and what were the responses, and how did the speakers reconcile their opinions or beliefs, the dialogue requires the speakers to be exceptional in their temperament and attitude. One speaker can cause difficulty in the process. Thus, how speakers approach the dialogue determines what success they will have in putting together an interesting discourse.

4. The first requirement for the dialogue, as in all public speaking, is that the speakers not merely have something to say but something worth saying. Many speakers are content to have something to say about everything, even if it has already been said or no one is interested in it, or it is not based upon the latest information, or they cannot be creative in their treatment of the topic. Dialogists must have the rhetorical aptitude to develop ideas, expand them, and demonstrate their applicability to various situations. Without the quality of rhetorical inventiveness, that is, the ability to discover how ideas can be presented effectively and to recognize the cultural restraints upon speakers by topics, themes, and ethics, the dialogists become monopolizers of their audience's time. Quite correctly, there is no redeeming value in such behavior. Those speakers who may not possess the special talent for creativity can depend upon preparation and attention to rhetorical strategies. For example, the speaker might attend to such things as how to find illustrations for his proposed discourse and what stylistic forms his language should take. Whereas the person with a natural ability will ordinarily cover these areas in the regular course of preparing his mind for the discourse, a person of lesser talents will have to give special attention to these factors.

The following is a brief example of a dialogue introduction. Two speakers were asked by a committee of a California school district to participate in a conference on Black English. They consented. During their preparations for individual sepeeches they discovered that it was highly probable they would cover some of the same territory, even though they may have had different opinions about

some of the data. After discussing it, they decided to give a dialogue
to combined audiences.

TOPIC: Black English in America
Introduction

Dialogist A: The subject that we have chosen to discuss with you is
extremely broad and highly controversial.

Dialogist B: It is as broad as the history of blacks in America, and
its controversy stems from the fact that it is a cultural and educational issues and is therefore political because it demands the
making of choices.

Dialogist A: We must seek to understand it because your teaching
depends so much upon it.

Dialogist B: We will talk about three aspects of Black English in
America: (1) its origin, (2) its significance, and (3) its educational value.

Dialogist A: These topics will not exhaust the subject, but they
provide a necessary overview for schoolteachers.

Throughout the remaining part of the dialogue, each person had
to provide information that would elucidate the topic. The dialogue
is more like a conversation in front of the audience rather than
two speakers dealing with two monologues. If one of the dialogists
had spoken for ten minutes on the origins of Black English and the
other for a similar length of time on the significance of Black English,
it would not have been a dialogue but more like two monologues.

In summary, the dialogue is an important discourse format, but
its presentation and effectiveness depend upon the cooperation of
two speakers possessed of personal attributes such as the ability to
work together on a single theme and a commitment to adequate
preparation. Four factors are specifically identified as being helpful:
intellectual qualities, discourse arrangement, personal attitudes, and
rhetorical aptitudes.

The speech

As we have already noted, there are numerous forms of public
presentations. The most commonly used term for public discourse
for the last two hundred years is *speech.* A speaker writes a speech,
presents a speech, or makes a speech. We listen to a speech or
turn off/on a speech. In this text we distinguish the basic discourse
forms as *speech* and *monologue.* However, speech is not used in

the traditional sense. For us a speech has to have *direction* and *expressive continuity* provided by the audience. On the other hand, a *monologue* is usually given by one person without interruptions from the audience. In both cases, however, the communicator must establish *purposiveness,* be *easily heard and seen,* and *challenge* and *retain attention.* To develop an intelligent monologue or speech a communicator must have a clear purpose in mind. When President Gerald Ford planned to give a monologue pardoning former President Richard Nixon of all Watergate involvement, he had to establish a clear and concise purpose for the communication. Failure to do so would have led to confusion for the audiences. A communicator should not speak if he or she cannot answer the question: "Why should I speak to this audience on this subject?" If one is able to answer this question soundly, then one will feel justified that one's remarks are worthwhile for an audience. A communicator must be easily heard and seen during a public discourse presentation. In Chapter 10 we present ideas for improving your presentation. Through the use of effective style and presentation a communicator should be able to secure and retain audience attention.

The speech is complete when the audience has participated in its development. Because the audience plays a major role in creating, developing, and expanding the speech, it takes on a radically different form than the monologue, which does not depend upon immediate audience participation for its success or effectiveness. As a discourse format, the speech provides the speaker and the audience with ample opportunity to contribute to the total discourse. Whereas the speaker is responsible for the *direction* of the speech, that is, choice of themes, general organization, and basic illustrations, the audience is primarily responsible for keeping the *continuity* on course, that is, audients provide relief words and expressions, augment the speaker's basic illustrations, and affirm his themes and organization. Thus, direction and continuity are the keys to a properly developed speech. Many factors influence whether a discourse will be a speech or not. A discourse meant to get an audience to laugh is an entertainment speech. It is a speech because the continuity carried by the audience in its vocal response to the speaker's direction is an organic part of the discourse. In effect the speaker and audience have an unwritten agreement that this type of discourse must be a joint production. The same can be said for the folk sermon in many black churches. An agreement exists, by reason of an unspoken convention, that the sermon is a participatory discourse prepared and delivered by the preacher and the audience. Failure of one party to the unspoken but clearly understood convention results in loss of continuity of direction. A discourse without continuity—the verbal responses that cement the speaker to the audience—is no more than a monologue, and a discourse with continuity but no direction becomes an extremely poor example of a speech.

The monologue

The monologue is the most traditional communication form. It is a relatively uninterrupted discourse. Applause, or *audience expressive continuity,* is not to be considered an organic part of a monologue. Most academic lectures, sermons, deliberative addresses, eulogies, and forensic presentations are monologues in that they are characterized as public addresses given by one person without interruptions.

Monologues may be given by anyone who has an *occasion,* a *subject,* and a *voice.* It is perhaps the simplest communication form to master because the natural human tendency to talk to friends or foes about something on one's mind is merely extended. Communication teachers, when speaking of this form, frequently ask students to imagine a person standing on a street trying to persuade another person. After he or she has talked for a while, another person stops to hear the message and soon other passersby stop too. Then the person talking moves to a corner and perhaps stands atop a handy fire hydrant in order to see all the people and for them to hear him. Suddenly you have a monologue. Thus, it becomes the extension of a one-sided conversation. In this case the monologist assumes the traditional role of teacher or disseminator of knowledge and information. People who stop by to hear him speak extend the concept of one-to-one communication into a kind of mass communication, one to many. Therefore, the monologist becomes a mass disseminator or persuader.

Whereas the traditional idea of a monologue as an entertainment form, usually associated with humor or drama, still persists, there is no essential difference between Winston Churchill's monologues and those by a performer. The purposes may differ, but purposes exist. In one case the purpose may be to arouse national spirit; in the other, to arouse a feeling of empathy for a fictitious character. Nevertheless, it is possible for both the politician's monologue and the performer's to have the same purpose. However, in most cases the monologue has a single purpose. In the confession of Nat Turner we get a good idea of a monologue occasionally punctuated by a question from Thomas Gray, an attorney. Turner was convicted on November 5, 1831, for leading an insurrection among slaves. His monologue appears below.

—You have asked me to give a history of the motives which induced me to undertake the late insurrection, as you call it. To do so I must go back to the days of my infancy, and even before I was born. I was thirty-one years of age the 2d of October last, and born the property of Benj. Turner, of this county. In my childhood a circumstance occurred, which made an indelible impression on my mind, and laid the groundwork of that enthusiasm, which has terminated so fatally to many, both white and black, and for which I am about to atone on the gallows. It is here necessary to relate this circumstance—trifling as it may seem, it was the commencement of that belief which has grown with time, and even now, sir, in this dungeon, helpless and forsaken as I am, I cannot divest myself of it. Being at play with other children, when three or four years old, I was telling them something, which my mother overhearing, said it had happened before I was born—I stuck to my story, however, and related some things which went, in the opinion, to confirm it—others being called on were greatly astonished, knowing that these things had happened, causing them to say in my hearing, I surely would be a prophet, as the Lord had shown me things that had happened before my birth. And my father and mother strengthened me in this my first impression, saying in my presence, I was intended for some great purpose, which they had always thought from certain marks on my head and breast—(a parcel of excrescences which I believe are not at all uncommon, particularly among negroes, as I have seen several with the same. In this case he has either cut them off, or they have nearly disappeared)—My grandmother, who was very religious, and to whom I was much attached—my master, who belonged to the church, and other religious persons who visited the house, and whom I often saw at prayers, noticing the singularity of my manners, I suppose, and my uncommon intelligence for a child, remarked I had too much sense to be raised, and if I was, I would never be of any service to anyone, as a slave. To a mind like mine, restless, inquisitive, and observant of everything that was passing, it was easy to suppose that religion was the subject to which it would be directed, and, although this subject principally occupied my thoughts, there was nothing that I saw or heard of, to which my attention was not directed. The manner in which I learned to read and write, not only had great influence on my own mind, as I acquired it with the most perfect ease, so much so, that I have no recollection whatever of learning the alphabet, but, to the astonishment of the family, one day, when a book was shown me to keep me from crying, I began spelling the names of different objects—this was a source of wonder to all in the neighborhood, particularly the blacks—and this learning was constantly improved at all opportunities. When I got large enough to go to work, while employed, I was reflecting on many things that would present themselves to my imagination, and whenever an opportunity occurred of looking at a book, when the schoolchildren were getting their lessons, I would find many things that the fertility of my own imagination had depicted to me before; all my time, not devoted to my master's service, was spent either in prayer, or in making experiments in casting different things in moulds made of earth, in attempting to make paper, gunpowder, and many other experiments, that, although I could not perfect, yet convinced me of their practicability, if I had the means.* I was not addicted to stealing in my youth, nor ever have been; yet such was the confidence of the negroes in the neighborhood, even at this early period of my life, in my superior judgment, that they would after carry me with them when they were going on any roguery, to plan for them. Growing up among them, with this confidence in my superior judgment, and when this, in their opinions, was perfected by Divine inspiration, from the circumstances already alluded to in infancy, and which belief was afterwards zealously inculcated by the austerity of my life and manners, which became the subject of remark with white and black.—Having soon discovered, that to be great, I must appear so, I therefore studiously avoided mixing in society, and wrapped myself in mystery, devoting my time to fasting and prayer. By this time, having arrived to man's estate, and hearing the scriptures commented on at meetings, I was struck with that particular passage, which says: "Seek ye the kingdom of heaven and all things shall be added unto you." I reflected much on this passage, and prayed daily for light on this subject. As I was praying one day at my plough, the Spirit broke to me, saying: "Seek ye the kingdom of heaven and all things shall be added unto you."

Question: What do you mean by the Spirit?

Answer: The Spirit that spoke to the prophets in former days; and I was greatly astonished, and for two years prayed continually, whenever my duty would permit; and then again I had the same revelation, which fully confirmed me in the impression that I was ordained for some great purpose in the hands of the Almighty.

---

* When questioned as to the manner of manufacturing those different articles, he was found well informed on the subject.

Several years rolled round, in which many events occurred to strengthen me in the belief. At this time I reverted in my mind to the remarks made of me in my childhood, and the things that had been shown me; and as it had been said of me in my childhood, by those by whom I had been taught to pray, both white and black, and in whom I had the greatest confidence, that I had too much sense to be raised, and if I was, I would never be of any use to anyone, as a slave. Now finding I had arrived at man's estate, and was a slave, and these revelations being made known to me, I began to direct my attention to this great object, to fulfill the purpose for which, by this time, I felt assured I was intended. Knowing the influence I had obtained over the minds of my fellow servants (not by means of conjuring and such like tricks, for to them I always spoke of such things with contempt) but by the communion of the Spirit, whose revelations I often communicated to them, and they believed and said my wisdom came from God. I now began to prepare them for my purpose, by telling them something was about to happen that would terminate in fulfilling the great promise that had been made to me. About this time I was placed under an overseer, from whom I ran away; and after remaining in the woods thirty days, I returned, to the astonishment of the negroes on the plantation, who thought I had made my escape to some other part of the country, as my father had done before. But the reason of my return was, that the Spirit appeared to me and said, I had my wishes directed to things of this world, and not to the kingdom of heaven, and that I should return to the service of my earthly master—"For he who knoweth his Master's will, and doeth it not, shall be beaten with many stripes, and thus have I chastened you." And the negroes found fault, and murmured against me, saying if they had my sense, they would not serve any master in the world. And about this time I had a vision, and I saw white spirits and black spirits engaged in battle, and the sun was darkened, the thunder rolled in the heavens, and blood flowed in streams; and I heard a voice saying, "Such is your luck, such are you called on to see, and let it come, rough or smooth, you must surely bear it." I now withdrew myself as much as my situation would permit, from the intercourse of my fellow servants, for the avowed purpose of serving the Spirit more fully; and it appeared to me, and reminded me of the things it had already shown me, and that it would then reveal to me the knowledge of the elements, the revolution of the planets, the operation of tides, and changes of the seasons. After this revelation, in the year 1825, and the knowledge of the elements being made known to me, I sought more than ever to obtain true holiness, before the great day of judgment should appear, and then I began to receive the true knowledge of faith. And from the first steps of righteousness until the last was I made perfect; and the Holy Ghost was with me and said, "Behold me as I stand in the heavens!" and I looked and saw the forms of men in different attitudes, and there were lights in the sky to which the children of darkness gave other names than what they really were; for they were the lights of the Saviour's hands, stretched forth from east to west, even as they were extended on the cross on Calvary, for the redemption of sinners. And I wondered greatly at these miracles, and prayed to be informed of a certainty of the meaning thereof; and shortly afterwards, while laboring in the field, I discovered drops of blood on the corn, as though it were dew from heaven; and I communicated it to many, both white and black, in the neighborhood; and I then found on the leaves in the woods hieroglyphic characters, and numbers, with the forms of men in different attitudes, portrayed in blood, and representing the figures I had seen before in the heavens. And now the Holy Ghost had revealed itself to me, and made plain the miracles it had shown me—for as the Blood of Christ had been shed on this earth, and had ascended to heaven for the salvation of sinners, and was now returning to earth again in the form of dew, and as the leaves on the trees bore the impression of the figures I had seen in the heavens, it was plain to me that the Saviour was about to lay down the yoke he had borne for the sins of men, and the great day of judgment was at hand. About this time I told these things to a white man (Ethelred T. Brantly) on whom it had a wonderful effect, and he ceased from his wickedness, and was attacked immediately with a cutaneous eruption, and the blood oozed from the pores of his skin, and after praying and fasting nine days he was healed, and the Spirit appeared to me again, and said, as the Saviour had been baptized so should we be also—and when the white people would not let us be baptized by the Spirit. After this I rejoiced greatly, and gave thanks to God. And on the 12th of May, 1828, I heard a loud noise in the heavens, and the Spirit instantly appeared to me and said, the Serpent was loosened, and Christ had laid down the yoke he had borne for the sins of men, and that I should take it on and fight against the Serpent, for the time was fast approaching when the first should be last and the last should be first.

Question: Do you not find yourself mistaken now?

Answer: Was not Christ crucified?—And by signs in the heavens, that it would make known to me when I should commence the great work—and until the first sign appeared, I should conceal it from the knowledge of men—And on the appearance of the sign (the eclipse of the sun last February), I should arise and prepare myself, and slay my enemies with their own weapons. And immediately on the sign appearing in the heavens, the seal was removed from my lips, and I communicated the great work laid out for me to do, to four in whom I had the greatest confidence (Henry, Hark, Nelson, and Sam). It was intended by us to have begun the work of death on the 4th of July last. Many were the plans formed and rejected by us, and it affected my mind to such a degree, that I fell sick, and the time passed without our coming to any determination how to commence, still forming new schemes and rejecting them, when the sign appeared again, which determined me not to wait longer.

Since the commencement of 1830, I had been living with Mr. Joseph Travis, who was to me a kind master, and placed the greatest confidence in me; in fact, I had no cause to complain of his treatment to me. On Saturday evening, the 20th of August, it was agreed between Henry, Hark, and myself, to prepare a dinner the next day for the men we expected, and then to concert a plan, as we had not yet determined on any. Hark, on the following morning, brought a pig, and Henry, brandy, and being joined by Sam, Nelson, Will, and Jack, they prepared in the woods a dinner, where about three o'clock, I joined them.

Question: Why were you so backward in joining them?

Answer: The same reason that had caused me not to mix with them for years before.

I saluted them on coming up, and asked Will how came he there, he answered, his life was worth no more than others, and his liberty as dear to him. I asked him if he thought to obtain it? He said he would, or lose his life. This was enough to put him in full confidence. Jack, I knew was only a tool in the hands of Hark; it was quickly agreed we should commence at home (Mr. J. Travis') on that night, and, until we had armed and equipped ourselves, and gathered sufficient force, neither age nor sex was to be spared (which was invariably adhered to). We remained at the feast, until about two hours in the night, when we went to the house and found Austin; they all went to the cider press and drank, except myself. On returning to the house, Hark went to the door with an axe, for the purpose of breaking it open, as we knew we were strong enough to murder the family should they be awakened by the noise; but reflecting that it might create an alarm in the neighborhood, we determined to enter the house secretly, and murder them whilst sleeping. Hark got a ladder and set it against the chimney, on which I ascended, and hoisting a window, entered and came downstairs, unbarred the door, and removed the guns from their places. It was then observed that I must spill the first blood. On which, armed with a hatchet, and accompanied by Will, I entered my master's chamber, it being dark, I could not give a deathblow, the hatchet glanced from his head, he sprang from the bed and called his wife; it was his last word. Will laid him dead with a blow of his axe, and Mrs. Travis shared the same fate, as she laid in bed. The murder of this family, five in number, was the work of a moment; not one of them awoke; there was a little infant sleeping in a cradle, that was forgotten, until we had left the house and gone some distance, when Henry and Will returned and killed it; we got four guns that would shoot, and several old muskets, with a pound or two of powder. We remained for some time at the barn where we paraded; I formed them in a line as soldiers, and after carrying them through all the maneuvers I was master of, marched them off to Mrs. Salathul Francis', about six hundred yards distant.

Sam and Will went to the door and knocked. Mr. Francis asked who was there, Sam replied it was him, and he had a letter for him, on which he got up and came to the door; they immediately seized him and dragging him out a little from the door, he was dispatched by repeated blows on the head; there was no other white person in the family. We started from there for Mrs. Reese's maintaining the most perfect silence on our march, where, finding the door unlocked, we entered and murdered Mrs. Reese in her bed while sleping; her son awoke, but only to sleep the sleep of death, he had only time to say, "who is that," and he was no more. From Mrs. Reese's we went to Mrs. Turner's, a mile distant, which we reached about sunrise, on Monday morning. Henry, Austin, and Sam went to the house, as we approached, the family discovered us and shut the door. Vain hope! Will, with one stroke of his axe, opened it and we entered, and found Mrs. Turner and Mrs. Newsome in the middle of a room, almost frightened to death. Will immediately killed Mrs. Turner, with one blow of his axe. I took Mrs. Newsome by the hand, and with the sword I had when I was apprehended, I struck her several blows over the head but not being able to kill her, as the sword was dull; Will turning round and discovering it, dispatched her also. A general destruction of property and search for money and ammunition always succeeded the murders. By this time my company amounted to fifteen, nine men mounted, who started for Mrs. Whitehead's (the other six were to go through a byway to Mr. Bryant's, and rejoin us at Mrs. Whitehead's); as we approached the house, we discovered Mr. Richard Whitehead standing in the cotton patch, near the lane fence; we called him over into the lane, and Will, the executioner, was near at hand, with his fatal axe to send him to an untimely grave. As we pushed on to the house, I discovered someone run round the garden, and thinking it was some of the white family, I pursued them, but finding it was a servant girl belonging to the house, I returned to commence the work of death, but they whom I left had not been idle; all the family were already murdered, but Mrs. Whitehead and her daughter Margaret. As I came round to the door I saw Will pulling Mrs. Whitehead out of the house, and at the step he nearly severed her head from her body, with his broadaxe. Miss Margaret, when I discovered her, had concealed herself in the corner formed by the projection of the cellar cap from the house; on my approach she fled but was soon overtaken, and after repeated blows with a sword, I killed her by a blow on the head with a fence rail. By this time the six who had gone by Mr. Bryant's rejoined us and informed me they had done the work of death assigned them. We again divided, part going to Mr. Richard Porter's and from thence to Nathaniel Francis', the others to Mr. Howell Harris', and Mr. T. Doyles'. On my reaching Mr. Porter's, he had escaped with his family. I understood there that the alarm had already spread, and I immediately returned to bring up those sent to Mr. Doyles, and Mr. Howell Harris; the party I left, going on to Mr. Francis', having told them I would join them in that neighborhood. I met these sent to Mr. Doyles and Mr. Harris returning, having met Mr. Doyle on the road and killed him, and learning from some who joined them, that Mr. Harris was from home, I immediately pursued the course taken by the party gone on before; but knowing that they would complete the work of death and pillage at Mr. Francis', before I could get there, I went to Mr. Peter Edwards', expecting to find them there, but they had been here also. I then went to Mr. John T. Barrow's; they had been here and murdered him. I pursued on their track to Capt. Newitt Harris', I found the greater part mounted, and ready to start; the men now amounting to about forty, shouted and hurrahed as I rode up, some were in the yard, loading their guns, others drinking. They said, Captain Harris and his family had escaped, the property in the house they destroyed, robbing him of money and other valuables. I ordered them to mount and march instantly; this was about nine or ten o'clock, Monday morning. I proceeded to Mr. Levi Waller's, two or three miles distant. I took my station in the rear, and it was my object to carry terror and devastation wherever we went, I placed fifteen or twenty of the best mounted and most to be relied on, in front, who generally approached the houses as fast as their horses could run; this was for two purposes, to prevent their escape and strike terror to the inhabitants—on this account I never got to the houses, after leaving Mrs. Whitehead's, until the murders were committed, except in one case. I sometimes got in sight in time to see the work of death completed, viewed the mangled bodies as they lay in silent satisfaction, and immediately started in quest of other victims. Having murdered Mrs. Waller and ten children, we started for Mr. William Williams'—having killed him and two little boys that were there; while engaged in this Mrs. Williams fled and got some distance from the house, but she was pursued, overtaken, and compelled to get up behind one of the company, who brought her back and after showing her the mangled body of her lifeless husband, she was told to get down and lay by his side, where she was shot dead. I then started for Mr. Jacob Williams', where the family were murdered—Here we found a young man named Drury, who had come on business with Mr. Williams—he was pursued, overtaken, and shot. Mrs. Vaughans was the next place we visited—and after murdering the family here, I determined on starting for Jerusalem—Our number amounted now to fifty or sixty, all mounted and armed with guns, axes, swords, and clubs—On reaching Mr. James W. Parker's gate, immediately on the road leading to Jerusalem and about three miles distant, it was proposed to me to call there, but I objected, as I knew he was gone to Jerusalem and my object was to reach there as soon as possible; but some of the men having relations at Mr. Parker's it was agreed that they might call and get his people. I remained at the gate on the road, with seven or eight, the others going across the field to the house, about half a mile off. After waiting some time for them, I became impatient, and started to the house for them, and on our return we were met by a party of white men, who had pursued our bloodstained track, and who had fired on those at the gate, and dispersed them, which I knew nothing of, not having been at that time rejoined by any of them—Immediately on discovering the whites, I ordered my men to halt and form, as they appeared to be alarmed—The white men, eighteen in number, approached us in about one hundred yards, when one of them fired (this was against the positive orders of Captain Alexander P. Peete, who commanded, and who directed the men to reserve their fire until within thirty paces), and I discovered about half of them retreating, I then ordered my men to fire and rush on them; the few remaining stood their ground until we approached within fifty yards, when they fired and retreated. We pursued and overtook some of them whom we thought we left dead (they were not killed); after pursuing them about two hundred yards, and rising a little hill, I discovered they were met by another party, and had halted, and were reloading their guns. (This was a small party from Jerusalem who knew the negroes were in the field, and had just tied their horses to await their return to the road, knowing that Mr. Parker and family were in Jerusalem, but knew nothing of the party that had gone in with Captain Peete; on hearing the firing they immediately rushed to the spot and arrived just in time to arrest the progress of these barbarous villains and save the lives of their friends and fellow citizens.) Thinking that those who retreated first, and the party who fired on us at fifty or sixty yards distant, had all only fallen back to meet others with ammunition. As I saw them reloading their guns, and more coming up than I saw at first, and several of my bravest men being wounded, the others became panic-struck and scattered over the field; the white men pursued and fired on us several times. Hark had his horse shot under him, and I caught another for him that was running by me; five or six of my men were wounded, but none left on the field; finding myself defeated here, I instantly determined to go through a private way, and cross the Nottoway river at the Cypress Bridge, three miles below Jerusalem, and attack that place in the rear, as I expected they would look for me on the other road, and I had a great desire to get there to procure arms and ammunition. After going a short distance in this private way, accompanied by about twenty men, I overtook two or three who told me the others were dispersed in every direction. After trying in vain to collect a sufficient force to proceed to Jerusalem, I determined to return, as I was sure they would make back to their old neighborhood, where they would rejoin me, make new recruits, and come down again. On my way back, I called on Mrs. Thomas', Mrs. Spencer's, and several other places; the white families having fled we found no more victims to gratify our thirst for blood, we stopped at Major Ridley's quarter for the night, and being joined by four of his men, with the recruits made since my defeat, we mustered now about forty strong.

After placing out sentinels, I laid down to sleep, but was quickly aroused by a great racket; starting up, I found some mounted and others in great confusion; one of the sentinels having given the alarm that we were about to be attacked, I ordered some to ride around and reconnoiter, and on their return the others being more alarmed, not knowing who they were, fled in different ways, so that I was reduced to about twenty again; with this I determined to attempt to recruit, and proceed on to rally in the neighborhood I had left. Dr. Blunt's was the nearest house, which we reached just before day; on riding up the yard, Hark fired a gun. We expected Dr. Blunt and his family were at Major Ridley's as I knew there was a company of men there; the gun was fired to ascertain if any of the family were at home, we were immediately fired upon and retreated, leaving several of my men. I do not know what became of them, as I never saw them afterwards. Pursuing our course back; and coming in sight of Captain Harris', where we had been the day before, we discovered a party of white men at the house, on which all deserted me but two (Jacob and Nat); we concealed ourselves in the woods until near night, when I sent them in search of Henry, Sam, Nelson, and Hark, and directed them to rally all they could, at the place we had our dinner the Sunday before, where they would find me, and I accordingly returned there as soon as it was dark and remained until Wednesday evening, when discovering white men riding around the place, as though they were looking for someone, and none of my men joining me, I concluded Jacob and Nat had been taken and compelled to betray me. On this I gave up all hope for the present, and on Thursday night, after having supplied myself with provisions from Mr. Travis', I scratched a hole under a pile of fence rails in a field, where I concealed myself for six weeks, never leaving my hiding place but for a few minutes in the dead of the night to get water which was very near; thinking by this time I could venture out, I began to go about in the night and eavesdrop the houses in the neighborhood; pursuing this course for about a fortnight and gathering little or no intelligence, afraid of speaking to any human being, and returning every morning to my cave before the dawn of day. I know not how long I might have led this life, if accident had not betrayed me. A dog in the neighborhood, passing by my hiding place, one night while I was out, was attracted by some meat I had in my cave, and crawled in and stole it, and was coming out just as I returned. A few nights after, two negroes having started to go hunting with the same dog, and passed that way, the dog came again to the place, and having just gone out to walk about, discovered me and barked, on which thinking myself discovered, I spoke to them to beg concealment. On making myself known, they fled from me. Knowing then they would betray me, I immediately left my hiding place, and was pursued almost incessantly, until I was taken, a fortnight afterwards, by Mr. Benjamin Phipps, in a little hole I had dug out with a sword, for the purpose of concealment, under the top of a fallen tree. On Mr. Phipps' discovering the place of my concealment, he cocked his gun and aimed at me. I requested him not to shoot, and I would give up, upon which he demanded my sword. I delivered it to him, and he brought me to prison. During the time I was pursued, I had many hairbreadth escapes, which your time will not permit me to relate. I am here, loaded with chains, and willing to suffer the fate that awaits me.

This confession by Nat Turner is in the best tradition of the monologue. It is complete, purposeful, and stylistically appropriate.

Among the various kinds of monologues we confront every day are the business monologues. If you are seeking to enter the public marketplace as a seller or consumer of goods, one of the most important things you should remember is that the purpose of business monologues is to sell goods and services. There are two basic kinds of business monologues: The "We're a Good Company" monologue and the "Our Product Is for You" monologue. Both are designed to increase profits for a particular business. Let us take a good look at how these monologues are developed.

The "We're a Good Company" monologue serves a basic premise of selling in that an effective salesperson must convince the potential buyer that you have a good company and a good product. By instilling a sense of confidence, goodwill, and respect for the product and the company, the monologist creates a good public relations image for the business. In order to develop goodwill, a business can emphasize the quality of its product, the expertise of its workers, and the general contribution of the business to the community. It is generally agreed that certain businesses have built-in monopolies and as such advertise their services or products only for goodwill. People who live in a highly technological society such as ours will need a telephone. But occasionally there are goodwill talks given by the telephone company, not necessarily to increase sales, but perhaps to make certain that when rates are increased, people will take the news a little easier.

Lecturers who speak before civic and other groups on the value of various utilities, military service, and industries give monologues designed to publicize specific benefits. Monologists should use indirection, that is, they must not try to sell products directly. Goodwill discourses are important to the selling function only because they create an attitude for the more direct approaches. Thus, rather than offering a product for sale or creating a demand for it, the monologist stresses services rendered for humanitarian purposes by his company, points to community participation by members of the business, and speaks about the economic value of his company in providing employment and experimenting in new and less expensive uses of raw materials. During a decline in public interest in the American space program, a cadre of speakers were sent across the country to explain to the public the benefits of space exploration. The speakers built up the public consciousness of the work being performed for society by the National Aeronautics and Space Agency. Whereas the public may have had difficulty understanding the enormous expenditures for moon exploration, it was a simple matter to point to the benefits of improved medical care.

The "We're a Good Company" line has been used by various

political parties prior to an election. The aim is to "soften" the public for the eventual pitch of the campaigner asking the public to vote in a certain way or for a particular candidate. It is not good strategy for the goodwill speaker to appear to be a salesman. The speaker must assume the role of a friend who reports to an interested public about the genial personalities associated with the management of the business, the common goals of the company and the public, and the broad social qualities that recommend the company as a good citizen. There are numerous examples of the goodwill monologue heard on radio and television daily. The electronic commercial, which utilizes the attraction power of top public figures, athletics heroes, former popular television newspersons, reporters, and even actors, has become one of the most widely recognized examples of the goodwill monologue. Whether it is American Airlines, Ford Motor Company, or some type of deodorant being presented on the commercial, many times the communication is only indirectly engaged in a selling function. Multinational corporations have found it to be good business to sponsor soccer matches in Ghana or Indonesia or wherever they are doing business. Some multinational corporations have been criticized for going too far in using financial influence to persuade foreign governments to purchase products. Most companies avoid illegal practices and use their influence for philanthropic ends. Coca-Cola regularly performs philanthropic activities to create a positive public image. In addition, the major United States oil companies recently campaigned extensively by emphasizing their environmental concerns, although there have been frequent instances of some companies polluting the environment. The reason for this type of campaign is to establish goodwill so that the salesperson's job will be made much easier because of name and product identification resulting from the consciousness developed in the audiences toward the company.

The "Our Product Is for You" monologue is the basic sales talk and represents the attempt to put forth the company's product in the best light. The sales talk is designed to influence the audience decision to adopt, purchase, or accept a given product. If it is not determined before for him or her, every monologist engaged in a sales situation must determine what specific aim she or he is trying to attain. Communicationists have generally agreed that a speaker must gauge a talk for the audience and that by understanding the audience's likes and dislikes, fears and loves, the speaker will be able to better present the case of his or her own product. For example, if you are trying to sell a new pocket-size digital calculator, you must determine if it is desired by your potential customers. Do they have knowledge of other brands of pocket calculators? Are they knowledgeable of the advantage of your brand? In sales, as in anything else, the best thing a speaker can have on his side is a quality product. If the product is no good, then the sales talk becomes demagoguery because the speaker is trying to represent something to the public that is less than honest. We tend to accept the view that the honest and sincere person generally succeeds in getting continual acceptance. When falsehood is discovered, people revolt and the seller is left holding the bad goods.

The key to sales success is to show the audience the utility of a product. This may be done before the audience knows the name of a product. By convincing the audience that a certain product will perform tasks beneficial to them, the speaker creates a demand for the product. Most of the technological inventions that have made life convenient in an industrial society are the result of someone showing a need. The sales talker must accentuate the positive. Many businesses provide manuals for salespersons involved in direct public sales. For example, Fuller Brush and Avon Products have almost perfected the positive presentation of their products. The basic approach is to make the buyer feel comfortable with the seller. You are perhaps aware of some of these direct public sales strategies: (1) confident manner, (2) use of free gift to create goodwill, (3) use of names (such as, "Good morning, Mrs. Jones. I have just been talking with your neighbor, Mrs. Smith. My name is Bob Hall."), (4) special price reductions for quick action, and (5) unique characteristics ("This product is different and better than any other").

In all cases of public communication intended to influence, the monologist must present the most favorable aspects of his or her product or ideas. What we have given you in this chapter are some key thoughts on the forms of contemporary public communication. However, it should be clear from our introductory chapter that all communication in our view must have good reasons. Thus, while a communicator seeks to show the favorable aspects of her or his ideas, he or she must give the audiences good reasons for accepting those ideas. This will mean that the ethical person should be aware of potential shortcomings of an idea as well as the advantages.

The formats for contemporary communication presented in this section are fairly common in complex societies. Each of you can look forward to spending a considerable portion of your time either presenting or listening to these types of communication. At least, we now feel confident that they will not take you by surprise. Furthermore, should you ever have to address an audience of any kind on any subject, you will have a choice of formats. The productive and humanistic art of sharing images with other humans can only be perfected through awareness of possibilities and the practice of skills.

FOR STUDENT APPLICATION

1. Listen to a radio or television sermon. What appeals were used by the preacher? What evidence was presented in support of the preacher's position?

2. Watch a television discussion program such as "Issues and Answers" or "Meet the Press." What were the major differences in participation between the moderator and the guest? Compare the duties and responsibilities of the moderator and the other members of the discussion group. What were the major differences that you observed?

3. Compare the one-person monologue with the two- or more-persons dialogue found in television commercials. Which form is the most frequently employed? Which do you think is the most effective?

4. Consider the last informal debate you observed. Did the monologue and dialogue forms remain throughout the debate or did the debate begin with the monologue form and emerge into a dialogue form?

5. Observe several television commercials. Did any of the commercials use an "expert" or "authority figure"? Do you think special expertise in one area, for example, sports, carries over into other areas such as automobiles?

6. Recall your experiences with "direct salesmen," those who call on people at their homes to attempt to sell various products. What are some of the techniques you have noticed such salesmen use? In what ways are the sales techniques of the direct salesman and the television advertiser different? In what ways are they similar?

Readings

BERLO, DAVID K. *The Process of Communication.* New York: Holt, Rinehart and Winston, 1960.

DANCE, FRANK E. X., ed. *Human Communication Theory.* New York: Holt, Rinehart and Winston, 1967.

MORTENSON, C. DAVID. *Communication: The Study of Human Interaction.* New York: McGraw-Hill, 1972.

ROSS, RAYMOND S. *Speech Communication: Fundamentals and Practice,* 2d ed. Englewood Cliffs, N.J.: Prentice-Hall, 1970.

3 Listening Intelligently to Contemporary Communication

WHAT YOU CAN EXPECT:

Chapter 3 discusses the importance of listening intelligently to contemporary communication.

This chapter suggests that we are in an age that has been described as "an age of information explosion." Since man's knowledge in terms of information more than doubles every ten years, it is essential for the contemporary public communicator and receiver to develop good listening habits. Only through an effort to increase our awareness of the reception of communication can we develop the good habits of listening intelligently, selectively, and efficiently to the many forms of contemporary communication.

Chapter Outline

The Prevalance of Listening
The Gap Between Listening and Thinking
Differences Between Reading and Listening Behavior
The Speaker-Listener and Listener-Listener
    Interactions

If we were attempting to make some statement about your typical, characteristic personal behavior and we wanted to be fairly certain that this statement would be accurate, we might say that you spend most of your waking hours being involved in some kind of communication. The probabilities that our statement will be accurate for your personal behavior are quite good because you spend approximately 80 percent of your time—yesterday, today, tomorrow, in fact, every day—engaged in some kind of *communicative behavior*. If we attempted another guess about your behavior, we might suggest that you spend about half of your communication behavior time involved in the *reception* of communication—that is, you probably spend about 42 percent of your communication behavior time *listening*. Listening is our most frequent communication behavior. We do more listening than any other kind of communication behavior. The importance of listening and the determination of how much time the average person spends listening has been the subject of research since 1926, when Professor Paul T. Rankin, of Ohio State University, pioneered listening research. But this fifty-year-old study is relevant today because Rankin's results have been confirmed several times, most recently in a 1969 research study.[1] Today, since it is estimated that Americans spend 360 million hours daily in front of their television sets, the amount of time spent listening is probably even higher.[2] Naturally, since we engage in listening behavior more than speaking, writing, or reading, we should be skilled listeners. But poor listening is perhaps a major barrier of communication effectiveness. One of the reasons for this is quite simple. Most of us have never had any formal training or an educational course in effective listening. In this chapter we set forth some informative material we have designed to increase your awareness of the importance of listening. Hopefully this material will help you to develop better, more effective habits of listening.

The Prevalence of Listening

You engage in more listening behavior than you may at first think. Assume a hypothetical college student named Susan. Let us follow Susan throughout a representatively imagined day and comment on her listening activities. Susan wakes up listening to the nice music of her radio alarm clock. The disc jockey tries to persuade

[1] Paul T. Rankin, "The Measurement of the Ability to Understand Spoken Language," *Dissertation Abstracts* 12 (1926), p. 847. Rankin's findings were recently verified by Larry A. Samover, Robert D. Brooks, and Richard E. Porter, in "A Survey of Adult Communication Activities," *Journal of Communication* 19 (December 1969), pp. 301–307.

[2] Robert J. Glessing and William P. White, *Mass Media: The Invisible Environment* (Chicago: Science Research Associates, 1973), p. v.

her to buy some product, then introduces the next hit record. Susan continues to listen. After a refreshing shower, she dresses and then prepares to eat breakfast. She may switch on the television set to listen to her favorite morning show. As she rides to school with her roommate on the bus, Susan listens to her portable transistor radio. She listens to her friend's conversation. At school Susan joins other students and they will spend most of their time listening to the professor. Susan goes home after a day of listening to her friends and professors and switches on her favorite stereo record. She listens to her records as she prepares to go out for a study date with her boyfriend. She listens to her boyfriend's discussion of his problems, and when she returns that evening, she listens to a TV show, her stereo, or her radio. We could continue making possible observations about this typical student named Susan, but our point hopefully has been made. People engage in listening behavior more than any other communication activity.

The Gap Between Listening and Thinking

Most people can "listen" and do a variety of other things at the same time. Some people, busy executives for example, have trained themselves to maximize their time by doing several tasks at once. For instance, some can add a column of figures and carry on a telephone conversation at the same time. Some professors are so proficient at typing that they can type and carry on a conversation simultaneously. Many people pride themselves in being able to do several things at once. Housewives, to use another example, are able to clean the house and "listen" to radio or television at the same time. But this ability can be irritating. Assume you are trying to talk to your father; he is reading the newspaper and says, "Go ahead, I'm listening." Or assume that during an appointment with your professor he continues to read or shuffle papers on the desk while you are attempting to discuss your progress in the course. Obviously, there are times when the ability to do several things at once can be annoying—even rude. But why does this habit of doing something else *while listening* seem so common? One possible answer is the fact that people can listen at the rate of approximately 400 words a minute, yet the average person speaks at a rate of about 100 words per minute. The "gap," which is the time represented by the difference in rate of speech and rate of listening ability, is generally "filled in" with other thoughts or behavior. We have found that this gap invites us to engage in poor listening habits. Ralph G. Nichols, a pioneer in listening research, suggests how you can put this extra time to work so that your listening becomes more effective and efficient. He lists four ways to fill in the gap and thereby become a good listener.

1. The listener thinks ahead of the talker, trying to anticipate what the oral discourse is leading to and what conclusions will be drawn from the words spoken at the moment.
2. The listener weighs the evidence used by the talker to support the points that he makes. "Is this evidence valid?" the listener asks himself. "Is it the complete evidence?"
3. Periodically the listener reviews and mentally summarizes the points of the talk completed thus far.
4. Throughout the talk the listener listens between the lines in search of meaning that is not necessarily put into spoken words. He pays attention to nonverbal communication (facial expression, gestures, tone of voice) to see if it adds meaning to the spoken words. He asks himself, "Is the talker purposely skirting some area of the subject? Why is he doing so?"[3]

Today, it is true that we live in an age of information explosion. It is estimated that available knowledge of man and his surrounding world *doubles every seven to ten years.* Therefore, we do have to be selective in our listening behavior because we simply cannot respond to all the information that is constantly bombarding our ears. And yet, as Ralph G. Nichols has observed, we generally do not learn how to listen in our school systems. Instead, teachers constantly try, from elementary school through college, to teach students how to read and write, when, in fact, people spend the greatest amount of their time not reading or writing, but *listening.*[4]

In short, although study after study has shown that of the four basic communication processes (listening, speaking, reading, and writing) we spend more time engaged in listening, you probably have never had so much as a single course in how to become a more effective listener! After a review of the state of listening education

[3] Ralph G. Nichols and Leonard A. Stevens, "Listening to People," *Harvard Business Review* XXXV (1957), pp. 85–92. See also Ralph G. Nichols and Leonard A. Stevens, *Are You Listening?* (New York: McGraw-Hill, 1957).

[4] See Ralph G. Nichols, "Listening to the Spoken Word," in Ernest G. Bormann et al., *Interpersonal Communication in the Modern Organization* (Englewood Cliffs, N.J.: Prentice-Hall, 1969), p. 170.

in America, Nichols suggests that there is general agreement among educators of the following five statements:

1. Most of us are poor listeners.
2. With training we could easily improve our performance.
3. Schools should definitely provide listening training.
4. To be an effective listener one must always be active and dynamic.
5. The effective listener is sure to be rewarded.[5]

In case you are not convinced by now of the importance of listening, we would like to mention two additional facts. In most of your college classrooms the average professor speaks somewhere between 75 to 85 percent of the time for that period. Research at Columbia University, which was later replicated at the University of Minnesota, indicates that university freshmen operate at a 25 percent level of efficiency when listening to a speech that only lasts 10 minutes.[6] If the students had listened to a much longer speech such as they do in a typical lecture class of 45 minutes to 1 hour, the probabilities are that listening efficiency would drop even lower.

But while it seems clear that ineffective listening causes serious problems in education, business, religion, marriage, and in almost all interpersonal relationships, consider our federal court systems. For example, during the famous Watergate trials the jurors had to base their decision of the innocence or guilt of their fellow man on their ability to listen to the evidence, testimony, and the complex legal instructions from the judge on how to apply the laws.[7]

Differences Between Reading and Listening Behavior

At one time or another you have probably had the following experience. You are reading a book, but after a while you realize that you have lost your concentration, so you go back and reread the part you missed. The same thing can happen in listening. Again, you have probably had the experience of alternately tuning in and tuning out the words of a professor. The problem here, however, is

---

[5] Ibid., p. 172.

[6] Ibid., pp. 184–185.

[7] For a review of listening research and our courts, see Jerry K. Frye, "An Analysis of the Problem of Listening to Federal District Criminal Court Jury Instructions: An Exploratory Study" (Master's thesis, Texas Christian University, 1970).

that when you realize you have missed a section of a lecture, you are unable to go back and "relisten."

In addition, whereas you have control of the speed when you are reading a book, the process of listening is source controlled. And the process of listening is hard work, whereas we have been conditioned to think of reading as easy work. Consider the phrases "relax with a book," "light reading," and "leisure reading." These same phrases cannot be substituted with the process of listening because listening is active, dynamic, and hard work. However, the process of listening is an investment that pays important dividends to the listener.

The Speaker-Listener and Listener-Listener Interactions

As a listener, you may be influenced by a speaker. You may buy a product, vote for a candidate, or modify your attitudes, beliefs, and values on the basis of the speaker's influence and ability to inform and persuade. However, you, as a listener, also influence the speaker. For example, the effective communicator will modify his message partly on the basis of information you give to him through your verbal and nonverbal reactions. An obvious example of the feedback is the negative booing of the audience; a less obvious example of negative nonverbal feedback is the frown or yawn of the listener. Of course, the verbal and nonverbal feedback can be positive indicators of the approval of the listeners, such as cheers and the standing ovation of applause.

But these reactions are obvious to even a casual observer of the public communication process. Less obvious, in fact, occasionally subtle, interactions occur *between* listeners themselves. The more readily identifiable behavior is sometimes called *conformity*. We tend to conform to the expressed behavior of those around us. So, for example, where others give an extremely favorable welcome to a speaker with a standing ovation, there is considerable pressure for us to join in, even if our heart is not in it. It is much easier to yell encouragement to the home team at home where you are one of many people yelling than at out-of-town games where you feel the constraints of being in a minority. Clearly, listeners are influenced by each other. At times, for example, when Orenthal James (O.J.) Simpson sets a new record, the reactions of those around you seem to infect you. Research suggests that enthusiasm is contagious. Whether it is at a football stadium, in a movie theater, in front of the home television set, or listening to a public speech, the listener-receivers tend to influence the perceptions, attitudes, beliefs, values, and behavior of each other. All this is not to say that audiences and listeners are one and the same; they are not the same at all. One can, for example, be a member of a particular audience and not be listening at all. But the active process of listening involves both speaker-listener and listener-listener reactions and influence.

The idea of focusing on the listener (the receiver or the audience) is a welcomed departure from either the source-oriented approach, the message-oriented approach, or the contextual (situational) approach. The analysis of listeners who make up the *audiences* for communication is the subject of an important book.[8] Another recent book notes that the process of listening involves active behavior and is subject to the same background of living experiences that affect other human behavior.[9]

Recently, the authors noted that the information explosion was occurring within our own university. We read with considerable interest the following news:

> The State University of New York has developed a statewide library network through which its members can make a computerized "search" of *more than one million book titles in less than ten seconds.*[10]

It is clear that with so much information being disseminated in books, magazines, television, movies, speeches, and in a host of other written and electronic devices, we must become selective of the information to which we expose ourselves. Obviously, it would be impossible to take in all of the available knowledge. Similarly with listening; we cannot possibly listen to all messages all the time. Rather, we must listen selectively to some of the messages some of the time.

We have indicated the significance of listening in the diverse day-to-day activities. Although we recognize that listening behavior, like any other human behavior, is ultimately complex and certainly

[8] Theodore Clevenger, Jr., *Audience Analysis* (Indianapolis: Bobbs-Merrill, 1966). See also Paul D. Holtzman, *The Psychology of Speakers' Audiences* (Glenview, Ill.: Scott, Foresman, 1970).

[9] Larry L. Barker, *Listening Behavior* (Englewood Cliffs, N.J.: Prentice-Hall, 1971).

[10] "Computers Link State Libraries," *The Spectrum,* Newspaper of the State University of New York at Buffalo (January 27, 1975), p. 5.

more complex than popularly believed, we hope that an increased awareness of listening behavior and the significant function it plays in the total communication process will stimulate you to seek additional information and to consciously attempt to become more effective listeners.

FOR STUDENT APPLICATION

1. Airline pilots, airport controllers, surgeons, and many others are often required to "take a break" and rest before working another shift. The basic idea is that one can be "really sharp" and alert only with adequate rest. Does this idea seem relevant to communication activity? The next time you are involved in a "heated argument," do you think it might be useful to "take a break" and "cool off" before making a decision? What about the cliché, "sleep on it"? Do such "rest periods" increase your effectiveness in communication? Why?

2. Read the following statement: "Although we see with the eyes and hear with the ears, we use all our senses to *listen* to another person." Do you agree that *listening* is more than merely hearing? How is perception related to listening? When you *listen*, is evaluation a part of the listening activity? Turn the picture off the television set but leave the sound on. Is there a difference between watching television and listening to television? What is the difference?

3. How many hours do you spend listening in your classes during a typical week? In what ways do you think you might benefit by more effective listening? What are the major listening problems you have experienced? Recall instances of listening problems and prepare to discuss solutions with other class members.

4. Have you ever tried to communicate with someone who refused to listen to your arguments? When a controversial topic is discussed, have you observed that some people tend to be on the offensive and others tend to be defensive? How do pro and con positions affect listening?

Readings

BAKAN, PAUL. "Some Reflections on Listening Behavior." *Journal of Communication* 6 (1956), pp. 108–113.

BARKER, LARRY L. *Listening Behavior.* Englewood Cliffs, N.J.: Prentice-Hall, 1971.

BROADBENT, D. E. *Perception and Communication.* Elmsford, N.Y.: Pergamon Press, 1958.

DEVINE, T. "Listening." *Review of Educational Research* 37 (April 1967), pp. 152–158.

DUKER, SAM. *Listening: Readings.* Metuchen, N.J.: Scarecrow Press, 1966.
DUKER, SAM. "Doctoral Dissertations on Listening." *Journal of Communication* XIII (June 1963), pp. 106–117.
FRYE, JERRY K. "An Analysis of the Problem of Listening to Federal District Criminal Court Jury Instructions: An Exploratory Study." Masters thesis, Texas Christian University, 1970.
NICHOLS, RALPH G., and STEVENS, LEONARD A. *Are You Listening?* New York: McGraw-Hill, 1957.
PETRIE, CHARLES R. "What We Don't Know About Listening." *Journal of Communication* XIV (1964), pp. 248–252.
PETRIE, CHARLES R. "An Experimental Evaluation of Two Methods for Improving Listening Comprehension Abilities." Ph.D dissertation, Purdue University, West Lafayette, Ind., 1961.
RANKIN, PAUL T. "The Measurement of the Ability to Understand Spoken Language." *Dissertation Abstracts* 12 (1926), p. 847.
RENWICK, RALPH, JR. "A Listening Course for High School Seniors." *The Speech Teacher* 6 (1957), pp. 59–62.
WEAVER, CARL H. *Human Listening: Processes and Behavior.* Indianapolis: Bobbs-Merrill, 1972.

4 Ideas for Contemporary Communication

WHAT YOU CAN EXPECT:

Chapter 4 focuses on the development of communicable ideas. We encourage you to seek ideas from your own cultural universe.

Our purpose in this chapter is to make certain that you know where to look for ideas and what kinds of ideas are *vital* and *interesting*. You should be able to present a monologue or speech on a topic from politics, multiculturalism, or education. We believe that this chapter will give you the kind of confidence you need for preparing your discourses.

Chapter Outline

Emerging Topics
    Politics
    Education
    Multiculturalism
Experience: The Universe of Interest
    Relevant to Subject
    Relevant to Communicator
    Relevant to Audience

Emerging Topics

"I don't have anything to talk about." This statement frequently represents the anxiety faced by a person who has been asked to present a speech, participate in a discussion, lead a panel, or debate an issue. If the request to give a speech or monologue is also accompanied by a topic or theme suggestion, the anxiety might become real frustration: "What am I to say on that subject?" During a college class in interpersonal communication, a teacher at a large university asked a student to "say a few words" about taxation of church property. The student protested that she did not have anything to say about the subject. As a way of introducing students to each other, the teacher had insisted that each one give a short monologue, hence she persisted, "It does not have to be as eloquent as an oration by Congresswoman Barbara Jordan." The student finally got up and spoke about religion and taxation. Asked afterward by the teacher why she had reacted so strongly to giving a brief talk, the student replied that she had never spoken in front of a group before and that she did not know whether churches were taxed or not. Informative public discourse requires that the communicator be knowledgeable.

However difficult it may seem to you at this point, when you finish this chapter, you should be able to deal with the exigencies of the selected topic. After all, the principle that guides effective speech communication—speaking from your heart the things you have knowledge of—can be adapted to most communication decisions. What a communicator does not have knowledge of or does not feel strongly about, he or she should endeavor to learn, or not speak. An audience can tell if you really are disinterested in or uninformed about your topic. It is not unusual for contemporary audiences to quietly leave their seats until a patently uninformed speaker has finished his discourse. A communicator who wastes the time of audiences by not having well-thought-out ideas contributes to the lack of communication skills in society. The advice of "put up, or shut up," usually applied to a person who talks a lot about odds on luck but never wagers, is applicable to a speaker who likes to occupy the podium but seldom has anything to say.

Politics

In *The Revolt of the Masses,* Ortega y Gasset outlined a theory of generation that explained for him why some generations were considering innovative and others traditional. On this account Ortega believed that the generation was the most powerful concept in history. What your parents or even your professors consider innovative, you find traditional, passé. Such theoretical formulation about history provides us with a clearer insight into politics as a source of public ideas. Politics is, as Richard McKeon, following Aristotle, understands, an organizing science because it establishes what the state will be, who shall govern, how economics will be organized, who will pay taxes, and even who will speak at what time.

Politics operates in this fashion regardless of the nature of the economic system. In fact, politics is the organizer of all economic systems. The idea of politics as an organizer of society, then, is one of the richer areas for contemporary rhetorical ideas. Students interested in speaking on the necessary reforms in the economic, social, and cultural order must give close attention to politics as a dimension of their discourse. For example, if you wanted to speak on the subject of taxation, particularly as it applies to the taxing of graduate assistants' stipends, you would be dealing in the realm of politics. Most people who speak about politics are quick to make statements like, "I don't know anything about politics," "That's politics," "Playing politics is a part of life these days," or "I am not political." What they are objecting to is not politics per se but partisan politics. There is hardly an individual in any society who is not touched by politics. You may not have a voice in politics, your party may be the one outside of power, or you may be a victim of political repression, but politics affects almost everyone. Thus, if you speak on prison reform or happen to be wearing a San Quentin or Attica number, you are involved in politics as an organizing system. Taxation of graduate assistants' stipends is a political act, and among the emerging topics in contemporary society are other political questions.

It is through the political mechanism, however cumbersome or crude or efficient, that social life is affected. Controversies over national policies, state regulations, and municipal ordinances lead to political topics that may be sources of ideas for your speeches. Simply because politics exists as a possible category for communication ideas is no reason for a communicator to march headlong into politics without understanding the nature and origin of the selected theme or topic. Preparation must follow interest.

Education

Perhaps no sector of society demonstrates the complex quality of the human brain more than the educational system. Cybernetics, nuclear technology, and bionics aside, the educational system reflects human beings at their most complicated level. Just take a few minutes to think of your education from prekindergarten through

high school to where you are now. You were properly recorded in
some kindergarten, given the right tests, physical and perhaps
psychological (depending on what school district you happened to
live in), and assigned to a teacher and class. Each year for twelve
or thirteen years in the United States and Canada you went through
this process. Once you left secondary school to go to college, you
were met with a totally different set of socialization experiences.
You saw a counselor or an adviser upon entering the college. That
did not disturb you too much because there were advisers and
counselors in secondary school. You then had to "go to the computer" for registration. In some cases it meant standing in a long
line waiting for the computer to "take your IBM cards." When the
cards were returned with no "class closed" designations, you were
ready to attend your first class. And when you stop to contemplate
the process, you think, "It is not over yet, I got three, maybe seven
more years if I get a doctorate." And it will not be over then. In
most countries education is a complex system within complex societies. What you experience processwise is only one part of the
educational system. There are bureaucracies, governing boards and
councils, teachers, instructional materials, clerical personnel, non-
teaching professionals, cafeterias, dormitory organizations, fraternities, sororities, and, perhaps, a communication research laboratory.

With such a multifaceted character, education provides the
communicator with numerous possibilities for ideas. A monologue
could be developed around transnational education, or the future
of elementary education, or locus of control theory, or reading
science. All of these ideas and others having to do with education
will continue to emerge as dominant themes in contemporary society. Keeping informed is one of the first laws of finding topics
and ideas for public communication. As you keep informed, you
will discover more possibilities in education.

Multiculturalism

Marshall McLuhan contends that the world is becoming a global
village. If it is, it will be a village with many tribes. One of the
emerging topics in contemporary society is multiculturalism. A
vast majority of all nations are multiracial or multiethnic, and often
both. Within each of these nations attempts are being made to
define the status or clarify the roles of the minority groups. In the

Soviet Union the Latvians, Ukrainians, Serbs, and Jews constitute sizable ethnic minorities. In Nigeria the Efiks, Rivers and Tiv are among 250 ethnic groups in a nation dominated by Hausa, Ibo, and Yoruba populations. In Israel the oriental Jews from Africa and Asia and Palestinian Arabs comprise minorities. Within the United States of America there are numerous white ethnic groups and sizable populations of Africans, Japanese, Chinese, native Americans, Puerto Ricans, Filipino, and Mexican-Americans. Almost every nation has a multicultural population. It is not possible in today's world for any communicator to be more than one hour by jet away from people of other ethnic or racial backgrounds. In fact, McLuhan's tribal village is nearer to reality than at any time in history.

Topics growing out of multiculturalism could extend from the United Nations to the problems of francophone and anglophone Canada. Each person has a wealth of information at his or her disposal on these subjects. Libraries, embassies, national consulates, foreign students, news magazines, and international centers can supply information on ethnic and cultural groups within nations. Perhaps no social issue in the United States has been treated so extensively as race relations. Information is abundant and no communicator need lack knowledge.

Our presentation of these three categories—*politics, education,* and *multiculturalism*—reflects the conviction that a student of public communication intending to speak on substantive issues can find good reasons for discussing any theme within these categories. They overlap to the extent that politics organizes education and multiculturalism, but they remain distinct enough to have their own areas. Given what we have just been saying, you should be ready to find ideas for your discourses. Where will you look first for information on a topic? We suggest that you start by looking at your personal universe of interest and then expand to other sources.

Experience: The Universe of Interest

The process of topic selection should involve a potential communicator looking at human experience as a major resource for choosing a subject. Three areas of experience are appropriate: (1) experience relevant to subject, (2) experience relevant to communicator, (3) experience relevant to audience. Most students have had experiences in each of these areas and many more by the time they reach college. From this reservoir of information the potential speaker can choose topics confidently, knowing that his experiences are his alone.

By the time a student is asked to make a speech or monologue in a communication class, he has given many brief talks to friends on a score of subjects from experiences. Each person's storehouse of topics is augmented by memory. From the city a person may bring experiences of a community organizer, a small league of baseball players, an interracial discussion group leader, a newspaper boy, a bar mitzvah, and of various other issues. From the rural area a student may have had experiences as a 4-H contestant, a cross-country skier, a livestock judge, or a hiking guide. We have mentioned only a few possibilities—they are more numerous than persons. Just give a few minutes thought to your past activities and many topics will come to mind. Of course, you may not be able to use all of the topics for your classroom assignments, but surely you will find some that can be transformed into interesting discourses.

What appears commonplace and pedestrian to you may be exciting and uniquely interesting to others. So you have never flown in a 747 airplane; you have never visited the West Indies; but you did spend a week in the wilderness of the Adirondacks or the Cascades, and you can tell us how not to pitch a tent when it is raining. Or you participated in several political campaigns for small political organizations and can give us your assessment of the American ethical and moral condition. While these ideas are a few examples of what you can do with your background, however uninteresting it seems to you, there are even more topics that will allow you to speak with confidence.

We rarely think of the opportunity to talk about books we have read, plays and movies we have seen, music we have heard, or jobs we have held. One of the most interesting monologues we heard in a class was when a student spoke of her job as editor of a fugitive political newspaper. Stories of harassment, difficulties with meeting deadlines, finding a printer, and getting ads kept our attention throughout the talk. Although the subject was rather intimate to her, it was interesting and alive for us. During the 1960s Alex Haley, coauthor of *The Autobiography of Malcolm X*, traveled around the United States lecturing on Afro-American genealogy. It became a classic oration, combining Haley's skill as a storyteller with his personal experience. The fact that he had found the village of his African ancestors after tedious investigations in London, Washington, and Bathurst, Gambia, made his public communication interesting, provocative, and informative.

Public discourses are required in almost every phase of professional life. The person who becomes a teacher, physician, communications director for a corporation, sales representative, or labor negotiator will be called upon to present discourses on general or specialized subjects. Newspapers and other information sources provide us with a vast amount of data on subjects as far ranging as medicine and the occult practices of India. Availability of topics and information should not prevent anyone in contemporary society from speaking on numerous topics. In addition to the press, electronic media bombard us with a catalog of economic, political, and military issues. Thus, the personal experiences of every professional person are truly limitless. Whereas our knowledge might be secondary, we live in an age when it is more than ever before possible to check our information with additional nonrelated sources.

The following two student speeches were given in communication classes very similar to the class that you are attending. These are speeches delivered to an undergraduate public speaking class at the State University of New York at Buffalo. This class consisted of 20 students representing a wide variety of individual interests and specializations. As you read these two speeches, notice how the topics emerged out of personal experiences and observations.

These speeches are printed by permission of Reva Betha and Rita Matter.

Using the Mass Media
by Reva W. Betha

The fact that we come here every Tuesday and Thursday is an indication that we want to become better informed—we want to acquire knowledge. Everyone has a right to knowledge—not just from textbooks and classroom lectures but from the world we live in.

You have a right to know what went on in Washington today, what went on in city hall, on the street where you live, and across the world for that matter.

Obviously, we can't run around the world gathering our own news.

We have to depend on someone else to inform us. We depend on mass media. By mass media I mean, of course, radio, television, and newspapers. Marshall McLuhan, in his book, "Gutenberg Galaxy," calls us a "print culture" because we are dependent on mass media for our information. How well does mass media do the job? When you pick up the newspaper, do you read the news, or do you read someone's views on the news?

It has been claimed that all news reporting is, inevitably, interpretation. Nadeau calls it "slanting."[1] Slanting is when a reporter reports the full story but colors it in such a way (by his choice of adjectives and adverbs, for instance) that he is able to manipulate the impressions and inferences you draw from the story.

The business periodical "Advertising Age" reports that newspapers derive 70 percent of their revenue from advertisers, and only 30 percent from subscribers.[2] So, who are the newspapers going to try to please? Not you and me, the subscribers! We only provide 30 percent of their revenue. Newspapers are in business to make money. They aren't going to print any story or take any position that would offend an advertiser. How are they going to please the advertisers? By withholding news, and by printing slanted versions of the news.

Television doesn't inform us any better. News viewing demands visual literacy. The nature of TV is such that to a viewer a program may appear as a continuously unfolding narrative, and we fail to see the quick film cutting that has been done.[3] This film cutting is called editing, so that the story we see is not exactly what the photographer photographed but what someone wants us to see. That "someone" is the network owners, the advertisers, or some powerful political group. If you would like to read about film cutting, an article can be found in the magazine, America, May 22, 1971 issue.

The media draws a curtain of obscurity around the news. Exaggeration (or at least emphasis) and selection are in the very nature of reporting. Objectivity in reporting, therefore, will best be achieved by having many viewpoints and reports available. They tend to be mutually self-correcting.

How do you receive the news? Do you watch the same TV news program every day? Are you among those people who believe if it wasn't on the 6 o'clock news, it didn't happen?

In Buffalo we receive news programs from the three major

[1] Ray E. Nadeau, A Modern Rhetoric of Speech-Communication, Reading, Mass.: Addison–Wesley, 1972, p. 26.

[2] Advertising Age, September 22, 1969, p. 51.

[3] America, May 22, 1971, pp. 541–542.

national TV networks, but we have only two daily newspapers.

If you really want to be informed, read other major newspapers, such as the *New York Times,* the *Washington Post,* the *Toronto Star,* and read news magazines, such as *Time* and *Newsweek.* Lift the curtain of obscurity. Look at the news from other viewpoints.

Dizzy, the Cockeyed Squirrel
by Rita "Reggi" Matter (Copyright © by Rita Matter)

Have you ever wondered what you would do to occupy your idle time, if you were suddenly stricken "immobile" with an incureable disease, and told that you had but nine months to live?

This is the problem that confronted my husband and me when his aunt came to live with us in mid-Summer of '71. She had been told by Physicians that she was suffering from an incureable disease called "Milo Fibrosis," which simply means, she had "no blood."

The nature of the disease is such that it also meant she would be subjected to an endless number of blood transfusions. At first, monthly; then, weekly; and finally, daily: until such time that her veins would collapse and she would be unable to tolerate the needed transfusions.

But, what could we do, we wondered, to help her through this trying period? Naturally, such bad news was not only emotionally disturbing to her, but created complete disinterest in life.

Believe it or not, a course that I had enrolled in that Summer, turned out to be a "blessing in disguise!" It was a Sociology course concerned with Animal Behavior. We were studying from a textbook by Roger Brown, and the various studies conducted relative to the Starling.

Behaviorists theorize that Starlings would seem to have an innate mechanism whereby they can learn to recognize their own species. By being able to do this, they can then determine how many Starlings are in a given territory. This process is called, *territorialism.* As a matter of fact, it is also believed that when we see Starlings gathering on roof tops at the end of a day, what they are literally doing is, *taking a head count,* to see just how many Starlings there are in proportion to the food supply. And, if there should be an over-abundance of birds, they are forced to migrate.

The content of the course intrigued me to such a degree that class discussion soon became the topic of conversation in our home.

I decided to fabricate a class project and enlist the assistance of our aunt. She would test the validity of these studies and make a mental documentation of the events of the day. Certain criteria would have to be met. The project was constructed and successfully resulted in *the creation of a new interest in life around her, an extension of life within her.*

But it wasn't until the Fall of the year, that we fully realized that each "season" presented a new experience, for one day, a little *squirrel invaded "our territory."*

As it happens, our home is situated on a corner lot which is completely surrounded by trees. HUGE fully-grown Maple trees border the corner, almost up to the driveway. At this point there sits an ENORMOUS Pine tree. On the opposite side of the drive grows a much shorter Pine, giving an asymmetrical look to the setting. This is because, a GIGANTIC Weeping Willow towers not only over the Pine tree, but over the drive, and over our home as well, almost serving as an umbrella.

When our aunt called to me one morning to *"quick! bring the camera!"* it was because the little squirrel was literally flipping from maple tree to maple tree, all around the lot, then, on to the GREAT Pine, over the driveway, and into the Willow. And, as if that were not enough, he dangled by his tail from a limb of the tree and tormented the dog who barked incessantly at his performance! Then back to the GREAT Pine he flipped, but this time, he began to BOUNCE, from limb to limb, (*as if on a feathered pillow*), from the top of the Pine to its very bottom! Up he scampered and down he bounced, over and over again! *He was having a ball . . . when all of a sudden,* he bounced so hard that he bounced *OUT OF THE TREE* and on to the concrete drive, and there he lay!

"What a pity," our aunt exclaimed, "he must be terribly hurt!" We thought of several things "I" might do to help him, but, since neither of us knew anything at all about squirrels, *we feared he might be dangerous!!*

We decided to "sit tight" and see what developed, when suddenly, *from out of nowhere,* a second squirrel appeared. 'ROUND and 'ROUND our playful friend he scampered, then, he would STOP, PEER at him and scamper around him again. Each time he stopped, he would peer at him from a different angle, as if to say, *"come on fella, get up, you can't be ALL THAT HURT!!"*

It seemed an eternity before the squirrel sprang to his feet, but when he did, he was so *"DIZZY"* he kept falling back down! It was hilarious!! When he finally managed to stay afoot, he *walked "COCKEYED",* down the drive, up past the Fitch's house and disappeared into the forest with his friend.

Several days passed, and when *"DIZZY"* did not return, we

believed that surely *he must have died!* Then early one morning, to our aunt's delight, he came scooting up the driveway, past our home and into our neighbor's yard; for behind their garage had been growing, all summer, FIVE beautifully tall sunflowers. They were at least 6 feet high!! Much taller than I!! As we watched curiously, he began *chewing the stalk at the base of the plant.* He chewed and chewed, until, we believed, he would not have the strength to chew anymore! It was a good days work before the beautiful sunflower toppled to the ground, but when this was accomplished, he simply scooted away and left it lying on the ground!

For FIVE days he repeated this process, and each time he would disappear into the forest leaving his day's work behind.

What could this *"silly"* creature possibly have in mind, we wondered? Surely he must have some sort of plan. We were soon to discover what that plan was to be, when on the morning of the sixth day, *"DIZZY" returned with a "helper."* We couldn't believe our eyes! To our amazement, they SUNK their teeth into the HUGE golden face of the Sunflower, and together they *tugged and pulled, tugged and pulled,* all the way across the big lot, down the driveway, past the Fitch's house, and into the deep woods!

For many days our aunt was entertained as she sat and watched our busy friends work feverishly as they *tugged and pulled* the Sunflowers home in preparation for the COLD Winter months ahead.

But before the cold had left the ground, when part of the "Good" had succumbed to Winter and Spring had yet to revive the rest, I reflected upon my experiences in the past. It seemed to me that the *"best"* of these should be shared with others, and this is what I have tried to do. So, if you should be walking through a bookstore one day, and you happen to notice a book entitled, *"DIZZY, THE COCKEYED SQUIRREL" by Rita "Reggi" Matter,* I hope that you will buy a copy of my book to read to your children.

There is a saying, "experience is the greatest teacher," but in order for you to find the topics in your experience, you must be an attentive listener, an avid reader, and a person who seeks information. Whatever your experiences, they can usually provide you with interesting subjects for classroom presentation. However, most communication occasions will demand more than just *any* subject—you will need an *appropriate* subject. This means that an additional task is required of the would-be communicator. Rather than select a topic merely because of personal experience, the communicator must find one suitable to the situation and subject as well.

Relevant to subject

The occasion may well provide a communicator with his or her best opportunity for choosing a topic for discussion. In some cases a person is asked to give a talk under the heading of a general subject or theme. If this is ever your case, then you can rely upon your experiences with that particular subject to help you discover an appropriate topic. Take time to think about the theme. Which of your experiences helps you to relate to it? Whereas your experiences may cover all that you have read and your professional activities, academic involvements, and social interactions, at every level, it is still possible that you may discover an area where your experiences have not carried you! If such is the case, then the best alternative would be to learn as much as possible concerning that subject before you attempt to give a speech about it. That means that you will learn *selectively*. When you deliberately set out to learn selectively about a subject, you will be on your way to doing your part for effective communication. The ability to learn selectively is the chief attribute of the communicator who is confronted with a topic he had little knowledge of heretofore. Telling a communicator to learn all he or she can about a subject is pretentious as well as impossible. We ask you to review as much of the subject as you possibly can, but learn *selectively* so that your time will be spent. Your audience prefers to hear "in depth" on one aspect of a subject rather than sitting while a speaker rambles on unrelatedly about the topic. John Dean, a former White House attorney during the embattled Nixon years, gave numerous speeches at high fees on one subject, "What Caused Watergate?" It was a subject he knew intimately because of personal and professional involvement. He conveyed a sense of moderation, sincerity, and plain speaking that interested his audiences. Too many communicators give the evidence of "much learning" in their discourses. What you learn, learn well; but no one expects you to learn everything about computer science before you give a speech on the Fortran. This kind of learning is experimental and helps you to prepare a topic from experience that is relevant to the subject. McCabe and Bender suggest the following benefits for the communicator who chooses an interesting subject.[1]

---

[1] Bernard McCabe, Jr., and Coleman Bender, *Speaking Is a Practical Matter* (Boston: Holbrook Press, 1968), p. 29.

Benefits for Speaker

1. Since he or she is already interested in the subject, the speaker is motivated to seek out an abundance of detailed information and ideas on the topic.
2. With this depth of knowledge, the speaker can easily use greater selectivity for the content of the speech.
3. By not being forced to exhaust all his or her knowledge during the speech, the speaker has a self-assuring cushion of reserve information.

Benefits for Listener

1. The listener is confronted by a poised, confident speaker.
2. The listener hears the delivery of a speaker who wants to communicate.
3. The listener learns from the knowledge of the speaker, thereby supplementing his or her own interest.

Relevant to communicator

Only *you* really know who you are. Your real aspirations, aims, hopes, and anxieties are only partially known to your most intimate relations. Because you know the most about yourself, you can see the value of looking into your background as a person, an optimist, a pessimist, a reformer, a revolutionary, a conservative, an athlete, a poet, or a budding philosopher for experiences that will contribute to a topic for discussion. To have something to communicate is one of the finest human privileges, and each of you is able to share with others some portion of your experience as a person. Thus, as a speaker, a communication source, you bring certain talents, skills, and experiences to the communication scene that will be helpful in formulating a topic. Furthermore, you bring experiences only you can share with an audience! Perhaps you were present at antiwar demonstrations or pro-administration rallies or antiracist marches in Boston. You might think that thousands of other people were also present at these public demonstrations and therefore you have nothing to say. However, no one had the particular experiences you had and you undoubtedly have something to say to the audience that only you can say.

Action experiences of the kind described above regarding the demonstrations are more common than we imagine; but as you develop ability to make it a part of your topic selection, other areas of knowledge and experience will also come to your aid.

The average person engages in some form of conversation about 80 percent of the time during the day. This means, of course, that a fertile source of topics for speech communication is the conversational activities we have with others. Were you to make a list of topics discussed between you and others in a single day, a variety of themes would emerge. The questions you ask, those asked of you, and those you overhear each day could provide a sufficient reservoir of topics for communication. Our daily conversations may cover a broad range of subjects, such as politics, religions, geography, ecology, and philosophy. Experiences relevant to the communicator are only the things that have happened to you or that you have caused to happen. In conversation with others you have the experience of a vivid or dull discussion on some particular subject. Having ears that retain events is an advantage for the person who wants to be a good speaker. Henry David Thoreau once wrote of "eyes that see in nature"; ears that retain conversation are just as important in topic selection.

An audience appreciates a communicator who seems interested in his or her own message. Enthusiasm can be contagious. You probably have met people, friends, relatives, or colleagues who always appear to be enthusiastic. You get a psychological lift from just being around them. Take two professors at a university who appear on the surface to be equally good teachers. One does the job of teaching rather nonchalantly, making certain that she or he delivers proper lectures and leads appropriate discussions. The second professor enthusiastically engages in teaching activities and is also available to students for after-class discussions, tutorials, research guidance, and general counseling. She or he demonstrates interest in all students regardless of their academic progress. Which professor would you prefer to teach you? The second, of course. It is a fundamental truism that an enthusiastic communicator makes an interesting communicator.

Relevant to audience

In addition to experience relevant to subject and to speaker, topics may be provided by experiences relevant to the audience. Speech communication is audience concerned. Topics for speeches are often derived from the nature of the audience to be addressed. Thus, when Malcolm X addressed a black group in Detroit purporting to represent the grassroots of the community, his subject was

"Message to the Grassroots," demonstrating rhetorical awareness and audience sensitivity. Subjects related to audiences are to be found in some of the great pieces of interpersonal communication. William Kunstler, defense lawyer for the Attica Prison brothers, might speak to a college group on "College Students and Law and Order." Such a topic becomes audience related in this case, whereas if given before a community ski cub, its derivation is *less likely* to be audience related. Politicians endeavor to master the art of finding topics relevant to audiences because what interests people does hold their attention. Attention retention is the first principle of audience control.

In using the audience as a topic source, the speaker relies upon his or her skill to make relevant comments on short notice. Comments growing out of the audience can be advantageous to the communication situation if the audience is unfamiliar with the speaker. *Audience texture,* by which we mean the total compositional characteristics of the audience, provides each speaker with clues to possible topics. Looking at the audience texture, the perceptive speaker can think of exciting ways to utilize the special features of the audience for topical selection. Inasmuch as all audiences contain several components, there is seldom an occasion when the creative speaker cannot use elements of the audience to build a topic or theme. Some of the areas within an audience that might provide topics are listed below:

Possible dimensions
Theme interest of the audiences
Political interests of the audiences
Sex of the audiences
Size of the audiences
Age of the audiences

We say possible dimensions because this list is not exhaustive; also, the speaker who concentrates solely on these dimensions has the capacity to become a demagogue. Lloyd Bitzer's concept of rhetorical situation is especially appropriate in considering themes and topics within audiences. The sincere communicator finds his topic in the exigence present within the rhetorical situation. Without an exigence there can be no rhetorical situation. (See our discussion of Bitzer's concept of rhetorical situation in Chapter 1.) Thus, when a Chicano spokesman presents his case for the investigation of police brutality in the barrios to interested listeners, a rhetorical situation exists. For the communicator to choose a topic related to audience composition but not to the exigence would be avoidance of the issue. In no case is the absolution of the issue justified in public discourse, particularly if the immediate effect of the neglect is to produce irrational behavior on the part of the audiences.

Finding topics in our experiences that are relevant to audiences does not mean that the communicator should never prepare until he sees the audience! The better speakers are always preparing; they read a news story, a journal article, a magazine editorial, see a movie, attend a political rally, and take mental notes as they do. However, it is possible to find a theme or topic in the audiences days or weeks before the speech is given, providing you know something fundamental about the group either through previous involvement or through established channels such as brochures, annual reports, and news releases. For instance, if you were asked to give a talk before the Chamber of Commerce, you should antici-pate certain interests and concerns before you meet the group. Similarly, if you were scheduled to speak before the board of regents or the board of trustees of your college, you should have some idea of their fundamental concerns by reference to charters, state con-stitutions, or by their consistent actions. However, in situations where the structure of the group is fluid and highly unstable in terms of shifting audiences, ideas, adherences, and allegiances, topic selection could not successfully be made days in advance. Whereas audiences such as the Chamber of Commerce and boards of trustees, among others, may have a fundamental stability that allows for topic selection in advance, at times prior topic selection does not work in these cases because of crisis events or spontaneous special happenings. The spontaneous mass-happening scenes, such as occur on college campuses, are more susceptible to an extemporaneous finding of topics. As was previously indicated, the effective com-municator is also a good student who knows the issues and studies the current literature and arguments relevant to the anticipated audiences.

Among the issues that must be considered are *audience interest* and *vital significance*. William James once wrote that people attend to what interests them and people are interested in what they attend to. This is nowhere any truer than in the relationship between a communicator and an audience. Thus, conscientious communicators will choose, if the choice is theirs, a speech topic that has meaning for the interests of the group addressed. In the event that people have come together in an audience around a central issue or exigence, it is incumbent upon speakers to address themselves to that interest. One mark of a perceptive communicator is the ability to ascertain what the exigence is and then how it fits into the world view of the audience. What is it that she or he knows that is of interest to the people? What special point of view can the communicator bring to bear upon the question at hand? Is the communicator qualified to deal intelligently with the problem that provokes the audience? What are people's needs, and how can one address them? How can one communicate more effectively a certain point to them? A college student in the communication department of a major university was asked to address a campus rally on the limits of free speech within a democratic society. When he accepted the invitation of the leading radical student association, he faced several problems: (1) What did he already know about this topic? (2) What personal resources could he call upon? (3) How would he isolate his topic? (4) What purpose would he try to achieve? Because his audience had already exhibited an interest in this topic his task was made exceedingly easier. He decided that he would entitle his talk "Free Speech: Students and Democracy." Then he would (a) narrow his subject to an area he could speak intelligently on, (b) call upon his Master's thesis research on free speech, and (c) demonstrate how free speech and democracy relate to students.

All of us face these kinds of difficulties when called upon to address an audience. As communicators you must make judgements about your *knowledge* of a given subject, the *special personal skills, talents,* or *experiences* available to you on certain issues, how to *isolate a topic,* and *what goals* you will try to achieve once you have secured the interests of the audience.

Just as you might react to a report that *your* house is on fire than to a report that *a* house is on fire in another city, so it is with topics of *vital significance* to audiences. You might get involved if the report indicated that the fire was in your next-door neighbor's house. But *your* own house would certainly cause immediate reaction. Audiences can sometimes be shown the vital significance of a topic where they had not seen the connection beforehand. When a communicator can make the necessary rhetorical connections, he may be able to provide audiences with reason to become vitally concerned. If the fire report to you had been that your neighbor's house is on fire and *your* house is likely to start burning at any moment, a clear connection will have been made to your vital interests.

There are some important questions to be asked by the communicator. What will discourse mean to the audience? How will it affect their behavior of condition? These types of questions seek to establish the significance of the topic for the audience. People are more inclined to listen to a talk that has particular bearing upon them than to one that has little or no relationship to their lives or livelihood. A member of the Black Student Union might find the choice difficult between a lecture on urban sociology or a speech on the subject "Black Students and the Educational Inadequacy of White Universities." Similarly, a Chicano student might spend an entire night working on posters announcing a speech by Cesar Chavez or Corky Gonzales. It is fairly safe to say, though, that few of the students would be especially eager to hear talks about the anxieties of housewives in suburbia. We give our energy to what we are interested in, particularly if the thing or event that interests us meets immediate needs, whether subsistent, political, or social. As we use our energy preparing for talks, so we give our attention to those communications that are *meant for us*. To say "meant for us" is to give voice to the emotion-cognitive elements possessed by each one of us at a given time. These elements may vary from one day to the next, but when a certain combination of these elements occurs, our discourses that speak to those needs are of more vital significance to us than at other times. All of us are inclined to be interested in those things that hold our attention, and more so if they are integrally tied to our conceptions of ourselves. The more the topic arouses strong sympathies in the audiences, the greater their interest. Winston Churchill understood this more than most speakers of this century.

In the event the audiences demonstrate indifference, the speaker or monologist has to state his vital significance. One good sign, then, that a talk does not have vital significance to an audience might be indifference. If it is not considered vital by an audience, then it is often impossible to arouse strong support for the topic. In this case, artificial creation of interest must be avoided because it only returns to haunt the creator.

While there may be several audiences in any given communication occasion, you usually can conjecture regarding the general attitudes of the audience as a whole. Inasmuch as the audience is the final arbiter regarding the talk, you should consider vital significance as a principal criterion for topic selection. For the most part the vital significance is clearly recognizable to an audience when the issue is initially stated, if well stated. Audiences that are not aroused by the well-stated theme of a discourse are signaling that what you are saying is not of vital significance. Each of us knows of cases where the communicator's topic was not vital to the audience. If you want to choose a topic that is of vital significance to your audience and do not succeed, this is often an indication that you have not understood the collective identity of the audience.

But while it is a fact that topics that have appeal to an audience's vital concerns will create more interest than those that have little or no significance for the audience, the communicator has to proceed with care. You should not become a captive of your audience. It is true, as Chaim Perelman and others have observed, that the audience often creates the speaker, but the communicator always has to stand beyond the boundaries of demagoguery that are so frequently the result of a communicator created by an audience. The sincere person is wise to get the best topic that can be found for the occasion and audience without "putting himself or the audience on" by slavishly trying to appeal to them when he or she knows there is no way to get immediate acceptance. Naturally, we all hope to have our ideas accepted but never at the cost of abnegating all ethical principles. Honesty and conviction are the cornerstones of a meaningful communication between human beings.

There is probably nothing so potent as an idea presented forcefully before an audience of human beings. Its force is not the power of guns and bombs, but of the rational-emotional responses of human beings. Questions are raised, thoughts are pondered, and answers are given, as reaction to ideas. Without the introduction and presence of ideas before audiences, the physiological responses would never occur. Each student of human communication has the potential to spark other persons to action by the power of ideas relevant to a particular subject, one's self, or one's audiences.

There is absolutely no reason for you to be without an interesting, or even vital, topic for any speech you are called upon to make in this class or in any other social, business, or political setting.

The ideas are out there like diamonds in the meadow waiting for you to find and make good use of them. You are on your way and we are right with you.

FOR STUDENT APPLICATION

1. The selection of a good topic is essential for effective classroom communication. The topic serves as a guide; it provides some direction to the communication event. Review the current issue of your school or community newspaper. Write a list of subjects that are prominent and share your list with your fellow students.

2. Read a local newspaper and list the front-page stories for one week. Contact the newspaper editor and ask how these stories were selected. What criteria did the editor use for the selection? Report your findings to your class.

3. Select a general topic that could be presented to a variety of audiences. List some ideas for communicating your topic to the following audiences:
    a. A college group composed of freshmen
    b. A college group composed of seniors
    c. A community women's social club
    d. A community group composed of businessmen
   What are some of the different ways you would approach your topic depending upon the type of audience?

4. Select any organization and determine the persuasive appeals used by that organization to increase its membership. What were the most frequent appeals used by the organization?

5. Review the full-page advertisements in popular magazines. What are the most frequent appeals found in the ads?

6. Select a specific category of advertised products such as food, automobiles, and cosmetics. Do you find similar persuasive appeals across different products? Collect five or more ads for the same general category, for example, collect five ads for automobiles. Do you find similar persuasive appeals used across different ads for the same product? Why do you think the appeals differ across categories, but contain similarities when the product category is the same?

Readings

BOULDING, KENNETH. *The Image: Knowledge in Life and Society.* University of Michigan Press, 1956.

GOFFMAN, ERVING. *The Presentation of Self in Everyday Life.* Garden City, N.Y.: Doubleday, 1959.

GOFFMAN, ERVING. *Behavior in Public Places.* Garden City, N.Y.: Doubleday, 1963.

TOFFLER, ALVIN. *The Culture Consumers.* New York: St. Martin's Press, 1964.

WEINBERG, MEYER. *TV in America.* New York: Ballantine Books, 1962.

5 The Contemporary Audience of the Speech

WHAT YOU CAN EXPECT:

Chapter 5 focuses on the contemporary audience of public communication.

This chapter provides the reader with information concerning the identifying characteristics of audiences, indicates how to utilize audience analysis, and suggests responses to your messages. The target of communication is the audience and how we try to help you communicate effectively to your target audience.

Chapter Outline

Just as a book without a reader is worthless, a speech presented by the most dynamic and most credible speaker is worthless without an audience. The term *audience* is taken from the Latin word *audire* meaning "to hear." But to many students the term *audience* remains a rather abstract, amorphous grouping of humanity to which a message is directed. The reception of communication has received scholarly attention, notably during the listening fad of the fifties and more recently in terms of psychological audience analysis.[1] Ineffective listening has been suggested as a major cause for breakdowns in the communication process of most interactive situations: parents-children, teacher-students, employer-employees, doctor-patient, male-female, husband-wife, blacks-whites, United States-Russia—the list seems endless. Another frequent communication gap occurs between the speaker and audience, and ineffective listening is often cited as the cause. The audience's influence upon a speaker, called "feedback," may be clearly seen in the effects of various listening modes, listener attention, and listener interest of a particular message or topic. In Chapter 3 we emphasized the importance of developing good listening habits and skills to increase the effectiveness of the communication process. The present chapter discusses the interactions of the speaker and audience and the major focus is on the audience's reception of the speaker's communication. The basic recognition of the importance we give to the audience has an ancient heritage. Aristotle noted in the *Rhetoric* that "a speech is the joint result of three things—the speaker, his subject, and the person addressed. . . ."[2] Thus, our discussion involves interaction relationships between (1) contemporary audiences and speakers, (2) contemporary audiences and the topic or subject, and (3) contemporary audience analysis.

Breakdown of Speaker-Audience Restraints

Even before the speaker is physically in front of his audience, there is a mental presence of that speaker in the minds of the audience. This is the familiar "sizing up the situation" process. These are audience expectations that occur before the speaker begins. Perhaps a familiar experience of students will help clarify. Imagine that it is the first day of class in your speech communication course. As

---

[1] One of the more popular works that received wide acceptance in the fifties was Ralph G. Nichols and Leonard A. Stevens, *Are You Listening?* (New York: McGraw-Hill, 1957). More recently scholarly attention is evidenced by Theodore Clevenger, Jr., *Audience Analysis* (Indianapolis: Bobbs-Merrill, 1966), and Paul D. Holtzman, *The Psychology of Speakers' Audiences* (Glenview, Ill.: Scott, Foresman, 1970).

[2] Lane Cooper, *The Rhetoric of Aristotle* (Englewood Cliffs, N.J.: Prentice-Hall, 1960), p. 16.

the students begin seating themselves, there are preconceived notions about what the professor will be like. Some of these preconceptions become attitudinal, that is, some become evaluative. The professor is young or old, is male or female, is new or established, is difficult or easy, and so on. During the chatter of making new acquaintances or reestablishing friendships, some of the preconceptions become reinforced. For example, perhaps you have heard that the professor is a young male, nice looking, but that he is also supposed to be difficult. If you hear these statements, or similar ones, your previous information is modified, reinforced, or altered in some way. As other statements are added, your informational storehouse increases and the total information you have is then compared with the professor when he appears. After the first day of class your *preconceived beliefs* about the professor are modified further in terms of what you *personally experienced.*

The speaker should always be aware of audience preconceptions. This awareness can help the speaker minimize the negative features associated with a particular topic or a particular viewpoint. Several factors that occur with sufficient frequency to merit careful attention are combined to constitute the "demographic characteristics" of your audience.

Demographic Characteristics of Audiences

The term *demography* was originally used to mean the study of people in terms of statistics concerning population, birthrates, death rates, marriage customs, health information, employment, and so on. Demographic analysis of audiences simply means to find out as much information about your audience as is possible and practical. Effective communication of messages can be facilitated by an understanding of audience membership. The age, socioeconomic level, educational level, sex, geographical representation, racial makeup, and religious views can have a significant impact on the reception of your message.

While we communicate routinely when we greet someone or when we talk during a meal, or merely visit with family and friends, there are occasions in which careful audience analysis will increase our effectiveness. We communicate in order to share our ideas with others, and often we communicate in order to attempt to persuade others to our point of view.

Who Is Your Audience?

One of the first important things we might mention is that the audience of a college speech class is an artificial one in several respects. Although the speech class audience has common characteristics of age, geographical similarity, and (hopefully) a common interest in communication, it is different from an audience in the "real world." For example, in order to distribute the allotted time equally, your instructor may arbitrarily limit your speaking time to a few minutes. Often students are asked to address themselves to assigned topics and, inevitably, members of your college audience will be more interested in some topics than in others. In many respects your classroom audience is a "captive audience" very different from a "real-world audience." We could list many differences and so could you, but the point here is that one of the major characteristics of effective communication is *adaptation*. How you adapt to your audience, regardless if it is the captive audience of the classroom or the real-world audience, will have a decided effect on how successful your communication will be. Thus, since adapting to your audience is vital, knowledge about that audience is necessary. Usually you will know the general composition of your audience before you speak. If you are invited to speak to the Young Democrats, the local historical society, or the local League of Women Voters, or the local PTA—in all these examples the membership of the organization is generally known. The breakdown of the speaker-audience constraints is easier when the audience composition is known ahead of time because you can plan your presentation specifically for that audience.

Audience Analysis

The *size* of the audience will have an effect on your presentation. Whereas it would be quite easy to be informal with an audience of 20 or 25, most speakers would become more formal with an audience of 75 to 100. The *sex* of your audience is an important consideration. For example, even in this age of women's liberation, a speech concerning automobile repair probably would require a different presentation to a predominately female audience than if the audience were composed of all males. Likewise, a presentation should be geared to the *age* of the audience members. Aristotle noted more than 2000 years ago that age was a factor to consider, that younger people tend to hold liberal views and that older people tend to hold conservative views. There are other variables to consider and the ones we have mentioned may not be critical for your particular presentation. The point to remember is that these various factors should be considered in the audience analysis process. We have already mentioned three: size, sex, and age. Other factors to be considered are: political affiliation, socioeconomic level, education, ethnic and cultural background, race, and religion.

Most attempts at audience analysis are far from exact or accurate. In the real world of practical affairs the closest approximation to accuracy in determining audience preconceptions are the professional pollsters, such as the Gallup Polls or the Harris Polls, but obviously such professionals would be appropriate only if your audience was a national one. However, even in the artificial situation of giving a speech to other speech students in the form of an assignment, audience analysis can help you to make a more effective presentation.

Using Audience Feedback

So far the focus of our discussion has centered on preparations and audience analysis prior to his or her public communication. But how does the contemporary speaker know if the audience members are *interested* in his or her message? And even if what you communicate is interesting, how do you know they *understand* your message? And if they are interested and understand, how do you know they *accept* the position you take in your message? The answer to these questions is that you cannot know, not for sure at least. But regardless of the fact that you can never "get inside the heads" of your audience, you can observe their reactions or responses to your communication. The positive (rewarding) or negative (punishing) reactions of your audience—their attention or inattention, smiles or frowns, applause or boos, and so forth—are called communication "feedback." Depending upon the audience and the situation, most of the feedback is provided by *nonverbal behavior,* such as facial expression and body movement, but feedback can be *vocal* reinforcement, such as "uh-huh," "mmmm," and "hmmm," or *verbal,* such as "yeah," "that's right," "right on," and "say it again brother." All forms of audience feedback, both positive and negative, provide the observant and sensitive speaker with the opportunity to make necessary modifications and adjustments of his or her message. Audience feedback thus provides the public communicator with instant evaluative reactions that can be used to increase message effectiveness.

Feedback adjustments range from the simple to the complex and the public communicator must develop receptiveness to the information supplied. For example, if some audience members in the back of the room indicate they cannot hear you clearly, it is quite simple to increase your volume; or if you are speaking too fast, you can consciously decrease your rate of delivery. However, the negative feedback of disagreement may be more difficult to correct. Perhaps you need to repeat a previous point, rephrase a statement, give additional clarifying information, provide a summary review of your major arguments, present an additional example or illustration, or add a new argument. If you are not entirely successful in overcoming negative feedback, remember that you may be misinterpreting the feedback. Misinterpretation is frequent, particularly since you are attempting to make inferences about internal states of feeling on the basis of overt physical behavior. But audience behavior remains the most practical aid to the contemporary speaker for adjusting the message to the needs of the audience. As we suggest in Chapter 8, the speaker who uses an outline effectively will be able to adjust to audience feedback, whereas the manuscript speech that is read or the memorized speech prevents the communicator from making feedback adjustments. We shall consider the advantages and disadvantages of different types of delivery in Chapter 10. In relatively informal extemporaneous communication settings you may find that the best approach for using feedback is to use the direct approach. Thus, you may want to create an informal atmosphere by stating "Feel free to interrupt me if you have a question," or "Let me know if I'm not being clear," or "Feel free to ask me for an additional example if you wish." Of course, one must be prepared to deal with such interruptions, and in more formal situations these may be inappropriate. However, even in formal situations you usually can omit such interchanges and yet provide the alternative of asking the audience for their reactions at the end of your presentation. Or perhaps you would want to provide time for a question and answer period at the conclusion.

One way or another you need to know how well your audience received you.

Of course, in those public communication situations where the receivers or audience members are not physically present, the feedback will be delayed. Delayed feedback is illustrated in the typical radio or television discourse as well as in all printed matter, such as magazines, newspapers, and books. The actual delayed feedback in these cases are the ratings, charts, market research, public opinion polls, fan mail, and special survey research. The delay obviously prevents immediate correction or modification, but even delayed feedback can be significant in the planning of additional public messages, which can be altered in accordance with the feedback.

The effective public communicator recognizes the importance of feedback and develops his or her perceptions to interpret audience feedback accurately. Conscious attempts to utilize feedback information increases the probability of effective communication.

Analyzing the Contemporary Audience

It has long been recognized that the process of communication is a reciprocal process involving the interaction of speaker and listener. In most communication situations the speaker will attempt to modify the audience's beliefs, attitudes, and behavior toward some predetermined goal. But the good speaker should consider not only himself but also primarily the needs or purposes of his audience. This means that you must analyze your audience so that you will be sensitive to their needs or purposes. Kenneth Burke calls this process the *identification* of yourself with your audience and the *identification* of your audience with you and your message.[3] While such identification approaches of establishing "common ground" between speaker and audience are often useful, we urge caution of introductory civilities, particularly if such civilities are not clearly honest; for example, when a person says, "I'm happy to be invited to this renowned institution and I'm both humbled and honored by your invitation to speak," or "Your fame is widespread; students here have both excelled in scholarship and sports," or "Your annual

[3] Kenneth Burke, *The Rhetoric of Motives* (New York: Prentice-Hall, 1950). For a summary of Burke's theory, see Daniel Fogarty, *Roots for a New Rhetoric,* Teachers College Studies in Education (New York: Bureau of Publications, Teachers College, Columbia University, 1959).

lecture series is highly valued in academic circles and I'll try to maintain those high standards in my remarks to you this evening." These introductory statements are flattering, but be careful of the quicksand of phony flattering civilities. Make sure that the first impression you create in your opening remarks is positive. Some attempted flattery can create negative impressions, which you would want to avoid; for example, the speaker who addressed a group of Afro-Americans by saying "You people sure can sing" or the speaker who attempted to identify with an Irish-American group by saying, "I'm not Irish, but people say I have an Irish temper." In both cases such statements probably were demeaning to both the communicator and the audience. A communicator can increase the effectiveness probability of his message by analyzing the audience, but phony flattery is perceived as dishonest.

So how can you utilize audience analysis to increase your chances of effectively communicating your message to others? We suggest that there are no absolute guidelines for conducting an analysis of the contemporary audience because every audience is "new," every audience is to some extent "different"; audiences are composed of people who are "constantly changing," and every new, different audience must be considered in terms of a particular communication situation. However, in general we believe that answers to the following questions may be helpful in most public communication interactions:

1. What is the general *age* level of your audience?
2. What is the *education* level of your audience?
3. How many people will attend the presentation (audience *size*)?
4. What is the dominant *religion* of your audience?
5. What is the *racial* makeup of your audience?
6. What is the dominant *employment* of your audience?
7. Is your audience composed of an *organized group*?
8. What are the *common interests* of your audience?
9. What are the *political views* of your audience?
10. Is your audience composed of more *males or females*?
11. Is your audience *for* or *against* your position on the topic?
12. Is the *situation* formal or informal?
13. Why is your audience meeting together (communication *purpose*)?
14. Where will the communication event take place (physical *setting*)?

15. What are the *time* limitations?
16. What is the *economic* status of your audience?

Although the list could easily be expanded, we believe the answers to these questions will generally help the speaker to analyze the contemporary audience. Thus, the list of questions is not intended to be a complete list. In addition, there will be some speaking situations that will make some of the questions less important than other situations. It is possible for some of the questions contained in the list to be unimportant for your specific communication situation. For example, the *sex* of your audience might be relatively unimportant if you were discussing the quality of your local community's drinking water. The *economic status* of members of your audience might not be important if you were discussing recent advances in cancer research. On the other hand, if you were asking for support of the Equal Rights Amendment, the *sex* of your audience members might be an important consideration, and if you were proposing an increase in social security taxes, the *economic status* might be important. In any given communication situation the characteristics of the particular audience should be known so you can modify your presentation and adapt it to your audience. An effective communicator will want to ask many of the questions we have suggested and attempt to analyze the contemporary audience before speaking to adapt the communication to the needs of the audience.

There are at least three major considerations for an audience analysis.

1. Plan your message so that you give members of your audience a sense of achievement or satisfaction.
2. Plan your message so that it appeals to the major or dominant groups connected with the audience.
3. Plan your message so that your information can be easily integrated with preconceived beliefs, attitudes, and values.

Achievement and satisfaction

Most humans derive some sense of achievement and satisfaction if the information they receive from a message can help them personally. Although it perhaps sounds selfish, each member really wants to know the answer to: "What's in it for me?" Thus, a speaker who clearly indicates how the content of his presentation will benefit members of the audience will be likely to receive the close attention of his audience.

Group memberships and affiliations

The speaker should attempt to discover the probable groups with which audience members are affiliated. People are frequently influenced to believe and behave in accordance with what they perceive to be in accordance with group norms. Even in this age of nonconformity it is difficult for most people to believe or behave counter to group norms. Each member of your audience probably belongs to several groups and often the goals of these various groups may be in conflict, but knowledge of group memberships and affiliations can help you design your message to be appropriate for the *dominant* group membership.

Preconceived beliefs, attitudes, and values

In 1957 Leon Festinger published a book called *Dissonance Theory.* Since that time his theory has received the support of hundreds of experimental studies. The basic idea has been called by various names (among others, "balance theory" and "congruity theory"), but the common principle is that there is a drive within humans toward consistency.[4]

Each of us tries to maintain a state of internal balance. If people we like have the same beliefs, attitudes, and values we have about objects or issues, then we have a feeling of balance; or if people we dislike have different beliefs, attitudes, and values than we have about objects or issues, we still have a balanced feeling. But if people we like have different beliefs, attitudes, and values or if people we dislike have the same beliefs, attitudes, and values as we have, then there exists a state of imbalance. For example, suppose the speaker is represented by *A;* the audience, by *B;* and the speech topic, by *X,* we would have the following situation diagrammed in Figure 3.

---

[4] For a review of related research in dissonance theory, see Chester A. Insko, *Theories of Attitude Change* (Englewood Cliffs, N.J.: Prentice-Hall, 1967), and Shel Feldman, ed., *Cognitive Consistency: Motivation Antecedents and Behavioral Consequences* (New York: Academic Press, 1966). For the origin of dissonance theory see Leon Festinger, *A Theory of Cognitive Dissonance* (Stanford, Calif.: Stanford University Press, 1957).

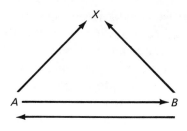

Figure 3

The model in Figure 3 applies the basic idea of balance in communication. This model, developed by Theodore Newcomb for interpersonal relationships, can be used in audience analysis.[5]

The speaker must keep in mind that the audience (B) has attitudes, beliefs, and values concerning the topic (X), and when the speaker (A) communicates to the audience, there will be some kind of feedback or response. This feedback or audience response can, of course, be either positive or negative. If the speaker considers the audience's probable beliefs, attitudes, and values, he will be more likely to receive positive feedback and his effectiveness will be more likely to increase.

The effective communicator constantly adjusts his message in accordance with the information he receives about his audience. The modification of his message continues even *during* his presentation as he adjusts his speech to the usually nonverbal feedback messages of his audience.

By adapting the message to the interests of the audience, the speaker will be more likely to obtain and maintain the audience's *attention.* James Winans has suggested that if one can get and hold attention, the probability of influencing your receiver is increased.[6]

The Boundaries of Audience Analysis

There are a number of limitations and boundaries in conducting an analysis of the contemporary audience. Suppose you are preparing a presentation for your classroom audience. Obviously you would not have the time or the resources to conduct an in-depth, com-

[5] Theodore M. Newcomb, "An Approach to the Study of Communicative Acts," *Psychological Review* (1953), pp. 60, 393–404.

[6] James A. Winans, *Public Speaking* (Englewood Cliffs, N.J.: Prentice-Hall, 1915).

prehensive analysis of all the possible variables connected to the interaction relationship. But you can carefully consider the time, place, occasion, rhetorical situation, possible preconceived attitudes, and general demographic characteristics of your audience. You can use the knowledge you gain from the analysis to design your message to appeal to your particular audience. Finally, by being aware of the importance of feedback and by adapting your message so that you demonstrate your reaction to that feedback, the message will be more likely to have the desired effect. The major way you will know if you have produced the desired effect during your presentation is your constant observation of the audience's *nonverbal* behavior. In fact, your own nonverbal cues are significant in producing an effective message and the next chapter will focus on a discussion of how these nonverbal elements affect you and your audience.

FOR STUDENT APPLICATION

1. How do you know that an audience has received your communicated message? Can you think of some ways to measure the effectiveness of your speech? Consider the politician who can measure his effectiveness in terms of *voting behavior*. But what about the preacher's sermon or a high school graduation speech? How can such speeches be assessed in terms of audience behavior?

2. Audience members resent wasting their time listening to a speaker who is not prepared. How can you demonstrate such preparation? Observe a speaking situation and look particularly for clues that indicate preparation. What did you find *demonstrated* the presence or absence of the speaker's preparation?

3. Work with two other members of your class and list elements of common interest among your class members. Compare your individual lists, then discuss your group's list with your class. What elements of common interest did you overlook? How can you judge the common interests of an audience?

4. Compare the differences in feedback obtained from the receiver in (1) a public political speech, (2) a television address, (3) a radio address, and (4) a casual conversation. What are the major differences? Discuss.

5. Recall the first day in this class and the other classes you are currently attending. In what ways were the audiences treated differently? Which approach did you prefer? Do you think the various instuctors used different techniques due to anticipated audience expectations?

6. Compare the verbal and nonverbal behavior of several different audiences (a classroom audience, a theater audience, a movie audience, a television audience, a radio audience, and a rock festival audience). What are the major verbal and nonverbal differences?

Readings

ANDERSON, MARTIN P.; NICHOLS, E. RAY, JR.; and BOOTH, HERBERT W. *The Speaker and His Audience: Dynamic Interpersonal Communication*, 2d ed. New York: Harper & Row, 1974.

BAUER, RAYMOND A. "The Audience." In ITHIEL DE SOLA POOL; FREDERICK W. FREY; WILBUR SCHRAMM; NATHAN MACCOBY; and EDWIN B. PARKER. *Handbook of Communication*. Skokie, Ill.: Rand McNally, 1973, pp. 141–152.

BAUER, RAYMOND A. "The Obstinate Audience." *American Psychologist* XIX (May 1964), pp. 319–328.

Clevenger, Theodore, Jr. *Audience Analysis*. Indianapolis: Bobbs-Merrill, 1966.

EISENSON, JON; AUER, J. JEFFREY; and IRWIN, JOHN V. *The Psychology of Communication*. Englewood Cliffs, N.J.: Prentice-Hall, 1963.

HOLLINGWORTH, HARRY L. *The Psychology of the Audience*. New York: American Book, 1935.

HOLTZMAN, PAUL D. *The Psychology of Speakers' Audiences*. Glenview, Ill.: Scott, Foresman, 1970.

SELDES, GILBERT V. *The Great Audience*. New York: Viking Press, 1950.

SCHRAMM, WILBUR. "Channels and Audiences," in ITHIEL DE SOLA POOL; FREDERICK W. FREY; WILBUR SCHRAMM; NATHAN MACCOBY; and EDWIN B. PARKER. *Handbook of Communication*. Skokie, Ill.: Rand McNally, 1973, pp. 116–140.

WOOLBERT, CHARLES H. "The Audience." *Psychological Review Monographs* XXI (June 1916), pp. 37–54.

ZIMMERMAN, CLAIRE, and BAUER, RAYMOND A. "The Effects of an Audience on What Was Remembered," *Public Opinion Quarterly* 20, (Spring), pp. 238–48.

6 Nonverbal Aspects of Contemporary Public Communication

WHAT YOU CAN EXPECT:

Chapter 6 focuses on the nonverbal aspects of contemporary public communication.

This chapter discusses the importance of nonverbal communication *generally* and then focuses on six *specific* elements of nonverbal communication significant to the contemporary public communicator.

Chapter Outline

General Aspects of Nonverbal Communication
Specific Nonverbal Elements
    Human Sounds
    Voice Qualities
    The Human Face
    The "Eyes" Have It
    The Hands and Body
    Time, Space, and Objects
Cross-Cultural Aspects

Much of our total information about the world around us is actually composed of nonverbal elements that we perceive through one or more of our five senses. Although the actual *verbal* aspects of the words and language you use are important, the *nonverbal* elements are very important also. A frequent cliché states that "Its not *what* you say, but *how* you say it." Like most clichés, there is some truth in this statement. We prefer to combine the verbal and nonverbal elements and state that how you say what you say can be significant for the public communicator. One word of caution before you proceed with this chapter: even though we talk of *nonverbal communication* and *verbal communication,* the two are not actually separated in human communication. When we communicate, we communicate as a whole person and our verbal and nonverbal cues are interrelated and used in combined, complementary fashion. We have a separate chapter here on nonverbal communication to enable us to examine it more carefully because it is often convenient to isolate a particular aspect of communication. But remember that all human communication is a process that in reality cannot be stopped, separated, or divided. In fact, some researchers suggest that you communicate nonverbally even when you do not want to communicate.

> . . . if it is accepted that all behavior in an interactional situation has message values, i.e., is communication, it follows that no matter how one may try, one cannot *not* communicate. Activity or inactivity, words or silence all have message value: they influence others and these others, in turn, cannot *not* respond to these communications and are thus themselves communicating. It should be clearly understood that the mere absence of talking or taking notice of each other is no exception to what has just been asserted. The man at a crowded lunch counter who looks straight ahead, or the airplane passenger who sits with his eyes closed, are both communicating that they do not want to speak to anybody or be spoken to, and their neighbors usually "get the message" and respond appropriately by leaving them alone. This, obviously, is just as much an interchange of communication as an animated discussion.[1]

Since nonverbal communication is so pervasive in our lives, let us take a closer look. We begin here with general aspects of nonverbal communication and later in this chapter will discuss some specific elements.

General Aspects of Nonverbal Communication

Nonverbal communication surrounds us all the time, and because it is with us all the time, many humans often overlook the signifi-

---

[1] Paul Watzlawick, Janet H. Beavin, and Don D. Jackson, *Pragmatics of Human Communication: A Study of Interactional Patterns, Pathologies and Paradoxes* (New York: Norton, 1967), pp. 48–49.

cance nonverbal elements play in human interactions. Just as a goldfish might be unaware of the water constantly surrounding its life, we all sometimes overlook the pervasive nature of nonverbal elements in our lives.

All of us are fairly skilled observers of others' nonverbal stimuli and we all make judgments every day that are based on these nonverbal stimuli. Another person's facial expression, gestures, body movement, posture, and even clothing often provide some clues about that person's attitudes, beliefs, values, and behavior. To the perceptive observer, sensitive to such clues, these nonverbal elements provide useful information. Of course, as in all communication interactions, some of these stimuli will in all probability be misrepresented, misinterpreted, or misunderstood. But such misinterpretation is a constant problem in communication—both verbal and nonverbal.

Assume a situation in which a communicator is addressing an audience and that you are a member of that audience. As a listener you will make judgments about the speaker and many of the nonverbal clues help you make those judgments based on your *perception*. As soon as you *see* the speaker, you note the speaker's sex, age, size, posture, movements, and clothing. When you *hear* the speaker's voice, you note volume, pitch, tone, rate, and accent. These silent messages when combined with the verbal message can help you make better judgments about the communicator's enthusiasm and sincerity for his topic within the rhetorical situation.

In particular, according to psychologist Albert Mehrabian, our perception of the communicator's inner attitude depends more on the nonverbal than the words themselves. Mehrabian's research suggests the following formula of a communicator's projected attitude:[2]

Receiver's image of communicator = 7% verbal + 38% vocal + 55% facial

Hence, if we accept the conclusions of Mehrabian's research studies and total the nonverbal elements (38 percent vocal plus 55 percent

[2] Albert Mehrabian, *Silent Messages* (Belmont, Calif.: Wadsworth, 1971), pp. 42–47. See also Albert Mehrabian and S. R. Ferris, "Inference of Attitudes from Nonverbal Communication in Two Channels," *Journal of Consulting Psychology*, vol. 31 (1967), pp. 248–252.

facial), we find that 93 percent of your communicative message depends not on the actual words you speak, but on how you say those words and on your facial expression, that is, the *nonverbal elements*. Thus, many of your impressions of a speaker are communicated without words. And while you have been perceiving the nonverbal elements of the speaker, he or she has been perceiving the nonverbal elements of the audience. Nonverbal clues are perceived by both the speaker and the audience simultaneously. Although first impressions can be deceiving, we all make observations of others as they are making observations about us and we are influenced by nonverbal cues.

A random listing of some of the different nonverbal stimuli serves to illustrate that we all do in fact interpret nonverbal communication in meaningful ways through our perceptual senses of sight, sound, smell, touch, and taste.

Nonverbal stimuli

1. dress (clothing)
2. gait (the way we walk)
3. touch (warm, firm handshake)
4. eye contact (interest value)
5. skin color (black, white, brown)
6. body build (muscular, husky, slender, fat)
7. eye color (blue eyes)
8. lips (smiling)
9. eyebrows (frowning)
10. black armbands (protest)
11. hairstyles (Afro, crew cut)
12. closed fist (defiance, protest, anger, victory)
13. time (early, late, punctual)
14. color (red = danger; green = go)
15. space, distance (close, distant)
16. drumming fingers on table (nervousness)
17. head nod (agreement or understanding)
18. blushing (embarrassment)
19. kiss (affectionate)
20. glance at wristwatch (it is time to go)
21. perfume (attraction)
22. facial features (physiognomy and person perception)
23. posture (optimistic, defeated, energetic, tired)
24. tone of voice (happy, sad, angry, scared)

25. distance (spatial relationships, seating patterns)
26. siren (danger)
27. smoke (fire)

Specific Nonverbal Elements

Nonverbal communication includes anything and everything that communicates without coded language or words. Although no universally acceptable definition of nonverbal communication exists, the term is generally defined as all communicative stimuli beyond the verbal words or language codes we use in communication. A recent book by Randall P. Harrison distinguishes four different categories of nonverbal communication: (1) human sounds, (2) the human face, (3) the hands and body, and (4) time, space, and object.[3] These four areas seem to us to be of particular practical value to the public communicator and thus deserve careful consideration. Public communicators should be aware of all the possible nonverbal elements that influence effective communication. Some of these elements will be under their control, some will not, but contemporary public communicators should realize the significance of nonverbal communication.

Human sounds

The human vocal mechanism is capable of producing an amazing variety of distinctively different sounds. Humans can speak, hum, sing, whistle, yawn, snore, sigh, sneeze, hiccup, burp, cough, pant, moan, whine, whisper, shout, scream, yell, laugh, and cry. You can probably think of more. Humans are quite good at producing these

---

[3] Randall P. Harrison, *Beyond Words: An Introduction to Nonverbal Communication* (Englewood Cliffs, N.J.: Prentice-Hall, 1974), pp. 97–157. During the past few years a number of different categories of nonverbal behavior have been suggested. For example, Paul Ekman and Wallace V. Friesen describe five categories: (1) adapters, (2) emblems, (3) illustrators, (4) affect displays, and (5) regulators in "The Repertoire of Nonverbal Behavior: Categories, Origins, Usage and Coding," *Semiotica*, vol. 1 (1969), pp. 49–98. Mark L. Knapp describes seven nonverbal dimensions of human communication: (1) body motion or kinesic behavior, (2) physical characteristics, (3) touching behavior, (4) paralanguage, (5) proxemics, (6) artifacts, and (7) environmental factors in *Nonverbal Communication in Human Interaction* (New York: Holt, Rinehart and Winston, 1972).

sounds and one reason is that they have had plenty of practice since speech is learned before writing. Of course, the public communicator uses only some of these sounds, hopefully only those most appropriate to producing the desired message. Generally, human speech sounds can be discussed under two headings: "paralanguage" and "voice qualities." The major term *paralanguage* includes the term *voice qualities.*

Paralanguage, a term coined by George L. Trager, simply means language about language. You will note that above we indented a few spaces to indicate a new paragraph and that we italicized some of the terms for emphasis. In addition, our written language is controlled by capitalization, punctuation, and other grammatical rules. You know that a period signals the end of a sentence and that the first word of a sentence is always capitalized. But how do you know when someone has finished a sentence orally? Paralanguage is the answer. For example, a vocal cue of inflection indicates you have finished a sentence. The inflection sounds different for a question. A rise in inflection suggests a question is being asked.

Another example of what we mean by paralanguage is the ability humans have to identify voices. If a friend calls you on the telephone, you know who it is by the sound of the voice. Experts who study voice identification suggest that the human voice can electronically produce a "voice print" on a machine called a "spectograph." Such voice prints are as individually distinctive as one's fingerprints. The major reason you find it quite easy to remember voices is because of their individualistic voice qualities. In addition, paralanguage helps us to understand the meaning of messages. For instance, consider this simple message: "These apples taste very sweet." If you repeat this sentence and emphasize a different word each time, notice the effects you create.

1. *These* apples taste very sweet. (One group of apples are *distinguished* from another group of apples.)
2. These *apples* taste very sweet. (The *apples* taste sweet but something else [lemons] does not.)
3. These apples *taste* very sweet. (Not only do the apples look good, but they also *taste* sweet.)
4. These apples taste *very* sweet. (These apples are unusual in that they are *very* sweet.)
5. These apples taste very *sweet.* (They could taste very sour, but these happen to taste very *sweet.*)

Everything in the five statements—word order, punctuation—is identical except the paralinguistic emphasis, and yet the different emphasis placed on each word created different interpretations.

Voice qualities

One of the requirements of successful singing groups is to find a distinctive sound. If that special sound is discovered, it can literally mean millions of dollars to that group. The variety of voice qualities is responsible for distinctive sounds. Some people sound energetic, enthusiastic, and happy; others sound tired, bored, and sad. Actually, the sound of a person's voice can supply a number of identifying features. For example, you probably can distinguish between a male's voice and a female's voice, a Texan's accent and a New Yorker's accent, a child's voice and an elderly person's voice. In addition, from the various voice qualities in the messages we hear, we all make judgments about a communicator. You might be able to infer that a person is frightened, calm, angry, happy, nervous, sad, and so on, from the sound of the voice. In fact, one psychologist who has studied these nonverbal elements has concluded that such vocal cues are generally used by receivers to indicate the speaker's emotional state.[4] Our voices are *idiosyncratic,* that is, our voices are peculiarly, personally, and individually distinctive. We recognize different voices because they *sound* different in pitch, tone, volume, rate, and intensity. The distinctive nature of our voices allows receivers to identify us and also allows for added vocal messages to the words we produce.

The human face

We depend on the human face to communicate most of the human emotions. Humans tend to facially display their happiness or sadness through their nonverbal expressions of smiles and frowns. For centuries the thespian happy face and sad face have been identified in stick figures. Today the "smile face" adorns posters, stationery, and ads. We have become accustomed to obtaining our interpretation of a person's emotional state from a quick glance

[4] Albert Mehrabian, *Silent Messages,* p. 43.

at his facial expression. Notice how simple changes of the mouth communicate the opposites of happiness and sadness and how the additional change of the eyebrows changes the sad face to the angry face. Of course, just because a person "looks happy" does not always mean that such a person is really happy. All of us become

a. The happy face

b. The sad face

c. The angry face

Figure 4

fairly good actors and actresses. Thus, if you wish others to get the impression that you are happy, you simply smile often or "put on a happy face." All communicators should be aware of the almost instantaneous communication potential of the human face, but the nonverbal and the verbal should complement each other. In Figure 5, notice how the verbal and nonverbal elements are contradictory.

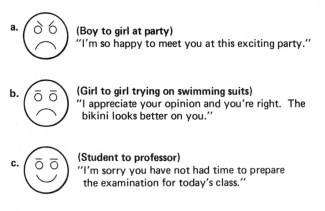

a. (Boy to girl at party)
"I'm so happy to meet you at this exciting party."

b. (Girl to girl trying on swimming suits)
"I appreciate your opinion and you're right. The bikini looks better on you."

c. (Student to professor)
"I'm sorry you have not had time to prepare the examination for today's class."

Figure 5

Given a choice between these verbal and nonverbal expressions of true feelings, we find that most people rely on the nonverbal. Thus, the silent messages tend to be trusted more because they are generally natural. We find that humans mistrust words and there is some support for the cliché "Action speaks louder than words." But again, "appearances can be deceiving" and we should all be cautious about the interpretation of all communicative stimuli. The best suggestion we can offer follows the advice of Kenneth Burke, who suggests that we use "all there is to use." Thus, by combining the nonverbal with the verbal information and giving careful consideration to the context of the rhetorical situation, we can increase the accuracy of our communicative judgments. The public communicator should make sure that the nonverbal facial expressions reinforce the verbal and that the nonverbal and verbal expressions are matched rather than contradictory.

The "Eyes" have it

The human face is the primary way we communicate our emotional feelings to others, and the *eyes* in particular are important for the public communicator. Generally, more frequent direct eye contact indicates more affection or interest. Members of the audience prefer speakers who maintain good eye contact, which is perceived as an indication of honesty, trustworthiness, and confidence. A speaker who avoids eye contact seems to be uncomfortable, and the audience may think he or she is attempting to deceive or hide something. Most people find that maintaining direct eye contact with a person you are attempting to deceive is quite difficult. Again, we must qualify this by saying that there are some people who can look you straight in the eye and still lie to you. But the major point here is that humans tend to depend a great deal on the eyes to convey and receive information, particularly of emotional states such as happiness, sadness, anger, surprise, fear, disgust, and pain.

The total facial features convey much of the emotional components of a message. The dominant features of the face are the eyebrows, eyes, and mouth. Notice the various changes between the messages conveyed by the changes in these various features.

For example, if we had a blank face, that is, an emotionless face, we would have to give more attention to the verbal message. In

Figure 6 the face is relatively blank or expressionless; thus, one has to rely on the verbal statement.

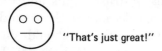

Figure 6

In Figure 7 there is conflict between the nonverbal expression and the verbal statement; thus, most people tend to rely more on the nonverbal expression for the true meaning. But since this conflicts with the verbal statement, we might conclude that this person is being sarcastic.

Figure 7

In Figure 8 both the verbal statement and the nonverbal expression match up; thus, there is reinforcement through the complementary interrelationship of verbal and nonverbal cues to make the whole impression more emphatic.

Figure 8

In the following series of faces, notice the slight changes seem to convey the statements. These facial expressions and the statements are said to be reinforcing or complementary.

Since we depend so much on the facial expressions for the meanings of our messages, the contemporary speaker should be aware of their importance and make sure that his and her use of facial expressions reinforce and complement the verbal message so as to make the total impact as effective as possible.

Happy
"I got an 'A' on my exam."

Happier
"I got a scholarship for
four years!"

Sad
"I lost my wallet."

Sadder
"I just remembered. That wallet
I lost had a $10 bill in it."

Angry
"I hit my *#!!! thumb with a hammer."

Devilish
"Aha, now that I own both Boardwalk
and Park Place, I betcha I'm going
to win this Monopoly game."

Figure 9

The hands and body

Movements of the body help to communicate meaning. The public communicator's use of hand and body gestures may help to silently emphasize or illustrate the important aspects of the verbal message. When we write a message, we employ a variety of techniques to call attention to important sentences. We may use CAPITAL LETTERS or *the important phrase may be italicized like this* for emphasis. And, of course, we use commas, semicolons, periods, question marks, exclamation marks, and other kinds of punctuation. When we present a message orally, we use gestures, tone of voice, inflection, and a variety of nonverbal punctuation. In addition, nonverbal gestures can complement the verbal message: "The snowball was this big!" or "I caught a fish this long."

Some kinds of movements are used so often that they become characteristic of a speaker. John F. Kennedy's pointing gesture is an example.

Ray L. Birdwhistell coined the term *kinesics*, which means "the study of body movements."[5]

The thumbing gesture of the hitchhiker, the "V" for victory or the peace sign, the pointing of the left index finger and quick rubbing motions of the right index finger ("shame on you"), the right index finger in a circular, clockwise motion beside the right temple ("crazy," "mixed up," "dumb"), clapping hands (applause), a handshake (greeting or farewell), the upraised fist are some of the many hand signals we employ.

The largest sensory device of the human body is our skin. From conception until death the human is surrounded by nonverbal tactile cues. Even within the mother's womb the embryonic human reacts to tactile sensations.

The major applications of the hands and body for the contemporary public communicator are *motion, posture,* and *gesture.*

Some researchers theorize that if we want to effectively communicate, we must obtain and maintain our audience's attention. One of the primary ways to obtain attention and then maintain it throughout your presentation is through action or *motion.* Movement indicates life and usually that which moves gets our attention. Suppose you are walking down a street and all of a sudden you see two men running. The running itself prompts you to ask yourself, "I wonder why they are running?" Since it it not likely that you would be able to ask the men why they were running, you would use nonverbal cues to suggest an answer. If, for example, you noted that one man wore ragged clothing, sported an untidy beard, and was carrying a purse, you might conclude that he was a purse snatcher. Your conclusion might be reinforced if you noted that the man chasing him wore a policeman's uniform. Notice that in this example the movement obtained your attention and that you used other nonverbal clues to interpret the situation. Observers perceive action and assign meaning to action. Thus, the animated speaker usually is perceived as confident, dynamic, informal, enthusiastic, lively, and interesting, whereas the motionless speaker is generally perceived as formal, boring, lifeless, dull, and perhaps insecure.

[5] Ray L. Birdwhistell, *Kinesics and Context: Essays on Body Motion Communication* (University of Pennsylvania Press, 1970).

Our *posture* is another nonverbal cue to our inner feelings. There are those who seem to drag themselves around, sit slouched over, and stand with shoulders drooping. Needless to say, such posture reflects a lack of energy or enthusiasm, a reluctance to communicate, and a general projected attitude of "I couldn't care less" about speaking to you. Although the opposite extreme of a rigid, formal, tight, intense, military posture should also be avoided, the public communicator should be aware of the effects of posture and attempt to communicate effectively by using a normal, relaxed posture that suggests confidence and interest in both the topic and the audience.

Almost all humans use *gestures* when they communicate. Some people seem to "talk with their hands," using almost constant hand gestures. There is a large variety of gestures, but it is not our purpose to suggest specific ones because we feel the best gesture is the natural one that emerges from your communication. The artificial gesture generally is poorly timed and thus ineffective. Good gestures should reinforce the verbal message.

Time, space, and objects

All humans differ to some degree with regard to how they treat time, space, and objects. You probably know some people who prefer to always be on time, desire wide open country space, and conserve objects. There are others who are always late, prefer the crowded city life, and consume objects.[6]

The temporal dimension is important to most of us. You probably have a watch. And today it is popular for the watch to not only indicate the hour, minute, and second, but also the month and day of the week (by both number and name). There is probably a clock in your classroom or nearby in the hall. You may have several clocks at home, such as an alarm clock, a clock radio, a decorative clock, a stove clock. We seem almost obsessed by time. Some people are early or right on time for dates, meetings, and appointments. We usually view this positively. Then there are those who seem to always be "running late," who consistently make others wait (doctors and lawyers, for example). Generally, the more important the

---

[6] An interesting discussion of some of these nonverbal elements can be found in the chapter "The Effects of Environment and Space on Human Communication," in Mark L. Knapp, *Nonverbal Communication in Human Interaction.*

person, the longer people will wait for that person. If you are on time, ahead of time, or behind time, you communicate to others that you are early or late and, depending on the situation, your use of time may create either a positive or negative atmosphere.

Thus, the temporal or time dimension of human interaction can be significant to the contemporary speaker. Some consideration should be given to the expected time to be allotted for the discourse. Audiences become impatient with a speaker who goes on and on past the specified time. Of course, time is critical if the message is prepared for radio or television. But generally, the public communicator should use time to indicate his or her respect for the interests and needs of the audience. Obviously, the speaker should be on time, in fact, we recommend an early arrival so that room conditions, visual aids, or any mechanical devices, such as overhead projectors and microphones, may be checked to make certain they are in working order. The more formal the situation is, the more important time becomes. By using time efficiently, you will demonstrate your value to your audience (no one likes to "waste" time). Just as humans typically become more anxious during timed situations (timed examinations, timed typing tests, etc.), the public speaker will always have a limited amount of time. Thus, careful preparation and practice is a requirement.

The spatial dimension also is important to most of us. Generally, in America, people avoid close contact in public. We are uncomfortable in subways, buses, elevators, and other public places where we are crowded together. Yet, as anthropologist Edward T. Hall, who coined the term *proxemics* for the study of space and distance, points out, an Arab would likely perceive public space quite differently.[7] As a matter of fact, each of us uses the space around us differently. The next time you go to your class notice where you sit. Why are you sitting in that particular place? Most people simply feel more comfortable with some seating positions than others. There is a different feeling created by sitting in the front row as compared with taking a seat in the back. Not only do you feel differently depending on your choice, but your choice suggests information to others. Perhaps those who sit in the front row of classrooms are more extroverted, friendly, interested, and confident. Research clearly suggests that the front center of the classroom is the "center

[7] Edward Twitchell Hall, *The Silent Language* (New York: Fawcett, 1959), pp. 116–128.

of activity" in terms of eye contact, interaction, and participation.[8] Space considerations supply the observer with information. For example, the person in charge, "the leader," usually sits at the head or end of the table. And once we have selected a seat, that seat somehow becomes "our seat." For instance, in the library we let others know that a certain seat is "ours" by placing some books or an article of clothing on it to "save our place" when we need to leave to get a book. Such ownership of space and the defensive behavior we use to protect it is sometimes called *territoriality*.[9]

The public communicator's use of space can reflect how you feel about your audience, your topic, and the occasion. A teacher may sit informally with a few students by arranging the chairs in a circle; but that same teacher may remain behind a lectern in the more formal situation of giving the commencement address. When space between the speaker and audience is increased, there is usually an increase in formality. Some speakers find that they can increase the interpersonal nature of interactions by leaving the lectern and walking among the audience members. Obviously, the topic and occasion often dictate how the audience expects the communicator to use space. The speaker would be expected to remain behind the lectern at a funeral service. In general, the communicator's choices of space will be guided by considerations of the topic, audience, and occasion.

The objects that surround us and the objects we possess tell something about ourselves. A man or woman sitting behind a desk in a room filled with law books is presumed to be a lawyer. Make the books medical and put a white smock on the person and you presume that person to be a doctor. Although some people cannot really afford it, they drive a large car like a Cadillac because of the status that object suggests. We place paintings in our rooms and encyclopedias or classical works on bookshelves partly because they "look nice." During the late 1960s and early 1970s long hair and mustaches became stylish. We associate a person who smokes a pipe as an intellectual and since professors like to be thought of as intellectual, you see many male professors smoking pipes. According to William Makepeace Thackeray, "the pipe draws wisdom from the lips of the philosopher, and shuts up the mouths of the foolish; it generates a style of conversation contemplative,

[8] Robert Sommer, *Personal Space* (Englewood Cliffs, N.J.: Prentice-Hall, 1969), pp. 110–120.
   [9] See Robert Ardrey, *The Territorial Imperative: A Personal Inquiry into the Animal Origins of Property and Nations* (New York: Atheneum, 1966).

thoughtful, benevolent, and unaffected." Although we do not suggest you smoke a pipe, particularly since it may not be healthy, it is interesting to note how a simple object like a pipe seems to communicate. The presence or absence of objects reflects information about people; clothing, jewelry, eyeglasses, cosmetics, furniture, and the size, shape, and color of objects—all contain influential messages.

The public communicator typically is limited in the amount of control he or she will have in terms of objects by the topic, audience, and occasion. But decisions about clothing, the use of a lectern, of notes, and of visual aids deserve careful attention.

Cross-Cultural Aspects

Although the human facial expressions of the smile (happy face) and the frown (sad face) are claimed to be universal nonverbal expressions by some researchers, we generally accept the view that our nonverbal communication is *culture bound*. By culture bound we mean that we learn nonverbal expressions from our particular culture and that when we cross over into other cultures, the nonverbal expressions we have learned may not be appropriate. For example, by touching our thumb with our index finger, we form the "A-OK" gesture. Generally, in America, this gesture is given to mean "everything is fine," "we're set to go," or something similar, and you have probably seen people give such a gesture at swimming events, car races, and other sporting events. But, according to Randall Harrison, this same gesture is interpreted as an insult to a young lady in some European countries.[10] Thus, you may be saying "everything is A-OK" and get your face slapped. The point here is that most of our *gestures*, mannerisms, and traits are dependent upon our culture. Since cultures are different, the nonverbal behavior we learn from our parents and peers is different. For example, if you have a business appointment in America, you may be asked to "wait a few minutes" (5 to 10 minutes) when you show up at the appointed place; but in Latin America the "wait a few minutes" may mean a waiting period of 45 to 55 minutes. The nonverbal element of *time* (arrival time, waiting time, etc.) is dependent upon culture. The popular view in the United States is that direct

---

[10] Randall P. Harrison, "Nonverbal Behavior: An Approach to Human Communication," in Richard W. Budd and Brent D. Ruben, eds., *Approaches to Human Communication* (New York: Spartan Books, 1972), p. 262.

eye contact suggests a high degree of interest and the avoidance of eye contact suggests lack of attention and interest; but our Nigerian graduate students pointed out to us that prolonged, direct eye contact suggests disrespect in their country. Americans clap their hands in order to applaud someone; but Russians hold their hands clasped together over their heads to indicate applause. In American business offices one's desk, bookshelves, and general working area is usually along the edges of the room; but in Europe the business-man generally puts his desk in the center of the room; "authority flows outward from the center" and "proximity to the center" is one indication of a person's status.[11] In the United States if you saw two men holding hands, this sort of touching suggests homo-sexuality; but in some Asian and African countries holding hands suggests friendship. In America when two men greet one another they shake hands; but hugging and kissing is the traditional form of greeting in some other countries. There are many other examples, but we should all remember that the nonverbal elements of our communication are largely learned from our particular background—they are culture bound.

In this chapter we have discussed only some of the many non-verbal means of communication that we feel are of primary im-portance to the public communicator. There are many additional elements and we hope that you will be stimulated to read more about nonverbal communication. Today's public communicator must be aware of the importance of nonverbal elements and control them advantageously to increase the effectiveness of rhetorical discourse. Finally, the audience members must be aware of the nonverbal elements of public discourse in order to accurately assess the com-municator's motivation and the meaning of the message produced.

FOR STUDENT APPLICATION

1. The next time someone in your class presents an oral report, focus on the nonverbal behavior of audience members. Generally, some look directly at the speaker, some take notes, some may be directing their eyes elsewhere, some may appear interested with an encouraging smile or a nod of their head, some may frown or appear bored. What effect does this nonverbal behavior have on the speaker? Is the "frown"

[11] Don Fabun, "The Silent Languages," in Joseph A. DeVito, ed., *Communica-tion Concepts and Processes* (Englewood Cliffs, N.J.: Prentice-Hall, 1971), p. 131.

a negative reaction to what the speaker is saying? Or is the frown due to a headache and totally unrelated to the speaker's report? How much of the nonverbal *behavior* is really consciously intended and therefore nonverbal communication? And even if the audience member is intentionally sending the speaker a nonverbal message, how is the nonverbal behavior used to communicate that message interpreted?

2. Notice that if I said to you "I like that *cat*," you would not know if I meant a person (he's a cool cat, man!), a pet kitten, or a roaring lion. You would normally understand the statement because of other things I might say, the meaning is made clear by the *context* or the statements surrounding this sentence. But what about nonverbal behavior? If I hold up two fingers, am I trying to say *peace, victory,* or *two?*

3. During the 1968 Olympics in Mexico City, several of the black athletes won medals. When they accepted their medals, they raised their clenched fists. Their nonverbal gestures stimulated much discussion by newspapers, newsmagazines, and television sports writers. Do you think such gestures would have had such an impact if the site had not been in Mexico City? Would the same gesture by white athletes have had a similar impact? Why?

4. A cliché states, "Action speaks louder than words." Obviously what we say is important, but the way be *behave* also communicates. The student who *says* he can solve a math problem but is unable to *demonstrate* his knowledge is clearly in a difficult communication situation. Can you think of some examples you have observed in which the *words* and the *behavior* do not match? Consider the areas of politics, education, and business organizations.

5. Suppose you receive a letter of invitation to a party. In the letter it is stated that your answer is requested in five days so that adequate space arrangements can be made. A week passes and you still have not replied. What does your "no response" communicate?

6. Communication involves much more than the utilization of words. Words are symbols. Words "stand" for something else. What are some significant symbols other than words? Consider the following statement: "All behavior is symbolic and, in some circumstances, even the absence of behavior communicates symbolically." List some examples of nonword symbols. What are some significant symbolic behaviors?

Readings

BIRDWHISTELL, RAY L. *Kinesics and Context: Essays on Body Motion Communication.* University of Pennsylvania Press, 1970.

DAVIS, FLORA. *Inside Intuition: What We Know About Nonverbal Communication.* New York: McGraw-Hill, 1973.

EISENBERG, ABNE M., and SMITH, RALPH R., JR. *Nonverbal Communication.* Indianapolis: Bobbs-Merrill, 1971.

HALL, EDWARD TWITCHELL. *The Silent Language.* New York: Fawcett, 1959.

KNAPP, MARK L. *Nonverbal Communication in Human Interaction.* New York: Holt, Rinehart and Winston, 1972.

HARRISON, RANDALL P. *Beyond Words: An Introduction to Nonverbal Communication.* Englewood Cliffs, N.J.: Prentice-Hall, 1974.

MEHRABIAN, ALBERT. *Nonverbal Communication.* Chicago: Aldine, 1972.

RUESCH, JURGEN and KEES, WELDON. *Nonverbal Communication: Notes on the Visual Perception of Human Relations.* University of California Press, 1956.

SCHEFLEN, ALBERT E. *Body Language and the Social Order: Communication as Behavioral Control.* Englewood Cliffs, N.J.: Prentice-Hall, 1973.

WATSON, O. MICHAEL. *Proxemic Behavior: A Cross-Cultural Study.* The Hague: Mouton, 1970.

7 Reasoning in Contemporary Discourse

WHAT YOU CAN EXPECT:

Chapter 7 directs you to reasoning in contemporary discourse. In this chapter you will be introduced to the fundamental concepts of argument in discourse.

The ability to present substantive arguments is an essential element in persuasive communication. In societies based upon cooperation through persuasion, the use of fundamental concepts in argumentation is important.

Chapter Outline

William Norwood Brigance advanced the idea of a genetic approach to persuasion by arguing that there were three levels of persuasion: *authority, experience,* and *reason.* Each level represented a successively higher state of proof.[1]

Brigance's view is provocative from a historical point of view, particularly with the rise of Darwin-

[1] William Norwood Brigance, "A Genetic Approach to Persuasion," *Quarterly Journal of Speech* XVII (June 1931),

ism in the social sciences. Winston Brembeck and William Howell advanced the notion that persuasion was "the conscious attempt to modify thought and action by manipulating the motives of men toward predetermined ends."[2]

In this section we treat controversy as an opportunity for persuasion. The controversial situation provides the communicator with an arena for his and her reasoning skills because the communicator must be able to convince the audiences to accept the position he or she is advancing. Controversy, then, is a legitimate area for reasoning.

What is reasoning? Perhaps each of you has had the occasion to say to a friend or colleague regarding someone you have had unusual difficulty in persuading to see your way, "I tried to reason with her," or "Reasoning did not seem to matter to him," or "I just as well might have thrown reason out of the window." We know from these expressions that reasoning has something to do with manipulating language symbols in some kind of order to produce sequential arousal. Reasoning might be identified as the human process of manipulating language symbols with the intent to arouse a sequential association in one's own mind or in the mind of others. We could also say that in reasoning a person associates the labels he has developed with various categories of human experiences. Put another way, you name an experience, thing, event, place, or person, and then apply that name to a certain class of experiences, things, events, places, or persons. The ability to establish clear and concise correspondence between your labels and your categories so that others are able to understand you is a characteristic of good reasoning. Once a person is able to make an association and can say, even if only to himself, "I understand," an *inference* has been made. Inference refers to the process of moving from established propositions and data to new propositions or a conclusion. One of the most influential treatments of inference appears in *The Uses of Argument* by Stephen Toulmin. The basic structure of Toulmin's theory of argument is that when we argue, we make an *inference* from *evidence*, or data, to a *conclusion*, or claim, by means of a connector of a *warrant*. In addition to this simple description, Toulmin proposes *backing* for the warrant, and a *qualifier* and a *rebuttal* for the conclusion. Thus the complete line of reasoning for Toulmin would look like the following figure.

---

[2] Winston Brembeck and William Howell, *Persuasion: A Means of Social Control* (Englewood Cliffs, N.J.: Prentice-Hall, 1952).

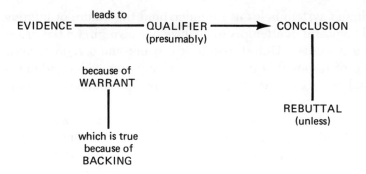

Figure 10

Thomas Scheidel in *Persuasive Speaking* reacts to Toulmin's concept of the warrant by saying that it "represents a relatively abstract generalization one has already arrived at or accepted, and evidence represents a fairly specific item of information. The inferential process attempts to subsume the specific evidence under the generalization of the warrant. Once this is done, an association is drawn between the evidence and other particulars (including the conclusion) also subsumed under the warrant. This association of particulars through the processes of categorizing and generalizing is the essence of inference."[3]

The example used by Toulmin illustrates the procedure by which a person may draw the inference that Harry is a British subject.

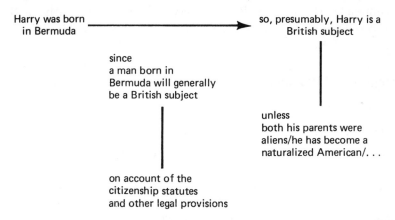

Figure 11

[3] Thomas Scheidel, *Persuasive Speaking* (Glenview, Ill.: Scott, Foresman, 1967), p. 36.

Toulmin's system helps us to understand the nature of inference and will be useful in attempts to analyze our own inferential process prior to a discourse. Unfortunately it can become a rigid structure incapable of responding to unstated assumptions, value judgments, and metalinguistics that are frequently not present in the spoken text.

Logical thinking does not guarantee that truth will be discovered; it only provides us with a sequential relationship among symbols. It is a mistake for you to think that if you know how to reason, you will also be led to truth. If your initial assumptions are false, no matter how rigorous your logic, the conclusion will also be false; that is, it is possible to have an argument that is formally logical but false.

Discourse in either its written or spoken form touches all of us. We are connected to each other by the linkage provided in human discourse. The reasonableness of that linkage is established by the clarity of ideas and cogency of arguments contained in discourse. All discourse deals with propositions. A proposition is a statement expressed or implied by a communicator in an attempt to secure the assent of his or her audiences. Many authors differ on class names for propositions, some identifying as many as seven possibilities and others as few as two. However, three broad categories of propositions are most generally accepted: *fact, value,* and *policy.* In fact, writers who classify more or less than these arrive at their classification system by subsuming·or dividing categories. Inasmuch as the propositions we have identified above have their own proof requirements we will discuss each category individually.

Categories of Proposition

Proposition of fact

Glen E. Mills once referred to propositions in this category as propositions of "criteria and application."[4] This is because Mills correctly sees what most writers call propositions of fact as constituting definition and classification. However, it is not necessary to further classify the area of fact as he does. Clearly, fact can be defined as that which is verifiable. Thus, in the statement "The

---

[4] Glen E. Mills, *Reason in Controversy: An Introduction to General Argumentation* (Boston: Allyn & Bacon, 1964), p. 43.

Watergate burglars are guilty of breaking and entering" we have a proposition of fact. It is classified in that way because it can be objectively verified. Two fundamental questions that must be raised and answered of propositions of fact are: (1) What did the subjects do? (2) Can what they did be definable as breaking and entering? Whereas it is possible to speak of propositions of fact that relate to past and future as well as present fact, the two key questions given above may be asked in each case with slight variations. For example, in the proposition "Bob Haldeman was disturbed about the playing of the Watergate tapes," the analyst must discover the requirements for establishing the alleged fact and determine if the data meet these requirements. In this way the controversial claim asserted about a past event must be submitted to the same process as a present event case. To illustrate the centrality of the fundamental questions in future fact, we can take the example of the proposition, "The election of liberal congressmen to the House of Representatives will intensify the demands for socialized medicine." We need to know what kinds of evidence are necessary to make the statement probably accurate and then we need to know if that evidence is available. Again, we are able to see how the examples underscore the need for the student of propositions of fact to ask questions of definition and application—that is, what is needed to define and once we know what is needed, do we have data available to support our view.

Before a communicator decides to present his or her opinions to an audience, he or she should have a formulation of the proposition of fact in his or her own mind. A communicator without an understanding of his or her own proposition is like a rocket ship without a gyro.

Proposition of value

The proposition of value makes an evaluative claim. It states a situation or an event that can only be subjectively verified. The following statements are evaluative and obviously controversial.

Communism is an unworthy philosophy.
Canadians are friendlier than Americans.
Arab oil policies are detrimental to world freedom.
Zionism is racism.
Physical education creates moral principles.

To analyze these propositions we must ascertain what kinds of criteria apply and whether or not the subject of concern meets these criteria. The criteria are subjectively determined, and this differs from propositions of fact where the criteria are objectively determined. Many arguments derive from the subjectively determined criteria of propositions of value. H. Rap Brown's statements that "America is the ultimate denial of the theory of man's evolution," "This country is the world's slop jar," and "America represents everything that humans have suffered from, their every affliction," are evaluative propositions.[5] Thus, the proposition of value, similar to the proposition of fact, asserts what *exists*. Whenever you express an opinion on the quality or merit of something, you are engaging in the proposition of value.

Proposition of policy

The proposition of policy is the most common type of proposition in deliberative bodies, public meetings, and intercollegiate forensics. It characteristically calls for policy change and uses the word *should* to imply that action should be taken but may not be taken. Propositions of this type differ further from propositions of fact and value in that they involve certain aspects of fact and value but also contain emphasis on *reasonableness, practicality, expediency,* and *action*. Thus, the proposition of policy proposes to establish a certain action as being within the bounds of reason. A communicator asserting this type of proposition must also seek to establish the expediency of such a plan. In preparing to present a discourse arguing that medicine should be socialized, a communicator would be trying to win approval for a method of operation she or he believes to be more expedient and practical than the method it is intended to supplant. A course of action is specified and a call for action is made. The following statements are examples of propositions of policy.

The OAS should lift the embargo on Cuba.
Television should be permitted in the Oval Office.
The abortion law should be changed.
The UN should debate the South African situation.
Hospitals should reduce their rates for rural people.

[5] Arthur L. Smith and Stephen Robb, eds., *The Voice of Black Rhetoric: Selections* (Boston: Allyn & Bacon, 1971), p. 305.

Issues

An issue is a vital question within a proposition. Strictly speaking, it is inherent in the proposition because it does not exist apart from the proposition. Furthermore, the fact that it cannot be separated means that it is vital and essential to the meaning of the proposition. Issues must be affirmed by someone if there is to be argumentation and persuasion. If you and a friend are interested in going to hear a lecture on multinational corporations, and in discussing whether to do so or not, you discover a disagreement with each other, you both present what you feel to be valid reasons for your attitude but you find that you are in opposition to one another. The question over which the opposing arguments clash is the issue.[6]

Issues may be classified as *common, waived, actual,* and *potential.* Common issues are found in a preliminary analysis of a proposition and appear in a somewhat universal form. As analytical tools, they are intended to apply to all propositions of a given variety. Thus, in a proposition of policy clash the communicator's proposal should be submitted to questions such as these: "Are there severe inadequacies and serious evils in the status quo?" "Are the problems serious enough to risk a change from the present course?" "Will the proposed policy provide a more desirable means of meeting the problem than the current policy?" "Is the proposed plan practicable?" Common issues for propositions of fact and value are worded differently. Each proposition of fact or value is comprised of a subject term and a predicate term. Common issues must always be found in these terms unlike in the proposition of policy where *should* or *ought* appears to indicate that something should but may not occur. Thus, in the proposition of fact example, "Zimbabwe is an old African nation," the first step in finding the common issues would be *definition of the predicate term.* This is also applicable to a proposition of value as in the following example: "Canadians are friendly." By establishing a definition for the predicate term, we are able to evaluate the subject term. The propositions should be submitted to questions such as, "What is an old African nation?" or "What is meant by friendly?" Even though the questions are specific to the proposition under discussion, the genre of definition is applicable in finding common issues. If criteria established by

[6] Charles S. Mudd and Malcolm D. Sillars, *Speech: Content and Communication* (New York: Intext, 1962), p. 42.

the advocate are satisfactory to himself or herself, and he or she believes they will be convincing to an audience, the next step is to apply them to the subject term. Once the analysis is completed, the advocate can make a judgment that the subject term is therefore as stated in the proposition.

As it is used for analysis of propositions of policy, this approach has some drawbacks.[7] It does not say anything about the subject matter of the proposition. If the proposition of policy is that the United Nations should establish a permanent mission in South Africa to monitor race policies, nothing specific is said about South African race policies when we ask a stock question about severe evils in the status quo. We do get a perspective on specific questions that should be asked about the proposition. Nadeau answered some objections to common issues by pointing out that they are not the end of analysis.[8]

Waived issues are those that can be deleted from a list of potential issues by the person opposing the proposition. While the opposition can require the affirmative to provide affirmation for every potential issue, it does not have to challenge every issue. Thus, in a controversy surrounding wage and price controls to protect the economy, the person opposing such action may present many potential issues as possible lines of attack. The affirmative must be able to answer each of the potential issues raised by the opposition. However, the opposition could simply waive or admit some of the issues initially raised. This is frequently a way for the negative to test the ability of the affirmative to provide answers rather than a serious attack on the affirmative. More importantly, it is the best method for determining if all the bases have been covered in analyzing the proposition. We are often surprised when someone raises an issue in debate or discussion that we had failed to consider and usually respond, "I never thought of that." What we mean, of course, is that it never occurred to us in connection with the proposition being debated.

Waived issues are potential issues that are admitted, usually in consideration of time, logical weakness, and interest. As a debate tactic, particularly in intercollegiate forensics, the most common instance of waiving occurs when the negative on a given proposition concedes that a need for action exists but offers a counterproposi-

---

[7] Robert P. Newman, "Analysis and Issues—A Study of Doctrine," *Central States Speech Journal* XIII, no. 1 (1961), p. 43.

[8] R. Nadeau, "In Defense of Deliberative Stock Issues," *Central States Speech Journal* XIII, no. 2 (1962).

tion as solution to the need. If an issue is admitted or waived, it can no longer be an issue in that debate. For example, if the proposition to be debated is "College fraternities should be abolished," the affirmative side may establish a need by saying that the selection procedures and standards are inadequate because they are based on money, narrow interests, prestige, and ancestry. In response to the need presentation the opposition or negative may admit the issue, that is, the opposition may concede that the selection procedures and standards are poor. Once this concession is made, however, the negative can offer a counterproposition that the "standards for admission into fraternities should be modified."

After concessions have been made by the negative and such waived issues deleted from the list of potential issues, the remaining issues are called actual or ultimate issues. They are the issues of debate, the key questions over which opposing sides clash. In a debate going on, or one that has ended, it is always effective for analysis to take a plain sheet of paper and draw a line straight down the center of it, making one side affirmative and the other side negative, placing all the opposing points opposite each other. Unattacked points would be opposite a blank spot. An illustration of this method is presented below. The proposition called for the amendment of an Illinois Banking Act to allow banks to open branches in their trade areas.[9]

Affirmative points	*Negative points*
Business development is retarded by inadequate banking facilities.	Chicago is a net exporter of bank loans.
Individuals are inconvenienced by a shortage of banks.	Very few communities are more than a few minutes from a bank.
Only large banks can provide specialized services.	
	Branches cost more than independent local units to operate.
Chicago banks are losing business because of having no branches.	
It would not lead to monopoly.	It would create a monopoly.

[9] Glen E. Mills, p. 62.

There were two actual or ultimate issues: (1) Is the present arrangement of banks in the Chicago area unable to render satisfactory service? (2) Would branch banking avoid the danger of monopoly?

All possible issues are potential. They exist within a given proposition and may be used by the affirmative or the negative. While they are the same for both sides, the affirmative may be required to answer every one. The negative can limit its own response to as few or as many as it chooses. It is always a good procedure in any controversy to list all of the potential issues; even though, if the controversy has not taken place, it may not be an adequate way of determining the actual issues. For a past controversy, however, this is a reliable method of finding issues that were actually debated.

Common Types of Argument

In the following section we introduce you to several common types of argument. During the course of your preparation for a speech or monologue meant to be persuasive, you will consider a number of ways to address the main issues. More likely than not, you will discover that you must resort to one or more of the common types of argument.

Argument from example

In the argument from example the conclusion is a general statement inferred from one or more examples.

> An inflationary condition exists in the United States. Prices of beans, rice, sugar, and corn have jumped 30 percent in the last month. Automobiles and services connected with the automobile industry have spiraled a record 20 percent in six weeks. These instances suggest an inflationary condition by asserting that when prices occur at a given rate of increase over a given time period, an inflationary condition exists.

The descriptive conclusion gives an accurate account of a condition, situation, or event. A communicator must have a clear grasp of what the examples demonstrate before he or she can state that they are typical of a certain class or category. In other words, the communicator has to know if the instances given are atypical or unusual. A speaker or writer must present examples that describe the general conclusion. In the example above it is conceivable that the argument might be attacked on the basis that it does not take into account the fact that there are other indices of inflation than the examples given. However, the speaker might use a supporting argument to strengthen the case.

Argument from definition to classification

A speaker who begins an argument against multinational corporations must first establish what constitutes a multinational corporation. Similarly, a person who wants to argue that a certain politician is a male chauvinist must define what constitutes a male chauvinist. Thus, to establish that a politician is a male chauvinist, the speaker must prove that the criteria for a male chauvinist are satisfied by the politician. Hastings, referring to this type of argument as criteria to verbal classification, believes that this form of reasoning has not been recognized previously as a separate and independent mode of argument.[10] Of course, the deductive argument could be thought of as an argument from definition to classification.

Argument from comparison

Many of our most effective arguments are made by comparing one event or thing with another. By demonstrating that situation one is similar to situation two, we are able to establish the probability that what is true of one will be true of two. The degree of certainty rests upon how similar the facts, circumstances, and contexts are in both cases. For instance, if we wanted to argue the benefits of a municipal convention center for Buffalo, we might point to Pittsburgh as a city of similar size, composition, and history. The benefits that accrued to Pittsburgh after completion of the convention center may be said to be probable for Buffalo.

Argument from cause to effect

There are two main categories of argument from cause to effect: (1) existing situations, (2) hypothetical situations. In a given discourse a speaker might employ both forms. Usually the first category

---

[10] Arthur Hastings, "Reasoning Processes," in Mills, *Reason in Controversy: An Introduction to General Argumentation*, p. 130.

is utilized for direct statements of assessment; the second category of cause-to-effect arguments is frequently used for emphasis. Whereas the factors that will produce the effect do not exist, their possibility of existence is the basis of prediction. A communicator may predict that certain policy decisions will affect the way we use gasoline; more specifically, the increase in gasoline prices will require a change in our automobile driving practices. Or it might be predicted that if Puerto Rico's political status is not changed, there will be more social and political disruptions on the island.

Argument from citation

This form of argument has been called argument from quotation and argument from testimony. It is properly the argument from citation, which covers personal testimonies, quotations, or references to documents or memorabilia. Much of the electronic media's commercial appeals are arguments from citations. Mrs. So-and-So of Fort Valley, Georgia, says this product is excellent for cleaning your wood floors. The weight of such arguments from citation depends on a number of factors, including the nature of the person's evidence and the accuracy of the report. In the political arena the argument from citation can often be seen in its most unabashed form. Almost every president after George Washington has cited a statement from his predecessor as supportive of a certain sentiment or argument of his.

Argument from authorities

In most situations where one person attempts to modify the opinions and behaviors of others it may be necessary to provide justification for ideas by citing persons in positions of authority. They are capable of making two basic types of statements to support argument: (1) statements of fact, (2) statements of opinion.

If the mayor of your town lists in the evening paper the categories of jobs that must be eliminated in order to balance the budget, that list with whatever accompanying numbers may be used in a presentation arguing the creation of more jobs. To a large extent the acceptability of the statement of fact is controlled by the audience of the authority making the statement. There are instances when the statement of fact may be correct but the audience refuses to accept the authority. According to a Gallup poll, college teachers ranked high on the scale of credibility among eleven professional categories. What this means is that a social scientist or an engineer is liable to be more credible to many audiences than an advertising executive or a politician. Acceptability has little to do with the individual person but a lot to do with what the audience believes about persons in a certain authority position. If an authority has a reputation for personal integrity and is in a position to know facts in a given situation, he or she is the most acceptable authority. As a communicator, you should always present your authority's qualifications when it is likely the audience will not know him or her.

Statements of opinion are usually less readily accepted by audiences than statements of fact. One reason this may be true is because statements of fact are usually based on *observation;* statements of opinion are based on *observed facts.* It is, therefore, a judgment as to what the facts mean. Observation may be verified but interpretation and judgment is strictly a matter of opinion. A communicator preparing a monologue or speech does not have to abandon his or her good senses because he or she wants to use statements of opinion from an authority. There are five questions that may be asked of the authority before using his or her statements.

1. Is the person quoted a currently recognized expert in the specific matter discussed? Joe Namath could be quoted in regard to professional football, but his expertise does not qualify him to discuss nuclear physics.

2. Does the person quoted have personal interest in the problem, or will he personally gain from a particular advocated position? The commissioner of baseball could not be very objective in comparing the relative status of baseball with that of football, hockey, basketball, or other American sports.

3. Is the person quoted currently in a position to have firsthand knowledge about the topic? The placement director of your college or university would likely have the latest information concerning employment for your school's graduates.

4. Does he have an image of fairness and honesty and would he likely be accepted by your audience? University audiences would likely be unwilling to believe or accept statements about American justice by Spiro Agnew, but probably would from a Supreme Court justice.

5. Is the person's statement consistent with other known facts or opinions?

When you have ascertained answers to those questions, you will be in a stronger position to establish your own case. In presenting any data in a speech, you should provide the source of data with which the audience is unfamiliar. If your sources are unimpeachable, the accuracy of your statements will usually be accepted by the audience. In terms of sources the Bureau of Labor Statistics ranks higher than the college newspaper; the *New York Times* higher than *Reader's Digest;* and *Encyclopedia Britannica* higher than the *American Mercury.*

Argument from sign

The argument from sign points to some symbol or phenomenon that almost always occurs in connection with some other condition. Cumulus clouds almost invariably mean rain. Flowers budding almost always mean spring is on the way. Reasoning, therefore, from sign a communicator demonstrates that certain phenomena occur with certain other phenomena. Causal relationships, that is, direct interaction of one phenomenon with another, are not attempted. The communicator assumes and seeks to have the audiences assume that if one condition exists, another will also exist. A flag at half-mast shows the death of a government official. The flag at half-mast did not *cause* the death; it simply points to the death of an official.

One of the principal problems faced by communicators is the assigning of too much weight to a symbol for the condition it is supposed to represent. A flag at half-mast may appear as neglect on the part of a flag keeper or it may represent something else of importance to a community or a nation. A sign may represent more than one other condition. Thus, cumulus clouds may also mean high humidity.

The preceding types of arguments represent the major kinds used in contemporary discourse. They are by no means exhaustive but are presented to give you an idea of how arguments are used in public communication.

The Universal Audience

Chaim Perelman and L. Obrechts-Tyteca writing in *The New Rhetoric* argue that communicators should address the universal audience in their discourse. For the student of communication seeking

to gain confidence to speak before the class, this may sound overwhelming. But one may speak to the universal audience while
speaking to his peers. The universal audience is neither bound by
occasion or time. A public discourse given in your classroom may be
addressed to the universal audience if your arguments will stand
the test of other reasonable audiences. One of the reasons there are
no great speeches from ancient history supporting slavery, incest,
or crime is because the universal audience does not accept slavery,
incest, or crime as supportive of the human personality.

John F. Kennedy's "Inaugural Address" contained a memorable
example of an appeal to the universal audience. He addressed all
citizens of America and, indirectly, all people of the world in 1961.
Thus, his address was meant not only for the literal audience of
several thousand in Washington, but for those worldwide, universal
audiences:

> And so, my fellow Americans: ask not what your country can do for
> you—ask what you can do for your country.
>
> My fellow citizens of the world: ask not what America will do for you,
> but what together we can do for the freedom of man.
>
> Finally, whether you are citizens of America or citizens of the world,
> ask of us here the same high standards of strength and sacrifice
> which all ask of you. With a good conscience our only sure reward,
> with history the final judge of our deeds, let us go forth to lead the
> land we love, asking His blessing and His help, but knowing that here
> on earth God's work must truly be our own.[11]

Martin Luther King, Jr.'s famous "I Have a Dream" speech also
contained appeals to the universal audience. More than 200,000
people gathered in front of the Lincoln Memorial at the nation's
capital heard King's universal appeals for justice, equality, and
freedom. For example, the last paragraph of King's address focused
on the universal audience of all mankind since it contained the
universal appeal for freedom:

> When we allow freedom to ring, when we let it ring from every village
> and every hamlet, from every state and every city, we will be able to
> speed up that day when all of God's children, black men and white
> men, Jews and Gentiles, protestants and Catholics, will be able to
> join hands and sing in the words of the old Negro spiritual, "Free at
> last! Free at last! Thank God Almighty, we are free at last!"[12]

[11] Davis Newton Lott, *The Presidents Speak* (New York: Holt, Rinehart and
Winston, 1969), p. 271.

[12] Smith and Robb, eds. *The Voice of Black Rhetoric: Selections,* p. 188.

Thus, where possible in a public communication situation, you should appeal to the universal audience. This can be accomplished even in the classroom by incorporating universal appeals into your message.

FOR STUDENT APPLICATION

1. Most people suggest that they are influenced by the weight of the *evidence* in the speaker's argument. How do you personally judge evidence? What is the difference between "good" or strong evidence and "bad" or weak evidence? List the kind of evidence you think is good and the kind you think is bad. Bring your list to class for an open discussion.

2. Read several brief "Letters to the Editor" in your local newspapers or in one of the United States newsmagazines such as *Time, Newsweek,* and *U.S. News and World Report.* How many different types of evidence do you find? What kind of evidence is most frequently found?

3. Consider any controversial issue such as the Equal Rights Amendment (ERA). Examine some articles in magazines and newspapers to discover the kinds of evidence used. What did you find? Do those who support the ERA use the same type of evidence as those who oppose the ERA?

4. Although it sounds contradictory, humans are both *alike* and *different* at the same time. For example, in terms of physiological needs (oxygen, water, etc.) humans are all alike, but in terms of individual experiences (culture, environment, etc.) we are all different. List some ways these similarities and differences affect reasoning.

5. Select a brief written account on a topic of your choice. Read the account and note statements of opinion. What is the author's basis for the expressed opinion? How many statements of opinion did you find that do not have supporting factual evidence?

6. Listen to a television discussion program such as "Issues and Answers" or "Meet the Press." Analyze the program in terms of the various kinds of reasoning employed. What was the most prominent type of reasoning employed? How many different types of reasoning did you observe? Which did you find the most effective? Why?

Readings

ALBIG, WILLIAM. *Modern Public Opinion.* New York: McGraw-Hill, 1956.
BARRETT, WILLIAM A. *Irrational Man.* Garden City, N.Y.: Doubleday, 1958.
BARZUN, JACQUES. *The House of Intellect.* New York: Harper & Row, 1959.

EHNINGER, DOUGLAS. *Influence, Belief, and Argument: An Introduction to Responsible Persuasion.* Glenview, Ill.: Scott, Foresman, 1974.

HUFF, DARRELL, and GEIS, IRVING. *How to Lie with Statistics.* New York: Norton, 1954.

NEWMAN, ROBERT P., and NEWMAN, DALE R. *Evidence.* Boston: Houghton Mifflin, 1969.

PERELMAN, CHAIM, and OLBRECHTS-TYTECA, L. *The New Rhetoric,* trans. John Wilkinson and Purcell Weaver. South Bend, Ind.: University of Notre Dame Press, 1969; originally published in French in 1958.

SMITH, CRAIG R., and HUNSAKER, DAVID M. *The Bases of Argument: Ideas in Conflict.* Indianapolis: Bobbs-Merrill, 1972.

TOULMIN, STEPHEN E. *The Uses of Argument.* London: Cambridge University Press, 1958.

ZIEGELMUELLER, GEORGE W., and DAUSE, CHARLES A. *Argumentation: Inquiry and Advocacy.* Englewood Cliffs, N.J.: Prentice-Hall, 1975.

8 The Structure of Public Communication

WHAT YOU CAN EXPECT:

Chapter 8 establishes the significance of order in public communication. It is our purpose to introduce you to the value of organizing your presentations.

The concept of order is applied in this chapter to the preparation of public discourse. We provide here theoretical foundations for organization, practical applications of organizational patterns and techniques, and some illustrated examples of outline forms.

Chapter Outline

Order in Messages

A carefully devised progression of ideas is characteristic of the commendable speech. In our view a commendable speech is one that possesses clarity, reason, and good sense. Clear organization coincides with our natural impulse to look for meaning in messages. Because valuable data may be missed or information confused due to faulty arrangement of ideas, this section seeks to provide the student with keys to a coherent arrangement of speech materials. Lomas and Richardson make an excellent point when they counsel, "clear organization helps the speaker remember what he wants to say and the listener understand and retain what he has heard."[1]

The appreciation of order, however fashioned, appears to be a universal trait of human beings. Classification of plants, animals, chemicals, and college students is a fact of our existence. We observe, classify, and label. In short, there is no one who is absolutely unfamiliar with the concept of order. For this reason, the idea of structure in public communication should be considered an essential ingredient in any recipe for communication interest and clarity. The notion that audiences appreciate random intellectual wandering is a half-baked notion with no substance in fact.

Some advice we have given in earlier chapters dealt with aspects of organization. In this chapter we seek to answer these questions: "How important is organization?" "How can organization help the audiences?" "What effects are produced by an organized message?" As we answer these questions in the succeeding pages, an orientation to organization should emerge for you.

It is possible to make some commonsense assumptions about organization and compare these with research findings. If you reflect for a moment, you might assume almost any types of organization would rate on the positive end of a bipolar scale. In other words, if you saw someone's house or office carefully organized, without saying anything vocally, you might think, "This person is well organized." On the other hand, if it were disorganized, you would have had a less positive attitude. However, most human beings assume that orderliness means efficiency, coherence, and logic. This general observation carries over to other situations. Automobile consumer guides frequently comment on how well organized the instruments on the dash of a car are arranged. Real estate agents point out the organized layout of the rooms of a house they show to a buyer and particular emphasis is often given to the organization of the kitchen. Efficiency in the business world often is related to the organization of workers, departments, divisions, branches, and

---

[1] Charles W. Lomas and Ralph Richardson, *Speech: Idea and Delivery* (Boston: Houghton Mifflin, 1963), p. 120.

offices. Consider the difficulty of selecting the particular book you desire at the library unless an organizational system of the general card file were available. Although there are many other examples, the point here is that organization per se is often perceived as positive. Thus, we might assume that if we were judging between two speeches, one organized and one disorganized, there would be almost a natural tendency to choose the organized speech over the disorganized one. We might also assume that the more organized the speech is, the easier that speech will be understood. Since we have already suggested that an organized speech might be selected by a judge over the disorganized one, we might suggest further that the more organized the speech, the better that speech will be rated or liked by the audience. Further, we might remember that during examinations we often group things together as a memory aide, and thus we might conclude that the more organized message will be more easily remembered than a disorganized message. And since organization suggests overt planning, we might assume that the audience will perceive the speaker as more intelligent, more trust-worthy, more competent, and more credible if he or she presents an organized message. In short, before we even investigate the research findings, we can make several assumptions that organized messages are:

1. positively perceived by the audience
2. easier to understand (comprehend)
3. easier to remember
4. assigned to the careful planning of the speaker and positively increase the speaker's image (ethos)

The order, structure, or organization of a message becomes a significant factor in how well people can remember items of in-formation and how well they can subsequently recall information they have stored.[2] Most students can testify that this is true with respect to the various instructors they have had. You probably can recall some professors whose lectures were so well organized that you found them easy to follow and you were able to take notes easily. However, you also can remember the frustrations of attempt-ing to understand and take notes from a professor whose lecture was little more than disorganized ramblings.

Our observations concerning the significance of organization of

[2] *Psychology Today: An Introduction* (Del Mar, Calif.: CRM Books, 1970), p. 362.

messages follows an ancient heritage. The classical works of Greek and Roman writers, particularly Aristotle and Cicero, advocate the utility of careful organization of message elements. Some of the prescriptive advice given more than 2000 years ago has been validated in modern experiments.[3] Of course, other prescriptive advice of ancient times simply is not valid for today's audiences. Although there are some unanswered questions concerning specific elements in the study of the effects of organization on message effectiveness and there continues to be some unresolved conflicts in contemporary research, we suggest that the beginning student should carefully organize his messages. Like human beings, organization can be very individualistic, so we recognize that each speaker must determine what type of organizational pattern is appropriate for the particular rhetorical situation.

Basic Patterns of Organization

Although you will need to determine which organization pattern is appropriate for your particular topic and rhetorical situation, there are a number of choices. The ancient Greeks advised that each speech should consist of at least three parts: the introduction or beginning, the body or middle, and the conclusion or end. Even today this pattern of *introduction, body,* and *conclusion* continues to serve us well. Generally, the communicator attempts to establish some "common ground" and rapport with the audience in the introduction; that is, he or she often indicates beliefs, attitudes, values, and behaviors that he or she holds in common with the audience members. For example, the local politician who indicates in a campaign speech that he or she too grew up in *this* town, attended church *here*, graduated from the *local* high school, and was employed for many years in *this* town, is establishing common ground with the audience. Typically, in the introduction the communicator also indicates the topic and position on that topic or at least an indication of where she or he is headed so that the audience members have a general notion of the direction. For an example of Booker T. Washington's technique, see the introduction below. He delivered this address to a crowd at the Atlanta Exposition in 1895.

---

[3] Wayne N. Thompson, *Quantitative Research in Public Address and Communication* (New York: Random House, 1967), pp. 65–71.

> Mr. President and Gentlemen of The Board of Directors and citizens: One third of the population of the South is Negro. No enterprise seeking the material, civil, or moral welfare of this section can disregard this element of our population and reach the highest success. I but convey to you, Mr. President and Directors, the sentiment of the masses of my race when I say that in no way have the value and manhood of the American Negro been more fittingly recognized than by the managers of this magnificent exposition at every stage of its progress. It is a recognition that will do more to cement the friendship of the two races than any occurrence since the dawn of freedom.

In formal speech situations where the speaker is formally introduced by another person, the introducer may indicate a communicator's experience, qualifications, and interest on the particular topic.

The middle, or body, sets forth the specific topic, the position of the speaker in relation to that topic, and the supporting materials that indicate why the speaker takes that position.

The end, or conclusion, usually recalls the major topic of the position taken and reviews the major reasons for that position. The audience members are generally asked to give serious consideration for the views expressed. Therefore, the conclusion typically contains a brief review or summary of the presentation.

But there are several patterns of organization beyond the basic foundational structure of introduction, body, and conclusion. Five patterns have been repeatedly employed by the great speakers: (1) the problem-solution pattern, (2) the cause-effect or effect-cause pattern, (3) the topical pattern, (4) the spatial pattern (5) the chronological pattern.

The problem-solution pattern

The speaker who employs the problem-solution pattern identifies the existing problem, describes reasons why that particular problem is significant to the audience members, and then offers a suggested method to solve the problem along with the reasons for choosing this solution. This pattern is based on the sound psychological principle that once a problem has been presented as personal, immediate, and relevant, there is a human tendency to seek a solution. Therefore, in the problem-solution format, the speaker identifies the problem that creates a need for change and then offers the audience his or her solution for that problem.

The cause-effect or effect-cause pattern

Buffalo, New York, is a highly industrialized city. Local environmentalists have at times criticized the air and water of the area. These environmental effects are then traced to the sources—the local industries—or the causes. Or if the speaker wishes to reverse the sequence, he or she could first point to the many industries (causes) and to their resultant production of polluted waste (effects). One of the effective aspects of either cause-effect or effect-cause patterns is that the speaker can serially build up an impressive array of either causes or effects, and by the time this listing is completed, there is a natural tendency to assign blame. The audience thus becomes an active participator in the communication and the probabilities of agreement with the speaker are often increased.

The topical pattern

The topical pattern allows the speaker to order the aspects, elements, characteristics, parts, and so on, of his or her topic according to his or her own preference of categories and hierarchies. For example, if your parents ask you to describe how you like your college courses, the order (most popular first or least popular first) and the ranking of the courses in terms of the importance you personally assign to them is very individualistic. Another student responding to the same question probably would respond differently. Or when elements of a topic can be categorized, the topical pattern may be used. For example, great literature can be topically arranged in terms of comedies, tragedies, histories, and so forth. Thus, the topical pattern allows the speaker to arbitrarily rank and order specific topics according to his or her personal estimate of clear and appropriate organization.

The spatial pattern

Usually this pattern is employed when speakers are attempting to get their audience to visualize a particular sequence. You probably have used this pattern unconsciously when describing the layout of your apartment in terms of its rooms and furnishings. The pilot may be instructed by the control tower to note the obstruction on a particular runway at nine o'clock. The pilot then mentally pictures the face of a clock and looks slightly to his left. At three o'clock the pilot would look to his right. The point here is that spatial pattern-ings often aid the listener.

The chronological pattern

The chronological pattern, as its name suggests, arranges message elements according to a particular sequence of time. The most obvious example of a chronological patterning is involved in giving biographical sketches in the college entrance applications. Or your instructor may ask you to present a brief biographical sketch to other members of your class as an aide for establishing a friendly personalized classroom atmosphere. Historical descriptions are often sequenced chronologically. For example, one could trace the history of America's space program by reciting the chronological achieve-ments leading up to the landing of men on the moon and further exploration.

In addition to these five patterns of organization, you may wonder whether your strongest argument should be presented at the beginning, middle, or end of your presentation. The question is a good one and has stimulated research for a number of years. The basic question is, "In what order should arguments be pre-sented?" Some research studies suggest strong arguments are more effective at the beginning of a presentation; this theory is referred to as a *law of primacy*. Other researchers claim that strong arguments are more effective at the close of a presentation and point to a *law of recency*.[4]

There are several reasons why the research on primacy-recency is contradictory. One is the number of intervening variables within each experiment. For example, where the receiver accepts the first argument and closes his or her mind to later arguments, we can say that this person has a closed mind.[5] Thus, if only one argument is given consideration, there would likely be support for the law of primacy. But if the person heard all arguments, there might be a tendency for the last strong argument to be more influential and

[4] Marvin Karlins and Herbert Abelson, *Persuasion: How Opinions and Attitudes Are Changed* 2nd ed. (New York: Springer, 1970), pp. 27–32 and Berlo and Gulley, "Some Determinants of the Effect of Oral Communication in Producing Attitude Change and Learning," *Speech Monographs* XXIV (1957), pp. 10–20.

[5] For an excellent treatment of this complex psychological phenomenon, see Milton Rokeach, *The Open and Closed Mind* (New York: Basic Books, 1960).

this would support the law of recency.[6] Interestingly, however, we have found no research that supports putting arguments in the middle, so we suggest that you put your strongest arguments either near the beginning or end of the body but avoid putting them in the middle.

Primacy-recency research is related to studies that focus on climax ordering (arrangement or arguments from weakest to strongest) or anticlimax (from strongest to weakest).[7]

Although the evidence is contradictory and although each speaker should carefully consider the particular rhetorical situation for exceptions, our experience suggests that those who present their strongest arguments last are often the most effective communicators.

To the beginning speaker, careful organization has an added dividend because it helps you remember the content of your message. The fact that you consciously selected a particular pattern of organization for the major ideas of your speech will generally help you remember the content.

We have discussed the foundational organizational pattern (introduction, body, conclusion), five specific patterns within that foundation (problem solution, cause-effect and effect-cause, topical, spatial, and chronological), and we have suggested a climactic ordering of the strongest arguments last based on our experience with beginning speakers.

Outlining Your Presentation

By now you understand the importance of ordering the message parts. In preparation for public communication you should begin to master techniques of outlining your ideas. In this section we emphasize the nature and efficacy of good outlining. In no case should communication, whether spoken or written, merely conform to a rigid formula at all costs. Yet most public communicators who seriously intend for their speeches to have an effect on audiences attempt to follow some type of structure. As we discussed in the

---

[6] See Gerald R. Miller, "Counter-Attitudinal Advocacy: A Current Appraisal," in C. David Mortenson and Kenneth K. Sereno, eds., *Advances in Communication Research* (New York: Harper & Row, 1973).

[7] Wayne C. Minnick, *The Art of Persuasion* (Boston: Houghton Mifflin, 1968), pp. 261–262, and Carl I. Hovland et al., eds., *The Order of Presentation in Persuasion* (New Haven: Yale University Press, 1957).

section on organizational patterns, order in communication is a valuable aid for the communicator and the audiences.

When a communicator chooses a given pattern of organization for materials, much of the structural work has been accomplished. If a person has chosen a topic, a purpose, and understands how best to achieve the communicative goal, it is fairly simple to proceed with the formal outline. When we read or hear a public communication, we expect to find movement from a beginning to an end. If the communicator has been attentive to the hearers or readers, the communication will be organized and each element will give the broadest opportunity for the development of the central idea.

The public communication is a work of art and, like great sculptures, the public communication is comprised of various elements of form and items of interest. Thus, even a stream of consciousness approach must lead somewhere and our ability to let others see where our art is directed remains significant for effective public communication. Instead of abandoning the items of a discourse to chance, the public communicator must develop a plan; that is, he or she must sketch the details of his or her thoughts on the subject. Without this procedure, the communicator is liable not to know where ideas fit together meaningfully.

There has been almost no improvement on the parts of discourse since the classical period in Western history. Plato, Aristotle, and Cicero generally agreed that a communicator had to do two things: (1) please his audience, (2) prove his case. From these considerations they proposed anywhere from three to five parts of a communication. The introduction and conclusion served to satisfy the audiences; the statement of the case, or narration, and the proof of the case were to satisfy the argument. What has evolved is an outline with three principal parts: beginning, middle, and ending, or introduction, body, and conclusion. Let us discuss these three divisions in more detail.

The introduction

The introduction should serve four chief functions in any public communication.

1. It should attract the audience's favorable attention.
2. It should stimulate and arouse interest in the topic.
3. It should prepare the audience for the communicator's central message. If the audience is disinterested, the introduction

must attempt to change them; if they are hostile, the introduction seeks to ease their hostility in order to get a fair
hearing.
4. It should indicate the purpose of the communication, that is,
it should state the communicator's thesis.

There are numerous ways to develop introductions, but even if
the communicators limit their method of development to the four
functions mentioned above, they will have a good assessment of
what their introductions will be capable of achieving.

The body

Introductions may accomplish the functions intended by the
communicator, but the discourse is more than an introduction. The
body is an essential part of a complete public communication. It
serves to develop the main ideas through an interlocking system of
supporting points. The communicator seeking to be effective should
concentrate on establishing support for a few main headings. In
addition to selecting the main headings, the communicator must
also be concerned with arranging them in the most useful order.
In considering how many main headings to choose, three factors
must be considered: (1) the audience, (2) the communicator,
(3) the discourse. In most instances audiences become restless after
ten or twelve points. Thus, an unnecessary task is placed on the
audience to remember all the major points. As to the communicator,
an outline with a large number of main headings indicates an
inability to consolidate ideas; therefore, many headings constitutes
an unfortunate decline in the communicator's *ethos*. Finally, few
subjects are likely to have as many main heads as the would-be
communicator might endeavor to develop. In that case the communicator prepares the outline with a view toward limiting the
major headings to that material which he or she has the strongest
supports and the most direct persuasive appeals. However, it should
be pointed out that each communicator must use the ability to
assess audiences to help determine when a topic should be introduced in a public communication.

The conclusion

The conclusion should serve two primary functions: (1) it
should refresh the memory of the audience about the communica-

tion; (2) it should cause the audience to desire to do something, even if it is only to hear more about or read more on the subject.

Principles of Effective Outlining

What we have been talking about so far is a systematic approach to developing a plan for public communication. Inasmuch as outlines serve both as blueprints and diagnostic aids for the communication, they indicate what a person plans to do. Outlines function as guides to the speaker much like a road map guides a traveler. A communicator should be able to determine after a discourse if particular problems arose because of faulty planning by a careful review of the outline. Thus, an outline is a significant instrument in communicating ideas. The requirements for a good outline construction presented below should be followed:

1. Use a clear purpose sentence. Many communicators fail to express clearly and completely their purpose.
2. Organize the outline into the three divisions discussed above: the *introduction,* the *body,* and the *conclusion.*
3. Use a uniform set of symbols to indicate main headings and each descending order of subheads. Whereas any consistent system can be used, the one in most common use is presented below:

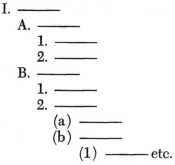

Indentation must also follow a consistent pattern in order to demonstrate logical relationships.
4. Consider each part of the outline as a separate entity. Thus, the main heads should possess numbers consistent with the numbers in their unit. Considering each unit as a separate entity will help most communicators to better remember their main points. It is the idea of remembering a few ideas within a unit rather than all the ideas of all the units.

Incorrect
    Introduction
  I. ———
 II. ———
    Body
III. ———
IV. ———
    Conclusion
  V. ———
VI. ———

Correct
    Introduction
  I. ———
 II. ———
    Body
  I. ———
 II. ———
    Conclusion
  I. ———
 II. ———

5. Each item in your outline should express only one idea.
6. Check main headings to see if they support the purpose sentence.
7. All subheads must develop the heads above them.

Types of Outlines

The sentence outline

Many communicators find the sentence outline to be the most useful kind of guide for their discourses. This type of outline helps communicators by summarizing in complete sentences what they plan to say about a given heading in the outline. Rules for indenting, developing, and numbering are like those already discussed. However, each unit in the sentence outline should be a positive summary of the ideas that the communicator will be expressing. In a sentence outline even the purpose statement becomes a sentence. You should make a thesis sentence out of the purpose. A clear sentence positively stated with only one independent thought should be characteristic of the entries in a sentence outline.

The topic outline

As mentioned in the discussion of the sentence outline, the directions for numbering, indenting, and developing the topic outline remain the same. Topic outlines are composed of entries that are incomplete sentences. Thus it simply lets you and your audience know what topic you will discuss; but it cannot, like the sentence outline, make a statement about how and what you will say on the subject. The topic outline does not organize specific content in the way that you will express it. Like all entries in a topic outline, the purpose statement is usually an incomplete sentence. Many communicators use the infinitive form of the verb to begin their purpose statement in a topic outline. The example below indicates how this system works.

Conservation of oil

PURPOSE: to convince the audiences that definite steps should be taken to conserve oil.
  I. Necessary for conservation
     A. Economic problems
        1. The astronomical cost to individuals
        2. The national expense
     B. Pollution of environment
        1. Oil spillage on sea
        2. Exhaust fumes in atmosphere
 II. Steps for conservation
     A. ———
     B. ——— etc.

The subject outline

The subject outline is a much shortened version of the topic outline. In most instances the main items are stated in a single entry. Many public communicators who give the impression that they are speaking without outlines are actually using subject outlines. The subject outline is nothing more than a brief note to yourself written in one-word form. For example, the outline on conservation of energy that was written as a topic outline above would be simply written:

Energy

Conservation
    Economic
    Environmental
Steps

Of course, in order to use such an outline a communicator must have familiarity with his or her topic. Martin Luther King, Jr., one of the more effective communicators of this era, frequently employed subject outlines. Use of this form allows one to speak on a broad subject with much more flexibility than is likely with a sentence or topic outline. The flexibility, however, is a potential disadvantage if the person employing the outline does not have in mind control points, that is, concluding or summary statements for each subject. In such cases one is liable to continue trying to communicate when the effectiveness of that point has been reached. A number of persons employing the subject outline make good use of the fifth classical canon of rhetoric, memory. They memorize the last sentence for a particular subject. This is fine as long as the person gets to the last sentence without wandering beyond the information.

Logical arrangement helps the audiences to appreciate your ideas. Thus, proper organization of a communicator's thoughts is an attribute that you will want to acquire. What we have presented in this section is an approach toward effective outlining. We have recommended that the outline be divided into three parts, *introduction, body,* and *conclusion.* Furthermore, we have suggested throughout this section that the public communicator must be concerned with coherence and organic wholeness. In the final analysis, a good outline is a measure of how much effort has gone into the structure of the discourse.

FOR STUDENT APPLICATION

1. Read a brief article in a newspaper or magazine. Now review the article and see if you can determine the main points. Locate the divisions of introduction, body, and conclusion. Can you prepare a one-page outline of the article?
2. Find any organizational chart. The administration of your school or your local city government should be able to provide you with such a chart. Review the chart and bring it to class for discussion.
3. From memory describe the arrangement of furniture in your room, apartment, or home. Use a diagram to illustrate the layout design of various rooms at home or in your school building.
4. Compare the organization of a casual conversation with any formal public communication. List the differences and discuss them with other members of your class.

5. Select a topic of your choice and prepare an outline of that topic using two or more patterns of organization. Which outline do you prefer? Which outline is preferred by other members of your class?

6. Read three recent presidential "inaugural addresses" and describe the pattern of organization used in each one. Ask another member of your class to read the same speeches and to describe the organizational patterns used. Now compare your findings. Did you both find the same patterns? Do you both agree about which pattern was the most effective? Discuss your findings with the rest of your class.

Readings

HOLM, JAMES N. *Productive Speaking for Business and the Professions.* Boston: Allyn & Bacon, 1967.

HOVLAND, CARL I. et al., eds. *The Order of Presentation in Persuasion.* New Haven: Yale University Press, 1957.

MANDLER, G. "Organization and Memory." In K. W. SPENCE and J. T. SPENCE, eds. *The Psychology of Learning and Motivation,* vol. 1. New York: Academic Press, 1967.

MONROE, ALAN H. *Principles and Types of Speech.* Glenview, Ill.: Scott, Foresman, 1964.

WALTER, OTIS M., and SCOTT, ROBERT L. *Thinking and Speaking.* New York: Macmillan, 1962.

9 The Style of Public Communication

WHAT YOU CAN EXPECT:

In Chapter 9 we provide a thorough treatment of style as a constituent of contemporary society. The student is presented with a rationale for the study and use of stylistic characteristics in public communication.

After reading this chapter, you should be able to vary your style as is appropriate for your audiences. Good style takes practice; practice takes patient work.

Chapter Outline

Symbols
Grammar
Representational and Instrumental
Techniques of Usage
    The Question
    Thematic Questions
    Rhetorical Questions
    Direct Quotes
Qualities of Public Style
    Simple Words
    Specificity
    Originality
    Cultural Usages
Figures of Grammar and Speech
Connectives

During the European Renaissance, rhetoricians, intellectual forerunners of contemporary communicationists, argued rather vehemently over the direction style should take in the preparation of discourses. The followers of Peter Ramus accepted the view that discourse had to have a *compositive* or a *resolutive* style. If a given communication lacked either one or the other, it was not merely disorganized, but lacking in the necessary aesthetic qualities that would cause it to demand attention. Thus, a public communicator who used the compositive, ascending-order method, concentrated on organizing the style of his discourse around the smallest units first, then the next largest, until the largest. To the contrary, the resolutive style was concerned with stylistic movement from the largest unit to the smallest. If such were the current practice or theory, few of our leading public communicators would meet the standards for public discourse. What is required of the contemporary communicator is an understanding and appreciation of style in language.

Language, generally speaking, is a set of symbols used by a number of people in accordance with a set of uniform rules that allows them to understand each other. While words constitute the primary symbol system, we must be aware of nonverbal symbols. (See Chapter 6 for a discussion of nonverbal symbols.) However, in this section we will speak primarily of the communicator's use of verbal symbols.

Symbols

We depend on symbols for knowledge of almost every piece of data that enters our senses. A symbol is something that stands for something else. This means that anything a group of people sharing a common set of rules for the use of symbols decides to make a symbol stand for can be done arbitrarily. There is nothing inherent in the symbol itself that requires it to stand for what it does. Symbols, therefore, are used to represent objects, events, ideas, feelings, and attitudes. In this way Afro-Americans have come to speak of Uncle Tom; native Americans, of Uncle Tomahawk; and Mexican-Americans, of Uncle Tomas, to represent a person who will do anything to save his own neck. Of course, the word is not the thing; it is a representation of the concept. Inasmuch as there is no necessary relationship between the symbol and the thing it stands for, it is called arbitrary. You are all familiar with at least one word that circulated among a group of your friends with a meaning that was known by the group. For this acceptance and knowledge of the word to have occurred, there must have been an implicit agreement to use the word in just that way.

The symbol must be related to a referent. There is no inherent meaning in a word. Ogden and Richards contended that a person's thoughts served as the bridge between what we identified as a symbol and its referent.[1] The son who received a telegram that his mother had recovered from a serious illness and who then framed the telegram and hung it on his office wall may have confused the symbol with the referent.

Meaning exists within us. When we decide to accept a certain word as powerful, weak, good, and so on, then the user of that word may whittle away at our defenses like a skillful woodsman. Berlo has understood that words may be transmitted between communicators but the meanings remain with each person separately.[2] The reason for this is because our meanings are wrapped up with our personal responses and reactions to the symbols. These vary from person to person. Effective public communication seeks to reduce the amount of ambiguity that exists between a communicator and his or her audiences. Wenburg and Wilmot say that "communication is a stirring-up process; the meanings we have for words determine the meanings we get from them."[3]

Grammar

We indicated above that language included for us both symbols and a set of rules for how one goes about using those rules. The specific rules may vary from one language to another, but all languages are dependent upon their grammatical elements for others to understand them. There are three parts of grammar that should be considered:

1. The rules that relate to accepted form and changes of words.
2. The rules that relate to the accepted order and pattern of words.
3. The rules that relate to transformations in language.

[1] Charles Kenneth C. K. Ogden and I. A. Richards, *The Meaning of Meaning*, (New York: Harcourt Brace Jovanovich, 1923), pp. 9–10.

[2] David K. Berlo, *The Process of Communication* (New York: Holt, Rinehart and Winston, 1960), p. 175.

[3] John R. Wenburg and William W. Wilmot, *The Personal Communication Process* (New York: Wiley, 1973), pp. 91–92.

Obviously there will be overlapping of these three grammatical elements of language. Grammar is nothing more than the conventions we have established and accepted in the use of a certain language. By examining Rule 1 above, we discover that some words are inflected to indicate variations in meanings. Note the following sentences for comparison:

1. Critics *tend* to make evaluations.
   Critics *tended* to make evaluations.
2. The man has become *thin*.
   The man has become *thinner*.

What these sentences show is how different meanings are created by *inflection*. Choice of the proper word makes it easier for the hearers to appreciate the communicator's message. There are, however, instances where failure to use a word or word forms in the conventional way does not interfere with meaning. For example,

She and *I* saw the car leave.
Her and *me seen* the car leave.

These two sentences mean nearly the same thing and few common users of English would have any difficulty understanding them. Yet they are different in that the second sentence does not conform to our accepted manner of usage. The user of such a sentence for a public discourse would probably call attention in a most negative way to his or her understanding of the grammatical elements in English.

Few aspects of culture change as frequently as language forms. Sometimes the change occurs because we get additional information about usage from specialized groups, such as, users of black English. At other times our words, as well as grammar, change because of deletions through lack of use; in this category are words that were in common use a few years ago (e.g., *spigot, parasol*) but are no longer common in the general American use of English. The public communicator should have a strong motivation to know and use the appropriate words in discourse. It also follows that the use of appropriate language should be conscious and deliberate.

Most importantly, the grammatical elements within a language should be seen as efficient vehicles to carry your thoughts. When rules for two or more languages are employed in the same discourse, it can be exceedingly disconcerting. The public communicator should use uniform rules of grammar throughout the discourse.

Lack of uniformity is the major fault in our employment of grammatical elements. Sometimes users of black English mix rules of grammar in their discourses. To the person who does not understand the accepted forms of black English, the discourse seems ungrammatical, much like the rules of German grammar would seem if applied to English. Proper use of grammatical elements is nothing more than using words in ways that are approved by the majority of people within a given language community. The public communicator should monitor that usage and attempt to satisfy the demands of his hearers.

Representational and Instrumental

A number of textbooks influenced by the early semanticists speak of words having two kinds of meanings: *denotative* and *connotative*. Usually denotative meaning is defined as logical, objective, extensional; and connotative meaning as emotive, subjective, and intensional.[4] Wenburg and Wilmot take a "fresh perspective" toward denotative and connotative meanings. For them, denotative meanings refer to the critical attributes of an object—attributes on which we all agree. Connotative meanings refer to the noncritical attributes that occur with regularity in our experience.[5] Wenburg and Wilmot added a dimension to our understanding of the different meanings of words.

Our view, however, is that as public communicators we must be interested in what words mean; but more appropriate to our capacity to communicate is the question of how words are used. Therefore, denotative and connotative meanings may help us understand how a given word is meant. This is often necessary information if we are to be able to analyze public communication. What we intend to discuss are the fundamental uses of words.

There are two broad categories of word uses: *representational* and *instrumental*. Representational refers to a public communicator's use of words to express something the receivers can understand by simply taking the language at face value. For example, if an ambassador speaking before the United Nations says, "At two o'clock

[4] E. Christian Buehler and Wil A. Linkugel, *Speech Communication: A First Course* (New York: Harper & Row, 1962), p. 244.

[5] Wenburg and Wilmot, *The Personal Communication Process*, p. 92.

tomorrow I will be in Abu Dhabi to negotiate for additional oil shipments to my country," the audiences can understand what he or she means by taking the words to represent what they should reasonably mean. Such use can include either denotative or connotative meanings, so long as the audiences can know what the words reasonably mean. It is true that meanings exist in people, but people must have reason to have the meanings they have. Thus, a connotative meaning, in the conventional sense, may be found in a representational use of language even though emotive and subjective elements are present. For example, when a public communicator says, "What we need to solve our waste problem is an angel of mercy," audiences can know what he or she reasonably means even though it is emotive and intensional. Audiences who share a particular cultural context, not necessarily the same religious community, will know what a communicator reasonably means by the word *angel*. This is not to say that the audiences will believe in angels; after all, there is no way to settle the argument precisely because it is emotive and intensional. Connotative meanings may also be representational if they are our personal uses of words typically considered denotative, for instance, "My car is a *lemon*" indicates that the car has many mechanical problems, or "John is yellow" indicates that he is a coward. Neither *lemon* nor *yellow* are denotatively understood to mean anything other than a fruit or a color. Thus, representational uses of language cut across denotative and connotative boundaries.

Instrumental refers to a communicator's use of language to express something that is not obvious by the choice of words. Language becomes a means of achieving an end that is not or cannot be openly stated. A female student may tell a male student that he looks good in his clothes, or that she had always wanted to tell him how much she appreciated his report in class. Language becomes an instrument where the communicator is saying, "I would like to have a date with you," or some other expression equivalent or similar.

Discourses of the political genre are frequently filled with instrumental language. When a person running for political office speaks before a Democratic club, he or she might invoke the names of Franklin D. Roosevelt and John F. Kennedy. Furthermore, the person might quote them and follow the quote with a statement of his or her own agreeing with the past presidents. What the person is saying is "Vote for me," or "I'm a good Democrat," or some similar statement.

Representational and instrumental uses of language are complementary to each other and may be used in the same discourse. The public communicator finds the appropriate uses of representational and instrumental language in a given rhetorical situation. Of course, cultural and background differences in people who use language may result in widely different choices of language. The objective is to use language in such a way as to make one's ideas understandable and acceptable.

Techniques of Usage

There are numerous techniques of language usage that are helpful to the public communicator. We will discuss a few of them in order that you may have an idea of how to use them in your communications.

Direct questions

The question is used primarily to obtain information, although it may be employed to impress and to clarify an idea. The *direct question* seeks to get an audience response to a question of information. Usually the communicator has reason to believe that the audiences know the answer to the question and that they will give a vocal response. In a speech or monologue, a communicator may ask audiences, "Who's the president of the United States?" and then proceed to discuss the elections or the biography of the president. Such direct questions serve to get the audiences involved in the communicative situation as participants rather than spectators. The traditional black preacher uses this technique effectivly by asking direct questions regarding the communicative event; "Can I get someone to pray with me?" and "Are you following me?" are typical of this type of question. The audience usually responds in a positive manner. Once the response is made, the preacher knows that the audiences have become participants in the communicative event. The direct question, therefore, is a technique for eliciting the vocal reactions of the listeners.

Thematic questions

This type of question seeks to organize the thoughts of the communicator and receiver into a specific category. It is called *thematic* because it concentrates on subject or term themes in discourses. For example, a speaker giving a speech on higher education might begin, "What is higher education?" Once he or she has discussed that question he or she might continue by asking, "What are the purposes of higher education?" and so forth. As a technique, the thematic question does not seek a vocal response from the audience like the direct question, but rather establishes a method for the speaker to organize ideas.

Rhetorical questions

The rhetorical question is one of the most common and effective techniques in communication. Its value is found in its directness and force. A public communicator may use the rhetorical question during a speech to persuade or inform; usually the speaker does not seek an audience response to the rhetorical question. It differs from the direct question in that the direct question requires a vocal answer; the rhetorical question does not. The direct question asks for information; the rhetorical question provides information. Within a discourse the rhetorical question is employed to force an audience to make a psychological decision. We have all been in situations where we have heard speakers present talks and they have delivered them with such force that we had to agree with them. It is this sense that the user of the rhetorical question wishes to establish.

Direct quotes

Direct quotes are frequently confused with the technique of testimony in a discourse. But although both use quotation marks, they perform different functions in a discourse. Testimony is the use of a quotation by an expert or authority to support one's own ideas. For example, a communicator might say that "such and such scientist says so and so about this concept or belief or idea." On the other hand, the direct quotation allows audiences to establish a familiar relationship with some personality. Booker T. Washington's famous Atlanta Exposition speech in 1895 contained an illustration with the quotation, "Cast down your buckets where you are." By using such a technique the speaker draws his audiences into the development of his or her discourse. The direct quote can establish personal warmth between speaker and audience.

Qualities of Public Style

We have been discussing elements of language and grammar in an effort to understand the use of various techniques of usage. Now our attention is turned to what it takes to master public communication style. Style can be learned. And while the old adage that "style is the man" has a ring of truth, the most effective speakers have always managed to acquire a desire to perfect their styles. Perfection of style is seldom achieved but there are public communicators who accomplish a great deal in the management of words. Each communicator should endeavor to acquire stylistic skills.

Simple words

Use of commonly understood words increases the communicator's effectiveness in most circumstances. There are, perhaps, a few exceptions that occur in given audiences. For example, it was frequently said of Martin Luther King's audiences that they understood him although some of the words he used were unfamiliar to them. One explanation for King's effectiveness lay in the overwhelming power of his *pathos* that usually was created by commonly understood words. Thus, if he used a word unfamiliar to his audiences, they could "read in" the meaning from the context. Such dramatic use of new and sometimes complex words helped to create a sense of suspense and anticipation. King's use of a combination of common words transformed his complex words into effective style.

We are not all as skillful as King, though we can improve with practice. Unless the use of complex words aid our discourse, simple words and more common expressions should be used. A communicator sometimes believes that large words add to style. Certainly, the judicious use of any word is of value to the communicator, but use of large and complex words in place of more simple and direct ones often hinders communication.

Specificity

There are times when a communicator wants to use general words, particularly if he or she is speaking of some large class of objects or things. For example, one may speak of *property* instead of *house* to indicate the generality of one's meaning. In most in-stances, however, informative communication seeks the specific term, the more well-defined word, the less general. Audiences tend to understand information much better if our choice of words is specific. As an illustration, we list below a group of words with different characteristics from the general to the specific.

Terms	Attributes
mode of transportation	vast group of things having in common the idea of mobility
vehicle	large class of objects that can be owned
automobile	large class of objects with same general use
sedan	class of objects having same general size and design
Smith's Cadillac Coupe deVille	one specific object with individual characteristics of size, color, shape, and owner-ship

These examples show clearly the value of specificity in com-munication. Audiences can focus more on smaller classes of objects because so many other possibilities have been eliminated. When a person says "the Johnsons' residence," we know that it is more specific than saying either "real estate" or "house." It refers to one specific object with individual characteristics.

What is true with nouns may also be true with verbs. Some verbs are general, such as *move;* others are specific, such as *walk, run,* and *ride.* In each case the individual may be said to move, but the audience gets a fuller picture when the communicator tells *how* one moved. A communicator is an artist who uses words like a plastic artist uses strokes of the brush. If the speaker wants to paint a more specific verbal picture, he or she uses words with greater specificity. Thus, *hobble* is more specific than *walk,* and *walk* is more specific than *move.* It is essential that the communicator select his or her words and terms carefully so as to fulfill the communicative pur-pose. When someone remarks, "I like an automobile better than a bus," she or he is probably conveying an idea about preference be-tween the two vehicles. But if the intention is to describe what kind of automobile one prefers, then the words would have to be more specific. The name of the game for the communicator is to make specificity coincide with purpose. In a significant way this corresponds to the classical conception of propriety.

Originality

There are few movies that we like to see repeatedly. Occasionally an excellent movie comes along with an unusually brilliant plot, excellent dialogue, and skillful cinematography and we say, "I sure could see that again." However, if we see the same movie three or four times, the plot, writing, and camera angles soon become dull. Certain words and phrases are like old movies. Once we have heard them or used them ourselves repeatedly, they lose their freshness. The effective communicator seeks to create or discover new useful combinations of words. It is only through originality that the communicator changes the pace of the speech and perhaps saves it from monotonous language. Communicators who do not think as they create their messages are liable to repeat hackneyed expressions. Barbara Cantwell and Molefi Kete Asante developed the list of hackneyed expressions that appear below:

dog eat dog	lay it on the line
secret of success	save his skin
which side the bread is buttered on	out of the woods
explore every avenue	the chips are down
upset the applecart	shoulder to the wheel
nail down the facts	nose to the grindstone
road to success	missed the boat
climb the ladder of success	clean bill of health
hit the nail on the head	in hot water
put your best foot forward	that'll be the day
don't put your foot in your mouth	play it by ear
	the long and the short of it
green with envy	off the top of your head
purple with anger	getting one's feet wet
like a bull seeing a red flag	as easy as falling off a log
key to success	carrying coals to Newcastle
sitting ducks	easy as pie
on the right track	work like a dog
last piece of the puzzle	with hat in hand
the powers that be	pie in the sky
bringing home the bacon	casting pearls before swine

a dose of his own medicine
method in his madness
ignorance is bliss
tilting at windmills
biting the hand that feeds
    you
a dark horse
paddle your own canoe
playing with fire
the bullet that choked
    Billy Patterson
being led up the garden
    path
throwing your cap over the
    windmill
give up the ghost
beating a dead horse
a bee in her bonnet
eating your words
gilding the lily
make hay while the sun
    shines
flying off the handle
on the horns of a dilemma
living high off the hob
tower of strength
motley crew
phony as a three-dollar
    bill
water over the dam
everything shipshape
in the same boat
sink or swim
in the public eye
not a dry eye in the house
special breed of cat
the bare facts
stand up and be counted
step on his toes
the tide is turning
handle with kid gloves
get out of hand
the guts of the matter
from head to toe

with a fine-tooth comb
bite the bullet
from the horse's mouth
not a leg to stand on
work together as a team
make it to the top
ball-park figures
out of our league
plain as the nose on your face
touch bases with owners
we had our ups and downs
rules of the game
can't get to first base
get caught off base
foot over foot like the dog went
    to Dover
hasn't a prayer
like a bolt from the blue
running around like a chicken
    with its head off
came the dawn
it's duck soup
throwing stones at the bar
busy as a bee
you can't fight city hall
hand in glove
life is not all beer and skittles
bold as brass
the shoe's on the other foot
the fair sex
checkered career
making a clean breast of it
look like the cat that ate the
    canary
the iron hand in the velvet glove
the handwriting on the wall
in a nutshell
the straw that broke the camel's
    back
within an inch of your life
by and large
hasn't a ghost of a chance
sold (or bought) for a song
dog in the manger

eating crow
strike while the iron is hot
if the shoe fits, wear it
picking a bone
it's always darkest before the
    dawn

chicken on Sunday; feathers the
    rest of the week
with bated breath
turn the clock back

Some expressions on the list are regional and may not be over-used in some English-speaking sections of the world. However, most of them, if not trite, are clichés that do not add vigor to the communicator's message.

Cultural usages

Some words and expressions are used more frequently by certain social aggregations of people than others. In cases where this occurs (e.g., the prison culture, the drug culture, or within certain ethnic and racial groups), persons within the culture are capable of understanding and communicating with no difficulty whereas others may find it nearly impossible to communicate. Below is a limited glossary of expressions from the black street culture.

A HIT   a puff of a cigarette or joint
AIN'T IT FUNKY NOW   it is really a good situation
ARE YOU SHITTING?   are you lying?
ASS-KICKING TIME   time to beat someone up

BITCH   to fuss
BLACKER THE BERRY THE SWEETER THE JUICE   expression used to
    describe a lovable person
BLADE   knife
BLOOD   a black person
BLOW YOUR MIND   confuses you
BULL-JIVING OF SHITTING   clowning

CAN YOU DIG IT?   do you agree or understand
CAT   man
CHECK IT OUT   see if it is OK
CHECK OUT YOUR MIND   think twice before doing or saying some-
    thing
CHUMP   a person who is disliked
CUTTING ZEES   sleeping

DIGGIN ON   liking
DIG YOU LATER   will see you later

DOING IT   really performing, as in dancing
DOOKEY   defecation

FOR DAYS   expression used when agreeing with something
FORK   natural comb
FRUTTI   homosexual
FUNKY   really good

GAS   really exciting
GAY   homosexuals
GET DOWN WITH IT   doing something really well
GET OVER   have sexual intercourse
GIG   party
GIVE ME FIVE   handshake of agreement
GON'NE WITH YOUR BAD SELF   you are really something
GOT ME IN A TRICK   a bad situation
GREENBACK   money
GUT BUCKET   pot of chitlings

HALF-ASS JOB   a job not finished
HALF-STEPPING   not doing what is right
HARD UP   will take and do anything
HIGH AS A KITE   expression used to describe one who is drunk or high
HIGH ON THE HOG   living expensively
H.N.I.C.   Head Nigger In Charge
HORSE   heroin

I BE DAMN!   expression of disbelief or anger
I BE FOR YOU   to side with someone
I CAN DIG IT   I understand or agree
I GOT TO GET SOME   must have sexual intercourse
I HEARS YOU   to agree with
I'LL CATCH YOU LATER   will talk to one later

JIVE-TIME NIGGER   one who is always acting up
JUMP ON HIM   tell him about himself
JUNGLE   black residence area

KEEP THE FAITH   keep hoping

LET IT SLIDE   disregard something
LET'S BLOW   let's leave
LID   hat
LOADED TO THE GILLS   same as high as a kite

MAKING GROCERY   buying grocery
MAKING IT   living as usual

MAKING TIME   getting through to the opposite sex
MAMMA   a young lady
MATCHBOXES   storage for marijuana
MEAN   really good-looking
MELLOW   state of delight
MESSED UP MY MIND   confused one
MISS ANNE   white lady
M'LADY   one's girl friend
MOTHER'S DAY   day one gets welfare check
MR. CHARLIE   white man
MY HEAD IS BAD   one is high and feels good
MY MAN   one's boyfriend
MY WOMAN   one's girl friend

NAPPY   kinky hair
NARCO MAN   narcotics man
NOSE IS WIDE OPEN   strung out over someone of the opposite sex

OUT OF IT   do not know what is happening
OUT-OF-SIGHT   really hipped
OVER YOUR HEAD   a level above one's intelligence

PARTY   have a good time
PEES   one's partners
PIGS   the police
PISS ME OFF   makes one mad
PLANTATION   university
PLAYED OUT   is no good
PLAYING IT COOL   not acting up
POPPIES   a drug
PUNK   homosexual

RAGS   clothing
RAP   to talk
RIDE   car
RIGHT ON   expression of agreement
RIPPLING   drinking Ripple (wine)
ROACH   the butt of a joint
ROD   a gun
ROLE PLAYING   acting as expected

SET   a party
SCORE   to obtain drugs
SCREW   sexual intercourse
SHACKING   living as man and wife
SHARP   good-looking
SHINE IT ON   disregard

SHORT   a car
SOLES   shoes
SHUCKIN' AND JIVING   same as half stepping
SIDE   record
SISTER   black girl
SLAVE   to work
SMACK   a drug
SOMEBODY'S JAWS ARE TIGHT   one is upset
SPLIBS   blacks
SPLIT   to leave
STICK IT IN YOUR EAR   same as kiss ass
STONED   same as high as a kite
STRAIGHT'N COMB   used to straighten hair
STRUNG OUT   same as nose is open
SWEET LUCY   wine
SWOOP   to go steady with another person's girl friend or boy-
    friend

TALKING OUT OF YOUR ASS   one does not know what he is saying
T.C.B.   Taking Care of Business
TELL ME 'BOUT IT   let me know about it
THE EAGLE FLIES   payday
THE HAWK   the wind
THE MERFY   conning and prostituting
THE MO   motel
THREADS   clothing
TIPPIN'   same as swoop
T.L.C.   Tender Loving Care
TORE DOWN   same as stoned
TURN ME ON   let me know about

UP YOUR ASS   expression of contempt or dissatisfaction

WASHING YOUR TEETH   brushing one's teeth
WEED   marijuana
WHAT IT IS?   what is one up to?
WHAT IT MEAN?   explain one's self
WHAT'S HAPPENING?   how are things going
WHAT'S THE BEEF?   same as what's happening
WHAT'S YOUR THING   what do you plan to do?
WHEELS   car
WHERE YOU COMING FROM?   explain oneself
WHIPPING A GAME   playing one for a fool
WHOOPDY   car
WRAP IT UP   finish

YEAH   expression of agreement
YOU AIN'T NEVER LIED   expression of agreement

Figures of Grammar and Speech

According to Cicero and Quintilian, figurative language included
any deviation, either in thought or expression, from the ordinary
modes of speaking.[6] Among the major deviations have been figures
of grammar and speech. Figures of grammar are those deviations
in structure and content that lend emphasis to discourse. Figures
of speech are those deviations that occur when we extend the literal
meanings of words and concepts. Thus, a *litotes*, or understatement,
such as "W. E. B. DuBois, author of over sixty books, was a fairly
productive writer," would be a figure of grammar. "Corporal Sanchez
was a tiger in the frontlines of Vietnam" would be a metaphor, a
figure of speech. Sheridan Baker classifies the figures according to
their function.

> *Alluding to the familiar* Example: Paroemia (applying proverbs
> to a new situation), "Man shall not live by bread alone." (He
> has just ordered steak.)
> *Building to climax* Example: Synonymy (using synonyms for
> emphasis), "A miserable, wretched, depressed neighborhood."
> *Intensifying* Example: Aposiopesis (stopping in midsentence),
> "And in the name of common sense . . ."
> *Irony* Example: Oxymoron (emphasizing a point by the irony
> of an apparent contradiction), "A wise fool, a fearful joy, a
> sweet sadness, a quiet orgy."
> *Overstating, understating* Example: Hypothesis (illustrating
> with an impossible supposition), "If salt lose its savor, where-
> with shall it be salted?"
> *Posing contrasts* Example: Chiasmus (crossing the terms of one
> clause by reversing their order in the next), "Ask not what
> your country can do for you; ask what you can do for your
> country."
> *Refining, elaborating* Example: Hirmos (heaping appositives to-
> gether), "All men, rich, poor, tall, short, young, old, love it."
> *Repeating* Example: Epistrophe (ending several sentences alike
> for emphasis), "They loved football. They ate football. They
> slept football."

[6] Sister Miriam Joseph, *The Trivium in College Composition and Reading* (South
Bend, Ind.: McClave Printing, 1948), p. 262.

Substituting Example: Prosopopoeia (personifying an inanimate
  object), "The stadium settled back for a lonely week."[7]

The important point for the communicator to remember is that
good use of figures can only come after much practice.

Use of the two most common figures of speech, *metaphors* and
similes, can add vividness and color to anyone's language, that is,
if they are not abused. If they are not used judiciously, they will
create a weak and ineffective discourse. Too many figures can
obscure the directness that gives a discourse stature and strength;
the proper combination, on the other hand, can hold the audience's
attention and interest. A *simile* usually compares two things with
the use of *like,* or *as.* The metaphor, similarly, compares two things
but omits the connectives. For example, "The woman is as restless
as a panther," is a simile. "The woman is a panther" is a metaphor.
Winston Churchill's use of metaphors has been amply recognized.
Buehler and Linkugel believe that "much of his oratorical greatness
lay in his ability to find exactly right figurative language."[8]

Connectives

It is impossible to communicate effectively without using some connectives. However, use of certain compound prepositions and con-
junctions can be troublesome and lead to confusion. The examples
presented below represent clusters that might be avoided:

Cluster	Substitute
for the purpose of	for
with a view to	to
with reference to	about
of the character of	like
with regard to	about
due to the fact that	since
in the event that	if
of the nature of	like
on account of	because
with the results that	so that
in the case of	if
from the point of view of	for

[7] Sheridan Baker, *The Complete Stylist* (New York: Crowell, 1966), pp. 330–
332.

[8] Buehler and Linkugel, p. 269.

Communicators generally utilize transitional connectives when showing (1) time relationships, (2) amplification, (3) logical sequence, (4) clarification by comparison or contrast. Examples of those connectives appear below.

Time relationships

beforehand	soon
later	therewith
subsequently	simultaneously
concomitantly	previously

Amplification

likewise	another
additionally	in addition
furthermore	besides
moreover	also

Logical sequence

therefore	because
since	consequently
accordingly	thus
on that account	hence

Clarification by comparison or contrast

conversely	however
yet	nevertheless
similarly	contrarily
congruently	inversely

Rudolph Flesch observes in *The Art of Plain Talk* that there are two sets of connectives: one for oral communication and another for written communication. A writer may use *likewise, furthermore,* and *moreover,* whereas a speaker may substitute *and* or *also.* While a writer may use *accordingly* or *thereupon,* a speaker suffices with *so* or *therefore.*

The mastery of connectives in public communication may be achieved by attention to two techniques: (1) compare written and spoken connectives and use the one that fits your discourse; (2) avoid excessive use of cluster connectives; when possible use a single-word substitute.

In conclusion, a communicator learns how to use effective style by reading and listening. If you read good prose and poetry, your mind will be exposed to a variety of language uses. By absorbing other communicators' styles a person may find resources for his or her own style. Listening to good speeches is also a natural way to discover new imagery, combinations of words, and expressive phrases. While you will not want to mimic the style of another, you will want to monitor style in order to learn for yourself. Finally, a communicator learns by doing. The more you speak, the better your style should become because certain stylistic features and devices will emerge as dominant in your overall communicative *ethos;* others will be eliminated from your stylistic repertoire.

FOR STUDENT APPLICATION

1. Compare the style of formal public communications with the style of a casual conversation with a friend. How are the styles different?

2. Listen to the television news on two different stations. Compare the two newscasters' style of presentation.

3. To what extent do various subcultures share a communicator's style? Consider groups composed primarily of (1) young members (16–20), (2) elderly members (over 60), (3) female members, and (4) male members. Does each subculture have its own distinctive style? Identify the various styles according to each subculture.

4. List some differences in the style of preachers, politicians, and teachers. Do you think that each occupation has its own style? What are some of the stereotyped style characteristics of each of these occupations?

5. Some people feel that the legal and medical professions have a "fancy-words style" of communicating. Do you think doctors and lawyers sometimes hide behind their "fancy words"? Why is their style more formal than other professions? Discuss it with other members of the class.

6. List as many differences as you can between a formal public presentation and an informal conversation. Are any of the differences you have listed primarily differences of style? Compare your list with other members of your class and discuss.

Readings

BLANKENSHIP, JANE. "A Linguistic Analysis of Oral and Written Style," *Quarterly Journal of Speech*, 48 (December, 1962), pp. 419–422.

BLANKENSHIP, JANE. *A Sense of Style*. Belmont, Calif.: Dickenson, 1968.

BRADLEY, BERT. *Speech Performance*. Dubuque, Iowa: Wm. C. Brown, 1967.

CHASE, STUART. *Power of Words*. New York: Harcourt Brace Jovanovich, 1954.

FLESCH, RUDOLPH. *The Art of Plain Talk*. New York: Harper & Row, 1946.

LUCAS, F. L. *Style*. London: Cassell, 1955.

MCEDWARDS, MARY G. *Introduction to Style*. Belmont, Calif.: Dickenson, 1968.

THOMAS, GORDON. "Oral Style and Intelligibility," *Speech Monographs* 23 (March, 1956), pp. 46–54.

10 Presentation of Public Communication

WHAT YOU CAN EXPECT:

Chapter 10 discusses the presentation of your communication message.

This chapter takes presentation of public communication seriously and attempts to provide the reader with suggestions for improving delivery. Our suggestions are placed in a general theoretical framework so that you will be able to use these ideas effectively.

Chapter Outline

Gerald R. Ford hired speech teachers to help him with the presentation of his public communications after he became President of the United States of America. Ford recognized the significance of his presentation of messages. Audiences demand that a communicator pay attention to visible and audible aspects of the communicative environment.

After a person has spent considerable time researching an idea, formulating an organizational plan, and identifying verbal strategies, the presentation of the message holds the key to whether or not all the effort is successful. Well-presented speeches can take care of themselves. Demosthenes, among the Greeks; Cicero, among the Romans; and Okomfo Anokye, among the Ashanti, all demonstrated a high regard for delivery.

Demosthenes spent years practicing projection of emphasis and enunciation of words. It has been said that his intense desire to speak well in public led him to place pebbles in his mouth and raise his voice against the sound of the sea's waves. This he did to achieve perfection in delivery. Cicero, the Roman orator, politician, and philosopher made style and delivery the principal characteristics of rhetorical discourse during his time. As a senator he was a practicing orator exhibiting the skills of delivery he wrote about as a theorist. Okomfo Anokye, the great priest of the Ashanti nation, was an *okyeame* (the best English translation is probably "orator-transmitter" or "medium") who lived in the early seventeenth century. Anokye would spend hours in the forest raising his voice against the wind. The giant baobabs and cotton silk trees were his audiences. Having developed his delivery after several months in the forest, Okomfo Anokye became the *okyeame* for King Osei Tutu. What each of these public speakers understood was that practice is essential to doing your best. Practice may not make perfect, but without it you are assured of mediocrity. In preparation to present a monologue or speech you should consider the following suggestions.

Some Elements of Delivery

Direction-indirection

Most textbooks emphasize the value of directness in presentation, arguing that the communicator should not signal a desire to withdraw from the auditors. There is obvious merit to a communicator concentrating his or her energies on audiences and causing them to concentrate their energies on him or her. However, directness may not be of value in every given case even within our contemporary society. Thus, a communicator must also understand the rhetorical value of indirection. In some instances a communicator may achieve greater resolution of an issue if her or she establishes the limits of the issue and gradually closes in upon it rather than attacks a point directly. Of course, this is a matter of rhetorical strategy; it is, however, an aspect of how one approaches audiences as a communicator. We might say that the typical direct communicator looks the audiences in the eye in order to give them the impression of taking them personally into consideration. We have learned in recent years from the work of Smith, Hernandez, and Allen as well as Cooke that Afro-Americans and Mexican-Americans may exhibit indirection in personal contact, such as an avoidance of eye contact with auditor-observers. Such behavior could erroneously suggest a lack of personal involvement, a withdrawal, or a lack of alertness to those who do not understand the cultural bases of this behavior. Problems occur because Euro-Americans generally associate eye contact with confidence. On the contrary, Afro-Americans frequently consider direct eye contact as evidence of dishonesty or an attempt to "pull the wool over someone's eyes."

As a communicator you must plan to exhibit the greatest respect for your audiences without taking them for granted by embarrassing actions. Presentation must be evaluated on the basis of the audiences' expectations. Most audiences expect the communicator to demonstrate poise and a well-integrated approach to physical action. When speaking to an audience, speak as if you are speaking to a friend. In this way you avoid furtive glances, glowering, and a complete lack of eye contact. A person speaking to a friend does not avoid eye contact but neither does she or he maintain it constantly. What is suggested is a relaxed but poised attitude toward presentation of the communication.

Spontaneity

While you will not be able to speak without notes on every occasion, a communicator should strive to give the impression of "first utterance." This is particularly difficult to do if you have given the speech or monologue more than twice. Usually when we speak without notes, however, we demonstrate more spontaneity than when using notes. The idea of "first utterance" captures what is meant by spontaneity. Spontaneity can imply speaking without any effort or premeditation. What we mean by spontaneity is the *quality of naturalness*. A communicator should speak as if words come without prompting. There are several sides to spontaneity. One is the obvious performance of the communicator, such as Dick Gregory, who gives the same basic speech over many times with excellent results. There may be a spontaneity in this case but it is a spontaneity growing out of familiarity. Some communicators are not able to make their speeches seem new and exciting after repeating them several times. Speakers like Georgia State Legislator Julian Bond and Senator Edward Kennedy appear to have the necessary alertness to make their speeches spontaneous.

What are the characteristics of presentation that make a prepared text appear spontaneous? There is no one quality that provides the presentation with spontaneity; many factors are significant. The prepared text itself may inhibit the speaker if the style of the text does not permit an oral style. There was a saying among Byzantine rhetoricians, "Some speeches are made to be heard and some are made to be read." A prepared text can be so poorly written or outlined that it is impossible for the communicator to give the impression of spontaneity. Another factor is the vocal flexibility of the communicator. To effect spontaneity you must make the idea sound as if it is being created at that moment. A person asked to describe his or her house could easily almost effortlessly give a description of the various rooms and entrances of a house. This occurs when we have information stored in our brains about the particular object. But in those cases where we do not have mastery over the information, our spontaneity is frequently difficult at best. There is a sort of haphazard spontaneity that accompanies ignorance. We do not counsel this approach to communication. Clearly, knowledge of your subject and an expressive voice are the two main ingredients in the recipe for spontaneity.

Phrasing

In vocal presentation of the speech or monologue, phrasing is a major element in securing and maintaining audience attention. Different communicators phrase differently. But communicators whose thought units or breath units do not allow the audience to grasp meaning may lose their audiences. Some speakers pause at the most inappropriate places. There is a story told about the Napoleonic Wars in Europe that illustrates what can happen if a thought unit is not complete. A crowd of people in a small town outside of London gathered at a little church to get news of Wellington's fight with Napoleon's armies. An announcement was made that a large sign would be hoisted upon the church with the news of the war. When the first crew of workmen came to hoist the sign, they brought only the part that read WELLINGTON DEFEATED. The people let out a thunderous gasp. They were saddened. Many in the crowd turned to go away but just then another group of workmen came with another portion of the news. Their portion read NAPOLEON AT WATERLOO. When the full message was seen, the news was WELLINGTON DEFEATED NAPOLEON AT WATERLOO. Here, you have a clear demonstration of how units of words can be used to affect audience behavior. Proper phrasing and pausing must be considered a part of vocal presentation. If you know the sense of what you are saying, you will have no trouble saying it sensibly.

Use of physical action

If you experience the shaking of your limbs during the communicative situation, you may use that to your advantage. Such trembling is nothing more than the homeostatic process of the body dissipating excess energy. The effective communicator is able to take this excess energy and use it in gesturing or in moving from place to place. Some of the most successful public communicators have been able to use this energy constructively. In this way they rid themselves of excess energy and also aid in communication. (See Chapter 6 for further discussion of nonverbal elements.)

Gestures and facial expressions

Gestures readily communicate meaning, from the rather simple hand signals a baseball catcher might use to signal the pitcher as to whether to throw a fast ball or a curve, to the complex sign language system utilized by the deaf. Gestures are used primarily to emphasize and illustrate the verbal part of a message. In his book *The Story of Language,* Mario Pei states that there are literally thousands of different meanings handled by gestural language.[1] Besides meaning, gestures also often add clarity. Historically there have been those who recognized the importance of bodily action in public speaking. Cicero and Quintilian suggested that effective

[1] Mario Pei, *The Story of Language* (Philadelphia, Lippincott, 1949), p. 13.

gestures and physical behavior often aided the speaker. Of course, there have also been several periods in which rule dominated and mechanically prescribed gestures and bodily movement have been advocated. This was particularly true during the elocutionary movement.[2] While we clearly do not suggest any prescribed set of rules, we do think that the contemporary speaker should plan appropriate gestures for his presentation.

Another important element in effective communication is facial expression. Since the speaker maintains the most obvious contact with the audience through eye contact, the importance of facial expression that reinforces meaning should not be overlooked. To neglect the visual contact by avoiding the eyes of audience members through looking at the floor, the wall behind the audience above eye level, the ceiling, or at your notes destroys the sense of communication and implies you are talking *to* your audience instead of talking *with* them.

Posture

So much has been written about posture by so many authors, we almost decided to say nothing on the issue. In fact, there is only a modicum of research information on how posture affects communication. Most of what we know about posture is from common experiences. For example, audiences usually have unfavorable reactions if a speaker slouches over the podium. But this accepted notion has never been proven to be true. We say that a person looks better if he or she has erect posture, but "looking better" may have little to do with speech effectiveness. Our advice on posture is simple and straightforward: be comfortable and make your audience comfortable.

The presentation of public communication is much like the delivery of the new cars each year to the local automobile dealers. The work has gone into the product and it is now in the showroom. *Delivery is the time of performance.* Cicero once remarked that delivery is the sole and supreme power in oratory.[3] At this time

---

[2] During the late eighteenth century, some proposed rigid detailed rules for pauses, accents, gestures, posture, and bodily activity in general. For a brief discussion of the movement and some of the most prominent advocates, see Lester Thonssen, A. Craig Baird, and Waldo W. Braden *Speech Criticism,* 2nd ed. (New York: Ronald Press, 1970), pp. 138–140.

[3] Cicero, *De Oratore,* trans. H. Rackham, 2 vols. (Cambridge, Mass: Harvard University Press, 1960), 2:169.

the communicator's knowledge of his or her subject, personal consciousness, and analysis of his or her audience must come together. During the delivery of the speech, visual and vocal information are transmitted to the audience. Accordingly, the audience sees and hears the speaker and one should strive to be effective in each area.

Communicator Apprehension

Theodore Clevenger has observed that *stage fright* is a misnomer and "the measuring instrument in a stage fright experiment is not only the measurement of stage fright, it is the definition as well."[4] "Researchers have used three different instruments to measure stage fright: the amount the speaker says she or he has, the amount the audience says the speaker has, and the amount a meter says the speaker has. These instruments operate with only moderate interdependence during the course of a public speech."[5] When we say stage fright, we give the impression that fear is present. Actually when a communicator stands before an audience to present a speech, she or he seldom experiences fear. Rather, anxiety is the key emotion. Fear is usually caused by a present or external stimulus; anxiety occurs because of apprehension of a probable loss or threat, or anticipation of a future situation. Therefore, *stage anxiety* is a more apt term. We accept Bert Bradley's definition of stage fright as "a normal form of anxiety, or emotional tension, occurring in anyone confronted with a situation in which the performance is important and the outcome uncertain."[6]

It is an abnormal state to have no feelings of apprehension. It is neither normal nor desirable.[7] Now that we have some idea about what stage fright is and what is normal and abnormal, how should we handle it? There are four elements in controlling stage fright.

1. A Proper Attitude
2. Extensive Communication Experience
3. Good Preparation for Speaking
4. Use of Physical Action

[4] Theodore Clevenger, "A Synthesis of Experimental Research in Stage Fright," *Quarterly Journal of Speech* 45 (April 1959), p. 135.

[5] *Ibid.*, p. 138.

[6] Bert Bradley, *Speech Performance* (Dubuque, Iowa: Brown, 1967), p. 31.

[7] Edward R. Robinson, "What Can the Speech Teacher Do About Student's Stage Fright?" *The Speech Teacher* 8 (January 1959), p. 10.

A proper attitude

We simply mean by this that you must understand what stage fright is and what it is not. This is done by recognizing that the physiological changes that occur can be helpful in presenting the speech. If you were asked by your professor to prepare a special speech to be delivered before the State Assembly your central nervous system would send a message to various organs indicating anxiety. With the proper attitude the speaker understands the physiological changes taking place and tries to counteract them by believing that these changes will increase his ability to speak effectively.

Extensive communication experience

Have you ever wondered why your best friend did not seem to exhibit signs of stage anxiety? Most likely your friend is an extrovert who makes friends easily, socializes well, and demonstrates considerable interest in self-expression activities. By getting a lot of experience, not necessarily in formal settings, your friend has been able to minimize the occasions of anxiety. When we are successful in a given situation, we are much more capable of going on to other situations. A series of successes can ensure a minimum of stage fright. A persistent attitude in the face of a few setbacks can greatly assist the struggling communicator. As the late Congressman Adam Clayton Powell used to say, "Keep the faith, baby."

Good preparation for speaking

When you know you have not prepared adequately, there is almost nothing that can counteract the apprehension. Good preparation is useful for decreasing anxiety. A speaker who knows the subject and has invested time in organizing the presentation is more than 90 percent ahead of the game. If you practice your monologue until you know the main points thoroughly, you will have the confidence needed to overcome anxiety.

Physical action

Physical action can be vocal and gestural. The human voice can be modified in several ways to enhance communicative effectiveness. The volume and rate can be increased or decreased for emphasis and effect, the pitch can be raised or lowered in accordance with the particular mood, and the tone of the voice can be modified to suit the emphasis desired. The integration of the flexible vocal aspect can be a considerable asset to the speaker. Insufficient variation of the voice produces the "deathly dull" monotone voice. Proper use of the voice and physical movement can minimize communicator apprehension.

The Use of Physical Space

The nature of the communication event and the rhetorical situation usually govern to some extent how much space is available. For example, if you visit your professor's office, the space available has already been largely determined. The professor may have arranged his office so that his chair is behind a desk that separates himself and visitors. Some believe this increases the status of the professor. Certainly it lends an air of formality to the office visit. Others may arrange the furniture in their office to facilitate an informal, more equal, lateral positioning of chairs. However, as the visitor, you have little control over the use of space during your communicative visit. The same basic situation holds true for the interview, small group, or public communication situation, but the experienced communicator takes advantage of opportunities to adjust physical arrangements wherever possible. For example, a minister in a large church with less than hoped-for numbers of the congregational flock might request that the members fill up the seats from front to back. Teachers of small classes have learned that a circular seating arrangement often increases student participation in class discussions.

Audio-Visual Aids

The use of audio-visual aids in public speaking is largely a matter of common sense, but there is some "know-how" based upon years of experience that can benefit the beginning student. Obviously, the added information perceived through the visual sense helps the audience to remember important aspects of your presentation. Unnecessary in some instances, in others the employment of well-prepared audio-visual aids can be an important ingredient in the effectiveness of the presentation. Often the use of a different medium to communicate to your audience provides the needed variety to sustain their attention. There are often cases in which a diagram, chart, photograph, tape recording, or film can communicate realism or dramatic effect, and provide vivid and accurate details that would be impossible through the verbal medium alone. The direct utilization of the senses allows one to learn and comprehend more readily. Consider the effectiveness of a verbal description of the Niagara Falls compared to a description plus the *sight* of a Niagara Falls photograph and the *sound* of the water, 700,000 gallons per second, cascading more than 182 feet to the rocks below.[8] One reason television is so popular is that it employs *both verbal and visual* mediums, bringing images of the whole world to those who must remain at home due to economic, health, time, and a host of other reasons.

Experience in the use of proper audio-visual aids is perhaps the quickest way to learn the do's and don'ts, but below are some of the suggestions that are frequently given to beginning public communicators.

1. Use audio-visual aids only when they will help the message.
2. Check accuracy of all charts prior to their use.
3. Check the operation of all electrical and mechanical audio-visual parts prior to presentation.
4. Remember that the judicious use of statistical charts is the best rule.
5. Vary your audio-visual materials.
6. Present your audio-visuals with confidence and poise. There is nothing so irritating as a communicator who does not know what to do with his *own* audio-visuals.

These are only a few suggestions that will help you overcome the major obstacles in the use of audio-visuals. Most universities and colleges now have instructional communication units and media centers where you will be able to find assistance with projectors, slides, video, and film. Make the best possible use of every available resource.

Types of Delivery

Contemporary communicators must be allowed great freedom in the type of delivery they will choose for their speeches. There are two fundamental types of delivery: (1) pretemporaneous, (2) extemporaneous. *Pretemporaneous* means "prior to the time"; *extem-*

---

[8] "Facts About Niagara Falls" (Niagara Falls Area Chamber of Commerce, 1975), p. 2.

poraneous means literally "out of the time." Thus, in pretemporaneous delivery a communicator utters a speech or monologue that has been created prior to the time of delivery. Two pretemporaneous forms are the *manuscript* and the *memorized* speech. In the extemporaneous delivery a communicator creates either all or most of the wording as he speaks, that is, *out of the time*. There are two forms of extemporaneous delivery: the impromptu and the note card.

Pretemporaneous

The *manuscript* for a public speech or monologue is a completely written text the speaker will usually read word for word. Jonathan Edwards, frequently considered alongside George Whitfield as the most effective American revivalist, delivered his powerful sermon, "Sinners in the Hands of an Angry God," from a manuscript. Abraham Lincoln's Gettysburg Address is perhaps the most widely known of all American manuscript monologues. Some communicators are so effective with the manuscript, you probably could not tell whether they use manuscripts or not. This is especially so if the manuscript is not seen. Numerous politicians speaking from a television studio employ prompters they read from by looking to the side of the television camera. Audiences at home often see these communicators as confident and folksy. Although the communicator does not use the manuscript in a way the audience is familiar with, it is nevertheless a message prepared rather precisely prior to the time of utterance.

In planning a manuscript you should use all of your creative writing skills. This does not mean you should produce a speech that will be filled with flighty expressions or words you have not made your own, either through use or rehearsal. It is one thing to write an essay and another to write a message to be given orally before an audience. The essential difference has to do with the style of the manuscript. A person writing a speech to be delivered at a political convention or in a church should concentrate on those elements of his or her own style that will make the words truly his or hers. A good beginning place in developing a manuscript responsive to your own style as a communicator and to the audience is to look at your own conversational style. Of course, you would not want to use the worst features of conversation, even with expletives deleted, but rather those features that exemplify your manner of speaking. You must remember to compose the manuscript in such a way that the audience can achieve *immediate* apprehension. Hence, while you should not write *exactly* as you speak, you should strive to utilize as much of your oral style as possible to make the manuscript easily apprehendable when presented orally. The following sample manuscript designed for reading aloud gives an idea of the oral style.

> These are serious times/and I mean real serious times/We have some fine individuals in our nation/old and young/black and white/Jew and Gentile/// But we have serious problems in health care/ young and old/black and white/ Jew and Gentile are dying because of inadequate health care///
> Yes/ these are serious times/ That's what I said/// But who's responsible?? You're the culprit!! Why you?? Because you consistently voted against propositions designed to correct health-care abuses/// What can you do??? Vote for progressive health-care legislation next year.

The *memorized* address is usually written in manuscript form and committed to memory. During the delivery of the speech the communicator attempts to use natural vocal inflection and physical movement to give a sense of spontaneity. If you plan to memorize your message, you should be aware of the dangers of this method of presentation:

1. A monotonous delivery
2. A loss of memory
3. A lack of interaction with audience

Because of the dangers outlined above, the memorized address is very rarely given in contemporary societies. Portions of a monologue or speech may be memorized but almost never the complete address. Although we believe that the memorized address should be used with caution, its selective use may encourage mental discipline.

Extemporaneous

The *impromptu* address is perhaps the most common form of public communication. Whenever you speak spontaneously without prior preparation, you are speaking impromptu. Some students like the impromptu address because they see it as a way of presenting a speech without much research. However, most students understand what communicators have always understood: good communication means informed communication. Accordingly, an impromptu address should be informed but spontaneous.

We all have had occasions to either give or hear impromptu speeches. We may have called them ad libs or off-the-cuff talks, but essentially they were composed at the time of delivery. In almost any human setting you may be called upon to give an impromptu address, in which case the following guidelines should be observed:

1. Establish your purpose.
2. State the main points for your listeners.
3. Seek illustrations for main points.
4. Reiterate your purpose and main arguments.

Because the impromptu is a surprise situation, the communicator must be wary of the tendency to talk beyond his or her knowledge.

If you are surprised with an impromptu situation, the first reaction should be to gain your composure by acknowledging that you have been requested to speak. The tendency to ramble through disconnected themes is the principal fault of impromptu speeches. You should exercise active listening behavior in order to know what has gone on before you speak and in that way you will be able to avoid rambling behavior.

The second type of speech or monologue delivered "out of the time" is traditionally called the *extemporaneous;* we refer to it as the *note card* delivery. The exact wording of this speech is presented at the moment of speaking, although some attention is usually given to the content prior to the delivery. Accordingly, it is the type of delivery that combines the best qualities of the impromptu and the manuscript speech. It has spontaneity because the words are not completely written out beforehand. It also has form because the communicator has given some thought to how best make a certain point or expound on a given theme. By recording main items or points on note cards, the extemporaneous communicator will have an opportunity to practice the talk and use the notes as a guide during the speech.

When you are giving this type of address, there are several guidelines to follow:

1. Get a clear understanding of what it is you have been asked to speak on.
2. Write an outline on note cards.
3. Practice each main point.

4. Be as natural as possible while delivering the monologue.
5. Depend on your skill rather than your memory (what we mean is do not memorize your extemporaneous speech).
6. It is all right if your audience sees the cards.

In summary, you see now that the presentation of the message is an essential aspect of communication. You should concentrate on developing spontaneity and using your natural communicator apprehension. It is rather simple to instruct you to relax, but we recognize that you will not be able to relax unless you are prepared to speak. Therefore, good presentation is based upon sound preparation.

FOR STUDENT APPLICATION

1. To what extent are you persuaded by television commercials that use celebrities such as movie stars, television stars, entertainers, and sports figures to promote certain products? For example, why do you think advertising agencies selected the American football star Joe Namath to endorse pantyhose?!

2. Many preachers inject a bit of humor in their sermons. Can you think of some positive or negative views concerning the use of humor in sermons? Think of some other public speaking situations where humor is often used. What effect did the humor have on you? How did other members of the audience react?

3. Does the way a person dresses or the person's general appearance affect the way you react to what that person says? Do you recall forming an initial impression of someone you met based on appearance? Did you change that initial impression after you knew the person better? Do you think your appearance is perceived positively or negatively by others? Why?

4. Prepare a one-page outline for presenting a topic of your choice. Indicate in the purpose sentence the specific course of action you expect from the audience. Now prepare a second one-page outline for a speech that will oppose the action desired in the first speech. How are the two outlines different? How are they similar?

5. When a speaker writes out a speech word for word and reads it, the speech will always sound written. People prefer to hear what the speaker has to say, not what he has written. Written and oral messages vary widely in style, structure, and rhythm. Consider, for example, the difference between writing a letter to a friend and talking to that friend in a casual conversation. In short, most speakers find it difficult to

make something written sound like something spoken. What does this suggest in terms of using notes for a speech? Can you recall going to hear a speech and ending up hearing someone read to you? How did you feel as an audience member? Could the problem be largely eliminated by the use of a topical outline?

6. Select any important argument you would like to present to your class. Now indicate two different ways to add information and clarity through the use of visual aids. Ask your class to evaluate which visual aid was the most successful. Why? Discuss.

Readings

COOKE, BENJAMIN. "Afro-American Nonverbal Behavior," in *Rappin' and Stylin' Out* edited by Thomas Kochman. Urbana: University of Illinois Press, 1974.

GOFFMAN, ERVING. *The Presentation of Self in Everyday Life.* Garden City, N.J.: Doubleday, 1959.

GOFFMAN, ERVING. Behavior in Public Places. New York: Free Press, 1963.

HASLING, JOHN. *The Audience, The Message, The Speaker.* New York: McGraw-Hill, 1976.

MILLER, GERALD R. *Speech Communication: A Behavioral Approach.* Indianapolis: Bobbs-Merrill, 1966.

MORTENSEN, C. DAVID. *Communication: The Study of Human Interaction.* New York: McGraw-Hill, 1972.

OLIVER, ROBERT T., ZELKO, HAROLD P.; and HOLTZMAN, PAUL D. *Communicative Speaking and Listening.* New York: Holt, Rinehart and Winston, 1968.

SMITH, ARTHUR L.; HERNANDEZ, DELUVINA; and ALLEN, ANNE. *How To Talk With People of Other Races.* Los Angeles: Transethnic Education-Communication Foundation, 1971.

11 Collective Communication

WHAT YOU CAN EXPECT:

Chapter 11 discusses "collective communication," that is, how you function and interact with others in groups and organizations.

All of us are members of a variety of groups: our family, our friends, at work, at school. Directly and indirectly much of our communication involves groups of other people. The information presented in this chapter is designed to increase your understanding of the function and process of group communication and how you can increase your effectiveness in groups through the communication process.

Chapter Outline

The Concept of Collective Communication
Patterns for Collective Communication Decisions
    PERT Sequence
    The Creative Problem-Solving Sequence
    The Ideal Solution Pattern
    The Single Question Form
    The Dewey Method
The Functions of Group Members
    Group Task Functions
    Group Building and Maintenance Functions
    Self-Centered Functions
Key Elements in Collective Communication
    Significant Topics
    Diversity
    Cooperation as a Key
    Consensus
Parliamentary Procedure
    Advantages of the Core Procedure
    Introducing a Motion
    The Chairperson
    Voting Procedure

The Concept of Collective Communication

We have been discussing how public communicators conduct themselves in the arena of public discourse. In this chapter we concentrate on how human beings interact as speakers and listeners in purposeful groups. Each participant interacts with other members of the group in order to resolve some issue. Thus, collective communication carries with it the idea that participants are seeking to arrive at a common answer to some problem. It does not imply what is called a "bull session" unless one means by that term a group concerned with the orderly presentation of ideas among knowledgeable persons for the purpose of finding appropriate solutions to a problem.

Collective communication presupposes that the participants will follow certain rules and procedures. How the rules are laid out and what the procedures will be are usually determined by the kind of group. L. S. Harms refers to two types of groups: the small group and the large group.[1] According to Harms, a small group system is organized by seven, plus or minus two, communicators; a large group system has fifteen communicators, or seven times two plus N communicators, or more. In each case the participants are eager to find the solution to a problem for which they share a mutual concern. In fact, to be successful, the group participants *must* share an interest in solving the problem. One individual may, as a juror might in an important trial, prevent successful collective communication. We have all seen hung discussions. They are usually the result of one or two individuals who have the ability to raise issues but are not willing to participate in the resolution of them.

We like the term *collective communication* because it implies a cooperative development of the ideas in a dynamic interaction setting. Without appreciation of some structure or procedure the group may be therapeutic but not very successful at coming to closure on an answer to the problem. Additionally, one person could conceivably use the group as his or her audience and affect the quality of the decision. Collective communication means that the participant tries to achieve general approval and acceptance of ideas as they are stated or as compromises, rather than using irrational appeals or unethical behavior to force opinions on the

[1] L. S. Harms, *Human Communication: The New Fundamentals* (New York: Harper & Row, 1974), pp. 96–111.

reluctant others. It is this concept that makes collective communication a valuable process in democratic societies. It could be said that directed talk, in the sense of collective communication, is responsible for most major decisions at the corporate, educational, and government levels in democratic societies. When we feel that constraints should be placed upon large oil companies that have little or no regard for ecological matters, or when we believe that education should be reformed, or that racism should be eliminated in the insurance industry, the small group becomes a forum for the formulation of policy. When policy decisions are made, they may be delivered to the person or persons who have the power to implement the group's decision. As advocates of the proposal, members of the collective communication may follow the idea through to implementation by providing persuasive speeches to support the group's proposal.

There appear to be several drawbacks to the collective communication process. First, by its nature, collective communication is slow. Because of its deliberateness, it is frequently denounced as being ineffective in modifying society. When we are outraged at some inequitable law or disturbed by an unjust policy, we tend to desire immediate redress. Collective communication usually mutes the clamor by sending our most emotional claims to a group or a panel for advice. Once a concern gets to a group, it may literally take weeks to be resolved or may simply disappear due to a lack of interest on the group's part or due to inadequate agenda planning by the chairman of the group. Persons unfamiliar with the collective communication process may see it as a stalling tactic. In the past, one of the persistent areas of conflict between black students and college administrators was the committee process. Students would present their requests or demands to the administrator, only to have them referred to a committee. Unable to understand why the administrator could not decide without a committee, many students rejected the committee idea. They believed that this was a strategy of delay and they usually knew they were correct. While collective communication may have been used in such a manner, it is an instrument that depends upon the users for its greatest efficacy.

A second drawback is that the group may not understand precisely its charge, or if it does not have a charge, it may not understand what issue is under discussion. Problems in issue perception arise because each participant may possess a different idea about what she or he is supposed to be discussing. This is why procedures and rules must be established so that participants have a perception of direction. However, beyond the rules of procedure must be the clear presentation of the issues. In some cases groups formed to discuss one issue or to resolve a given crisis find themselves looking at different issues altogether. For this reason we believe that understanding the principles of collective communication will help you in almost every organizational setting, particularly if you learn to use the group as an instrument to solve problems, not to prevent them from being solved.

The fundamental principles of collective communication contribute to our total understanding and allow us to participate in another dimension of public communication. Responsibility and experience will probably lead most of you at one time or another into either an educational, civic, or business group. As participants, you will have to formulate policies, attempt to win approval and acceptance by the other participants or the organization as a whole, and demonstrate a willingness to compromise. Effective collective communication depends upon three basic elements: (1) informed participants, (2) a thorough consideration of the facts, (3) orderly procedures. John Geier found that a participant who was perceived as uninformed was usually eliminated from effective influence in leaderless discussion groups.[2] There is no substitute for information. A participant must collect accurate and valid information to have a voice in the group's decision. As a participant, you should always check your information for accuracy. Biased information, faulty statistics, and opinions stated as facts can lead to useless argument and bad decisions. Our advice to every participant is to *collect* and *check* your data prior to the discussion and you will be an asset to a reasonable decision. Once a participant has a stock of information and ideas on the subject, the next step is to thoroughly evaluate the facts. Think of a group of politicians considering tax-reform measures without studying the tax structure. You would certainly question the validity of any proposal made by such an uninformed group. Orderly procedures for arriving at a conclusion must be agreed upon in advance of the discussion to have a meaningful impact on the discussion progress. Thus, information, con-

    [2] John G. Geier, "A Trait Approach to the Study of Leadership in Small Groups," in Robert S. Cathcart and Larry A. Samovar, eds., *Small Group Communication: A Reader* (Dubuque, Iowa: Brown, 1970), p. 414.

sideration of the quality of facts, and orderly procedures are key elements in effective collective communication.

Each of these elements is dependent upon the other in some way so that ignorance is no blessing for the collective communicator because it leads to a lack of consideration of all the facts on an issue. On the other hand, if an orderly procedure is not adhered to, the group can degenerate into a directionless aggregation of persons.

Patterns for Collective Communication Decisions

How a group organizes its talk, regulates its participants, and achieves a group solution is what we discuss in this section. There are a number of patterns for group problem solving. Some of these patterns are the results of empirical testing; others are derived from commonsense knowledge. Our intention is to provide you with the most common patterns for problem solving. You may not recognize any of these patterns in their complete forms because modifications occur and are probably more prevalent than the pure forms. Furthermore, John K. Brilhart's assessment of the modification of problem-solving patterns is explicit:

> A group assigned to evaluate and choose from a list of alternatives would need only a limited analysis of the problem if that had been done by a prior group, but would need an outline to guide the setting of explicit criteria, evaluating the list of ideas, and arriving at a final decision.[3]

Among the patterns for problem solving that may be employed is the Program Evaluation and Review Technique (PERT). PERT provides the group with a method for developing an operations plan. Accordingly, PERT can be applied to any program proposal that needs time. PERT will measure whether or not the program will be completed on schedule, allow the group to review its program to detect errors, and reveal to an administrator the kind of decisions he might be asked to make. PERT was developed by the United States Navy in 1958 to solve some problems of coordination in the Polaris guided-missile program.[4]

[3] John K. Brilhart, *Effective Group Discussion* (Dubuque, Iowa: Brown, 1974), p. 110.
[4] Gerald M. Phillips, *Communication and the Small Group* (Indianapolis: Bobbs-Merrill, 1966), p. 89.

PERT sequence[5]

I. Group completes discussion. Group has defined problem, discovered facts, made statement of causes, determined authority, limitations, and goals, suggested solutions, selected a solution, phrased the solution as a program.

II. Group specifies final event that signals completion of their program.

III. Group lists events that must happen before the final event and assigns reference numbers.

IV. Immediate, necessary, precedent events are determined for each event.

V. A PERT diagram is drawn showing connection of events. Extraneous and redundant events are deleted.

VI. Activities are listed between each pair of events.

VII. Group makes best, worst, most likely time estimates for activities. Estimated time calculated for each track. Variances are calculated for each event.

VIII. Expected completion time is calculated by summation for each event. Where activities converge, maximum expected completion time is used.

IX. Scheduled completion date is determined. Latest allowable time is calculated for each event. Where activities converge, minimum latest available time is used.

X. Slack time is calculated for each track to final event. Critical path is drawn based on path with least slack.

XI. Probability estimate of satisfactory completion is made based on critical path.

PERT has been criticized as being too complicated for most everyday problems of collective communication. It works best in highly complex situations involving construction of major buildings, development of technological systems, and coordinating the making of a documentary film. The following four patterns are among the most practical for collective communication. We have adapted them from Brilhart and Larson.[6]

[5] Gerald M. Phillips, "PERT as a Logical Adjunct to the Discussion Process," *Journal of Communication* 15 (1965), pp. 89–99. Also see extended discussion in Phillips, *Communication and the Small Group*, pp. 88–105.

[6] John K. Brilhart, *Effective Group Discussion* (Dubuque, Iowa: Brown, 1974), pp. 110–113; and Carl E. Larson, "Forms of Analysis and Small Group Problem-Solving," *Speech Monographs* 36 (1969), pp. 452–455.

The creative problem-solving sequence

I. What is the scope of the problem (current state, obstacles, goals)?

    A. What are we talking about? Is the problem question or assignment clear to us?

    B. What limits should we place on our consideration of the problem? Are we to plan and take action, to make a policy decision, or to advise?

    C. What has been happening? What information do we have about the problem? (This is often called the fact-finding phase of discussion.)

        1. Who is affected, how, and under what conditions?

        2. What seems to have gone wrong? How do we know?

            (a) How serious do we consider the situation to be?

            (b) What additional information do we need? How can we obtain it?

        3. What present or past steps have been taken to remedy the problem, and what were the results?

    D. What would be a desirable situation?

        1. What outcome would we like to achieve?

        2. What is our goal?

    E. What factors seem to have contributed to the problem?

        1. What are the obstacles to achieving the desired goal?

        2. What has caused the present situation?

    F. Can we state the problem clearly in terms of our findings, the causes, the goal, and obstacles to achieving it?

        1. Do we have a set of subproblems that should be tackled one at a time?

        2. If so, in what order should we take them up?

II. What might be done to solve the problem?
List *all* ideas that group members suggest without evaluation.

III. By what specific criteria shall we judge among our possible solutions?

    A. Are there any absolute criteria that any solution must meet?

    B. What relative standards shall we apply? (List and rank these values and standards by group agreement.)

IV. What are the relative merits of our possible solutions?

    A. What ideas can we screen out as unsupported by un-contested facts?

    B. Can we combine and simplify our list of possible solutions in any way?

C. How well do the remaining ideas measure up to the criteria?
V. How will we put our decision into effect?
   A. Who will do what, when, and how?
   B. Do we need any follow-up or check procedures?

The ideal solution pattern

This pattern is especially suited to discussion of problems that will affect different groups of people with different interests, or that must have the support of various types of people with different concerns and values. For example, a change in traffic law would be of real concern to motorists, police officers, insurance companies, and businesses, at least.

I. What is the scope of the problem? (The rest of this section of the analytic outline would be very much like that for creative problem solving.)
II. What would be an ideal solution from the point of view of each interested person or group? (A separate question, then, for each group:)
   A. Democrat
   B. Republican
   C. Socialist
III. What *can* be changed in the present situation?
   (That is, what solutions are possible? What could be done?)
IV. What solution best approximates the ideal?
   (Here the group synthesizes and decides on the final solution to apply or recommend.)
V. How will we implement this solution?

The single question form

Larson is most responsible for this pattern.

I. What is the single question which, when answered, means the group knows how to accomplish its purpose?
II. What subquestions must we answer before we can answer the single question we have formulated?
III. Do we have sufficient information to answer the subquestions with confidence?
   A. If "yes," what are our answers? Then go to V.

     B. If "no," the group continues to IV or adjourns to look for
        answers.
  IV. What are the most reasonable answers to the subquestions?
   V. If our answers to the subquestions are adequate, what is the
      best solution to the problem?
      (You will notice that this format calls for a thorough analysis
      of the issues in the problem, then a search for answers to
      them, followed by the construction of a solution. A final step,
      of course, will often be VI.)
  VI. How will we implement this solution?

The Dewey method

In his book, *How We Think*, John Dewey developed five stages
of reflective thinking: (1) a felt difficulty, (2) its location and
definition, (3) suggestion of possible solutions, (4) development
by reasoning of the bearings of the suggestion, (5) further observation and experiment leading to its acceptance or rejection; that is,
the conclusion of belief and disbelief. Reflective thinking is different
from intentional thinking in that the first begins with a problem
and seeks a solution; the latter begins with a solution and seeks
the best means of persuading others to accept it.[7] An example of
the two forms of thinking might be the issue of financing airports.
A collective communication topic may be, "What is the best method
to finance airports?" On the other hand, a collegiate debate squad
may argue the proposition, "Resolved, airports should be financed by
gasoline taxes." Although both would be discussing the same issue,
one invites reflective thinking and the other intentional thinking.

Dewey's reflective thinking stages do occur in some instances,
but they are more the products of contrived situations than actual
discussion procedure. Sometimes a participant within a collective
communication has no felt difficulty but is interested in the topic
and willing to add hers or his knowledge to the discussion. Our view
is that the five-stage reflective idea makes good reading but poor
collective communication. Most participants in a discussion will
approach it knowledgeably and with an anticipated outcome. For
example, if the issue is whether the United States should recognize
North Korea, most participants in a collective communication will,

[7] Charles W. Lomas and Ralph Richardson, *Speech: Idea and Delivery* (Boston:
Houghton Mifflin, 1963), p. 241.

because they are knowledgeable, have a certain opinion in their minds regarding the answer. Certainly they may withhold their opinions until it is time to present alternatives, but it would be incorrect to suggest that their suggestions for solutions developed during the discussion. What usually happens during a discussion is that a person with views tries to substantiate those views by presenting supporting arguments. Rarely will you find a knowledgeable person who goes to a discussion without an attitude toward the issue to be resolved. This is the reason why we say Dewey's system probably exists under conditions of extreme control and not in usual collective communication.

The patterns of problem solution presented in the preceding pages are meant to give you clear guidelines for your own group discussions. Experience with the different patterns will help you to become a more effective collective communicator. Each discussion group, whether small or large, must consider the pattern most appropriate to its objective.

The Functions of Group Members

Kenneth D. Benne's and Paul Sheats' 1948 article on "Functional Roles of Group Members" has been adapted in numerous textbooks on discussion. Because we believe that their treatment of the functions of group members is one of the most comprehensive, we have adapted their categories for our discussion.[8] There are three broad categories of functions: (1) group task functions, (2) group building and maintenance functions, (3) self-centered functions.

Group task functions

These behaviors provide information, ideas, and the energy for effective discussion:

1. *Idea initiating* proposing new ideas, new goals, possible solutions.
2. *Information seeking* asking for facts, clarification or infor-

---

[8] Kenneth D. Benne and Paul Sheats, "Functional Roles of Group Members," *Journal of Social Issues*, 4 (1948), pp. 41–49.

mation from other members, or suggesting that information is needed.

3. *Information giving*   offering facts and information, personal experiences and evidence that is pertinent to the group purpose.

4. *Opinion seeking*   asking for convictions, opinions, beliefs, values, and judgments of others.

5. *Opinion giving*   stating own belief, opinion, judgment, value, or conviction.

6. *Elaborating*   developing an idea expressed previously, explaining, clarifying with examples, illustrations, and explanations.

7. *Coordinating*   developing, describing, or clarifying relationships among facts, ideas, and suggestions, or suggesting an integration of ideas, proposed solutions, and activities of two or more participants.

8. *Orienting*   clarifying purpose or goal of group, defining position of group in relation to its task, suggesting direction for the discussion to take, suggesting procedure for the group to follow.

9. *Energizing*   prodding the group to greater activity, stimulating activity, reminding of importance of task or time available.

10. *Recording*   keeping written record on paper or chalkboard, serving as group memory, preparing reports and minutes of meetings.

Group building and maintenance functions

These behaviors establish and maintain cooperative relationships, cohesiveness, and a group orientation:

1. *Supporting*   agreeing, praising, indicating warmth and solidarity with others.

2. *Harmonizing*   mediating differences between others, finding common ground of values or beliefs, reconciling disagreements, conciliating, suggesting compromises.

3. *Tension relieving*   joking and pointing out humor in a situation that relieves tensions among members, reducing formality and status differences, putting others at ease.

4. *Gatekeeping*   encouraging others to speak, stopping the overly talkative and dominating from interrupting or blocking others from speaking, opening channels of communication.

5. *Norming* suggesting standards of behavior for members, challenging unproductive ways of behaving in group, "punishing" behaviors that violate group rules of conduct.

Self-centered functions

The following behaviors seek to satisfy individual needs at the expense of the group or other individuals; most of them are harmful to group cohesiveness and to accomplishing the group task.

1. *Blocking* preventing progress toward group goals by constantly raising objections, repeatedly bringing up the same topic or issue after the group has considered it and rejected it (it is not blocking to keep raising an idea or topic the group has not really listened to or considered).
2. *Attacking* attacking the competence of another, name-calling, impugning the motive of another instead of describing own feelings; joking at expense of another; attempting to destroy "face" of another.
3. *Recognition seeking* boasting, calling attention to one's own expertise or experience when it is not necessary to establish credibility or relevant to group task; relating irrelevant experiences; game-playing to elicit sympathy or pity.
4. *Horseplaying* making tangential jokes; engaging in horseplay that takes the group away from serious work or maintenance behavior.
5. *Dominating* giving orders, interrupting and cutting off, flattering to get own way, insisting on own way.
6. *Advocating* playing the advocate for the interests of a different group, thus acting as its representative, apologist, or advocate counter to the best interests or consensus of the current group.
7. *Jiving* presenting information that has the appearance of acceptability and reasonableness, but in actuality is false.

In a collective communication situation, participants soon discover each other's strengths and weaknesses. The emergence of specialists who are looked to when the group reaches a certain point or discusses a given issue is a natural tendency within groups. In order for any collective communication group to be successful, honest mutual respect must exist between participants. Such an atmosphere insures the cooperation of the group's members. Ernest G. Bormann and Nancy C. Bormann recommended that a group seeks to do the following:

1. Develop a strong identity as a group and a group tradition or history. This can be done by developing nicknames for the group, insignia of membership, referring to past events with pride and pleasure, holding ceremonies and rituals, and emphasizing the high quality of accomplishments.
2. Stress teamwork and give credit to the group. Avoid talking about what you did personally for the group, especially if you are the designated leader.
3. Recognize contributions to the group goal by members. Low-status members especially need reward and praise from other group members, *not* criticism, if they are to develop the loyalty that make them more productive and dependable.
4. Show human concern for the people who make up the group, providing warmth, affection, and direct attention to personal tensions and problems that members indicate.
5. Support both disagreement and agreement, which basically means working for a norm of open expression of disagreement or support for ideas. When conflicts are settled, signs of solidarity such as joking, laughing together, compliments of people who supported rejected ideas that helped build a better group solution, and comments such as "Let's get behind this" are needed.[9]

Key Elements in Collective Communication

Whatever subjects occupy the mind of the public communicator are also subjects for collective communication. If a topic can be advocated by a speaker, it can most assuredly be discussed by a group of persons. To insure that the discussion will proceed orderly and meaningfully, a well-phrased topic should be chosen. Although good phrasing establishes clarity of a topic, it is not necessarily a guarantor of a good topic. We can think of any number of topics that may be well phrased but would lead to limited and perhaps unfruitful discussion.

Significant topics

You would probably seek to choose a subject for collective communication that contributes to the education of yourself and your

[9] Modified and adapted from Ernest G. Bormann and Nancy C. Bormann, *Effective Small Group Communication* (Minneapolis: Burgess, 1972), pp. 32–38.

colleagues. Issues affecting society, the nation, and the world are always good topics for discussion. Our own neighborhoods can provide us with significant topics related to water pollution, school desegregation, crime, and the new civic projects. You need not deal with world famine or the crisis in oil for every discussion. However, a discussion on whether or not you and your roommate should buy draperies is of little educational significance of itself. If you are a college student, seek to discuss issues that go beyond your campus; if you are a business employee, seek issues that extend beyond your business. Of course, we recognize that there are occasional issues in any sector of our lives that become significant by the impact they have outside the group.

Diversity

While we do not encourage collective communicators to become debaters, we do suggest that there should be some difference of opinion. A group that simply verbalizes words expected of it because of its composition does not provide any real education to the receivers of the collective communication. Thus, the Baptist Student Union, if committed to admitting every Baptist, would argue that the union could not accept atheists as members. There would be no ground for differences. Another example, taken from politics, would be that a collective communication group of Democrats would not argue that Richard Nixon was a better president than Lyndon Johnson. Most real values occur in groups where some differences exist because it allows for all parts of a topic to be covered. Such diversity animates discussion and produces substantive points of view. Whenever a communicator succeeds in raising issues that are basic to himself or herself, the results will usually be either strong support or opposition from group members. What is achieved, however, is an increase in the possible solutions.

Cooperation as a Key

The assumption of democratic government is that people are free to assemble together and work cooperatively to achieve some goal that is the mutual concern of the members. Whatever topic is under discussion, participants should seek to cooperate on the solution of the problem. During most of your life you will be work-ing with others for mutual benefits. Throughout our society, groups are constantly functioning. In fact, the very word *society* suggests this grouping of humans. The discipline of sociology studies how humans interact with one another in a number of group settings. You are a member of your family group, peer group, work group, social group, entertainment group, and others. Perhaps the most obvious groups can be seen in education; for example, your class-room group. In businesses there are groups. Typically, the mere fact that one is an employee means involvement in labor, management, and union groups.

Our government is composed in large part of groups: from the familiar local city council to the county, state, and the federal government groupings of legislative, judicial, and executive divi-sional groups. Whether you are consciously aware of it or not, our society is composed of a wide variety of diverse groups. One of the purposes of this chapter is to indicate the general function of groups and to describe the most frequently utilized procedure of groups so that the individual members are treated fairly and equally.

Consensus

Group members meet together for a variety of purposes: to discuss mutual problems, to interact and socialize, to obtain in-formation, to propose solutions. In general, these purposes are accomplished through two methods: consensus and parliamentary procedure. Personal preferences are relinquished when the welfare of the group becomes more important. The overall group aims are the achievement of its goals. The goal of a social club or a com-mune may simply be to interact and provide companionship that seeks happiness and avoids friction. Whenever the members of a group agree without formally voting, we can say that these general, overall goals were achieved through consensus. However, although general goals are often arrived at through consensus, there often is a need to become specific. A group might generally agree that funds should be raised to be given to some needy charity. The conception, birth, and development of this general decision may be accom-plished through the method of consensus. But *which* needy charity should receive the funds? This specific goal becomes a final decision-making activity that lends itself to the time-tested principles of parliamentary procedure.

Parliamentary Procedure

One of the fundamental building blocks of modern democracy is the tradition of one man one vote and majority rule. This tradition demands a sense of individual rights and personal responsibility. Parliamentary procedure was developed to protect the three essential parts of groups: (1) the individual, (2) the minority, (3) the majority.

The degree of formality for a group depends largely on both the type of group and the size of that group. The more formal the group, the more complex the rules that are employed. For example, most of the Watergate related hearings and investigations from both the House of Representatives and the United States Senate were guided by a complicated set of rules and regulations. In contrast, some of the groups in which most of us hold membership simply do not require the complex rules. However, most groups follow a simple, basic set of rules generally referred to by the label "parliamentary rules." Parliamentary procedure is typically chosen as the basic set of rules to follow. A complete set of those rules has been handed down for many years through a book called *Robert's Rules of Order.*

Only very formal groups really need the complex procedural rules set forth in this rather difficult book. We believe that most groups do not need to concentrate on complex rules but that a *basic core* of parliamentary procedures can be helpful to most groups. This *core procedure* is simply a useful label for what we have found to be needed by most groups we have observed.[10] In short, a less detailed procedure is required for the average group.

Advantages of the core procedure

If groups follow the core procedure, we believe there will be the following advantages: (1) individual members will be able to

---

[10] The phrase "core procedure" has been used by several writers dealing with parliamentary procedure. Our use of "core procedure" and its discussion follows Hugo E. Hellman, *Parliamentary Procedure* (London: Macmillan, 1966), pp. 7–10.

participate with equality among other members; (2) the business or goals of the group will be attained more quickly; (3) there will be more precision and less confusion in group meetings.

The following five points are the basic order of business for group meetings that constitute the core procedure:

1. Sign-in sheet (written record of attendance).
2. Record of previous meeting ("minutes").
3. Complete unfinished business from last meeting.
4. Consideration of new business.
5. Set directions for activity of members before next meeting.

Introducing a motion

Generally, if you want to propose something to the members of your group, you get the attention of the person in charge and say, "I move that. . . ." You will need the support of at least one other member to second your motion (this is to prevent wasting time on a motion that might be the sole interest of one person). Once seconded and accepted, your motion is open for discussion. At this point no other motions can be introduced. Sometimes during the discussion an improvement is discovered. In order to modify the original, a "motion to amend" must be made. You again obtain the attention of the chairperson and propose your amendment, which then must be seconded, discussed, and passed. The following example indicates the order of a motion and amendment:

1. Original motion (directed to chairperson): "I move that we donate $50 to charity X."
   Supporter (also to chairperson): "I second the motion."
2. Amendment: "I move that we donate $25 to charity X and $25 to charity Y."
3. Amended motion: $25 to charity X and $25 to charity Y.

The amended motion simply is the general idea contained in the original with a specific change: instead of giving a larger donation to one charity (original motion), the sum is divided between two charities (amended motion). Notice how the smooth and clear manner of transacting business is due primarily to the orderly sequence of the core procedure. It allows for the meeting to proceed without one member having an unfair advantage over other members, time is used to efficiently attain the group's goal, and there is less confusion in meetings. The following five basic steps to introduce a motion should become routine:

1. Obtain the attention of the chairperson and get permission to speak.
2. State your motion.
3. Obtain the support of another member who seconds your motion.
4. Have an orderly, open discussion of the motion by the membership.
5. Each member has the opportunity to vote for or against the motion.

Notice that parliamentary procedure is largely a matter of *orderly* procedure. There is an *order* to the meeting itself and an *order* to procedures within that meeting. Order is a natural concept to humans and allows them to make progress in their everyday affairs at home, at school, and at work. Perhaps the major reason parliamentary procedure is used by organizations is the fact that it is based on *order*.

The chairperson

One of the first actions of an organized group is that of electing a chairperson from among the membership. The members have a right to nominate anyone, including themselves, for the office of chairperson. After everyone has had an opportunity to nominate candidates, the membership votes for each candidate. The candidate receiving a majority vote is elected as chairperson.

One of the chairperson's most important duties, in fact, primary responsibility, is to preserve order. The chairperson makes sure that the five steps of the core procedure and the five steps in introducing a motion are followed faithfully, and that each member is given the opportunity to speak, *one at a time* in an orderly manner. Speakers must get the chairperson's attention and be recognized before they speak. Order eliminates the confusion involved when more than one member want to speak. The chairperson sees that *order* is maintained from the beginning statement, "This meeting will now come to *order*," to the end, "This meeting is adjourned."

In addition to maintaining order, the chairperson has the power to appoint members of the organization to committees with subordinates in charge or "chairing" those committees. In short, the chairperson usually exerts strong, active, energetic leadership; therefore, the nomination and selection should be given careful, serious consideration by all members. Good leadership of an organization will increase the probabilities of efficient, fair, and successful activity.

Voting procedure

Every member of an organization has the right to vote for or against any motion. In effect, a vote simply asks if you favor or oppose the motion. If you are for it, you vote affirmative; if you oppose it, you vote negative. Voting takes place after the motion has been discussed openly and fully by the members. When everyone has stated his or her position of support or opposition, the chairperson will suggest that the members end discussion and vote. If all are in agreement, then voting takes place. If someone objects and wants more discussion, the group must decide what to do. Otherwise, discussion might take up too much valuable time. If two-thirds of those present feel that the motion has been discussed enough, the chairperson tells the objecting member something like this: "I'm sorry, but the necessary two-thirds of our membership has decided we have had enough discussion. Now we must make our decision and vote for or against the motion." The members then vote and the motion is either passed or rejected.

FOR STUDENT APPLICATION

1. Consider the various classes you attend now and those you have attended in the past. Some teachers lecture, other teachers direct open discussions, still others break their classes into small groups. What effect do these various teaching methods have on you? If you are like most students, you have strong feelings about which method you prefer. But *why* do you prefer one method over another? Do different methods exert different controls over your behavior? Which method is most comfortable to you? Which method do you prefer? Why?

2. Think of any recent group discussion in which you participated. Who was the leader? Why do you think that particular person became the leader?

3. In groups composed of five class members, select a topic for a fifteen-minute in-class discussion. Who was the most verbal member? Who was the least verbal member? How do you explain the difference between the vocal and the quiet member? Do you think their involvement would change much if the group had selected a different topic for discussion? Why?

4. What are some of the additional duties and responsibilities of a group member and the group leader? Compare your answer with other class members and discuss.

5. Join four other students in your class for a discussion of some significant improvement in the way your school can better serve its students. The specific topic can be determined by your group's members. For example, perhaps your group feels the need for some additional course that is not now available. After the topic has been selected, engage in three discussion sessions of about twenty minutes each. Continue your deliberations throughout the sessions. At the end of the third session prepare a written "consensus statement" that reflects your group's specific suggestions for change. The group's leader will then present the consensus statement to the entire class for general discussion.

6. There are many groups and organizations at your school and in your community. These groups and organizations often hold meetings that you could attend. Obtain permission to attend any such meeting and observe the group process at work. Report your observations to members of your class and compare your observations with theirs. Here is a brief list of possible groups: city council, county board meeting, government (city, state, federal) legislative meetings, college faculty and administrative meetings, student association meetings, and professional associations (heart association, cancer society, medical association, legal association). Your instructor will be able to suggest additional possibilities.

Readings

BORMANN, ERNEST G. *Discussion and Group Methods: Theory and Practice*, 2nd ed. New York: Harper & Row, 1975.
DEWEY, JOHN. *How We Think*. Boston: Heath, 1933.
FIEDLER, FRED E. *A Theory of Leadership Effectiveness*. New York: McGraw-Hill, 1967.

HOLLANDER, EDWIN P. *Leaders, Groups, and Influence.* New York: Oxford University Press, 1964.

Robert's Rules of Order, rev ed. Glenview, Ill.: Scott, Foresman, 1969.

SHAW, MARVIN E. *Group Dynamics: The Psychology of Small Group Behavior.* New York: McGraw-Hill, 1971.

SMELSER, NEIL J. *Theory of Collective Behavior.* New York: Free Press, 1963.

12 The Miracle of Communication

WHAT YOU CAN EXPECT:

In Chapter 12 we emphasize the miracle of communicating with anyone.

Now that you have spent a considerable amount of your academic time studying ways to become a commendable communicator, we are ready to turn you loose on a waiting society.

Chapter Outline

The Stage Is Set
The Act Is Over

The Stage Is Set

If you have ever seen a play, you are aware that the first thing most people look for when they take their seats is the stage. They want to know if the stage is set. If it is, they want to know how it was set and perhaps even when will it change. Well, communication is something like a miracle occurring on a stage.

When we engage in conversation with a friend, give a monologue to a large gathering, or give an interview as an expert, we are acting on a stage. To say that communication is like a miracle is to announce the enormous difficulty most people have communicating efficiently with others. Even when we think we communicate, we frequently find that we are misunderstood. Think about the times you have really reached a peak communication experience with a friend. How was it? It was almost as if the other person knew what you were attempting to communicate before you did or *vice versa*.

The stage is whatever situation we happen to be in at the moment. We are acting on a stage as we write these lines. If you understand what we are communicating, then the miracle has occurred again. The stage may be a man and a woman talking in the meadows, a priest speaking in a church, a politician campaigning for office, our teacher coming across the video screen, or an international conference on energy conservation. Whatever the specific situation and circumstance, when a message is transmitted and received the communicative process has begun.

Much of the advice given in the earlier chapters dealt with the acquisition of specific skills in preparing for communication. We asked you to consider good reasons for speaking, methods of reasoning, and how to organize your message. This was all in preparation for setting the stage. When the stage is set, then the actors can come out and speak their parts in an effort to effect communication with their audience.

The Act Is Over

In the closing pages of this book we should tell you that once you have employed the best skills along with the most reasonable arguments for a worthy position, you have done what you could to communicate. Even so, you might discover that your views are so diametrically opposed to those of your audience that you will not be able to arrive at complete satisfaction in your communication. Although we have not made an extensive discussion of humor, it is worth remembering that a carefully chosen humorous story may be successful where an argument might not be. Humor amuses while establishing goodwill.

As you have the opportunity to communicate, you should not forget that with increased opportunity for success comes increased opportunity for failure. Andersch, Staats, and Bostrom understand this well when they tell us that those who seek to understand foreigners all too frequently have communication problems with their coworkers, neighbors, husbands, and colleagues.[1]

Certainly we assume that by now you have gained more confidence and will be able to handle your own messages better. But as communicator you are both speaker and listener. As it is impossible to communicate without a receiver, you must complete the act by becoming a good listener.

There is an enormous pressure, it seems, that leads each of us to expect others to hear and understand us while we fail to hear and understand them. This tendency to trade in confusion is a strong human compulsion. You know the line, "I'm right, that's why I must be *heard*." Well, we would be surely disappointed were you to close your act with such an attitude.

---

[1] Elizabeth G. Andersch, Lorin C. Staats, and Robert N. Bostrom, *Communication in Everyday Use* 3rd edition, (New York: Holt, Rinehart and Winston 1969), p. 116.

FOR STUDENT APPLICATION

1. When you are considering a problem, your "thinking process" is sometimes called *intra*personal communication. When you "talk to yourself," you become both the source and receiver. Can you construct an
   *intra*communication model? How would such a model compare with
   existing communication models? What elements would be similar?
   What elements would be different?

2. In any dyadic (two-person) communication, two individuals try to
   share meanings. However, your past experiences may be significantly
   different from another person's past experience. The overlap of meanings is sometimes illustrated as follows:

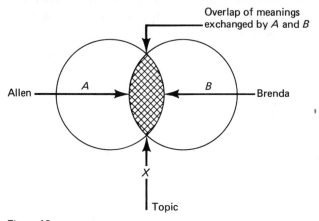

Figure 12

Although Allen (A) and Brenda (B) may discuss any topic (X), the
amount of shared meaning is limited. Such a situation is characteristic
and commonly observed in everyday communication situations. Try
this: talk with another person about some event you shared. For
example, perhaps you viewed the same movie. Typically, there will
be differing amounts of agreement about the movie: the quality of
the story line, the effectiveness of the actors, the appropriateness of
the music, and so on. Consider that two people discussing an event
(e.g., a movie, an automobile accident, a painting) may have quite
different reactions because of different past experiences. To what
extent can you communicate to another person how you feel? The
answer is, "never completely."

3. To what extent do different neighborhood experiences, different ages,
   different sex, different economic conditions, different religions, dif-

ferent races, and so on, affect how much we can communicate (share) with one another?

4. Sometimes you and I interpret the same symbol differently. For example, the following symbol can be perceived differently:

$$B$$

Without *context* I could say the symbol represented the letter B and you could say it represented the number 13. However, the *context* tends to shape our perceptions and there would be a decreased amount of variance in our interpretations if the *context* was provided: 12, *13*, 14 or A *B* C. Can you think of other situations in which the communication is affected clearly by the *context*? Bring at least two examples to class for an open discussion.

5. Consider several team efforts in sports. For example, think of the various relationships of teamwork in football, basketball, and hockey. Consider the aspects of the team effort in terms of cooperation, competition, leadership, and unity. In what ways are these aspects comparable to social groups?

6. Describe as many groups as you can that can be distinguished on the basis of common symbols. For example, why is it important that all members of some groups dress alike? List as many different symbols that tend to identify group membership. Consider dress, music, slogans, gestures, and other symbolic membership behavior. Discuss your list of group symbols with others in your class and prepare a master list of group symbols and group affiliations.

13 Selected Speeches

JOHN F. KENNEDY *(1961–1963)*
Inaugural Address, January 20, 1961
Capitol Steps, Washington, D.C.

Fellow citizens:

We observe today not a victory of party but a celebration of freedom—symbolizing an end as well as a beginning—signifying renewal as well as change. For I have sworn before you and Almighty God the same solemn oath our forebears prescribed nearly a century and three-quarters ago.

The world is very different now. For man holds in his mortal hands the power to abolish all forms of human poverty and all forms of human life. And yet the same revolutionary beliefs for which our forebears fought are still at issue around the globe—the belief that the rights of man come not from the generosity of the state but from the hand of God.

We dare not forget today that we are the heirs of that first revolution. Let the word go forth from this time and place, to friend and foe alike, that the torch has been passed to a new generation of Americans—born in this century, tempered by war, disciplined by a hard and bitter peace, proud of our ancient heritage—and unwilling to witness or permit the slow undoing of those human rights to which this nation has always been committed, and to which we are committed today at home and around the world.

Let every nation know, whether it wishes us well or ill, that we shall pay any price, bear any burden, meet any hardship, support any friend, oppose any foe to assure the survival and the success of liberty.

This much we pledge—and more.

To those old allies whose cultural and spiritual origins we share, we pledge the loyalty of faithful friends. United, there is little we cannot do in a host of cooperative ventures. Divided, there is little we can do—for we dare not meet a powerful challenge at odds and split asunder.

To those new states whom we welcome to the ranks of the free, we pledge our word that one form of colonial control shall not have passed away merely to be replaced by a far more iron tyranny. We shall not always expect to find them supporting our view. But we shall always hope to find them strongly supporting their own freedom —and to remember that, in the past, those who foolishly sought power by riding the back of the tiger ended up inside.

To those peoples in the huts and villages of half the globe struggling to break the bonds of mass misery, we pledge our best efforts to help them help themselves, for whatever period is required —not because the Communists may be doing it, not because we seek their votes, but because it is right. If a free society cannot help the many who are poor, it cannot save the few who are rich.

To our sister republics south of our border, we offer a special pledge—to convert our good words into good deeds—in a new alliance for progress—to assist free men and free governments in casting off the chains of poverty. But this peaceful revolution of hope cannot become the prey of hostile powers. Let all our neighbors know that we shall join with them to oppose aggression or subversion anywhere in the Americas. And let every other power know that this hemisphere intends to remain the master of its own house.

To that world assembly of sovereign states, the United Nations, our last best hope in an age where the instruments of war have far outpaced the instruments of peace, we renew our pledge of support—to prevent it from becoming merely a forum for invective— to strengthen its shield of the new and the weak—and to enlarge the area in which its writ may run.

Finally, to those nations who would make themselves our adversary, we offer not a pledge but a request; that both sides begin anew the quest for peace, before the dark powers of destruction unleashed by science engulf all humanity in planned or accidental self-destruction.

We dare not tempt them with weakness. For only when our arms are sufficient beyond doubt can we be certain beyond doubt that they will never be employed.

But neither can two great and powerful groups of nations take comfort from our present course—both sides overburdened by the cost of modern weapons, both rightly alarmed by the steady spread of the deadly atom, yet both racing to alter that uncertain balance of terror that stays the hand of mankind's final war.

So let us begin anew—remembering on both sides that civility is not a sign of weakness, and sincerity is always subject to proof. Let us never negotiate out of fear. But let us never fear to negotiate.

Let both sides explore what problems unite us instead of belaboring those problems which divide us.

Let both sides, for the first time, formulate serious and precise proposals for the inspection and control of arms—and bring the absolute power to destroy other nations under the absolute control of all nations.

Let both sides seek to invoke the wonders of science instead of its terrors. Together let us explore the stars, conquer the deserts, eradicate disease, tap the ocean depths and encourage the arts and commerce.

Let both sides unite to heed in all corners of the earth the command of Isaiah—to "undo the heavy burdens . . . [and] let the oppressed go free."

And if a beachhead of cooperation may push back the jungle of suspicion, let both sides join in creating a new endeavor not a new balance of power, but a new world of law, where the strong are just and the weak secure and the peace preserved.

All this will not be finished in the first 100 days. Nor will it be finished in the first 1,000, nor in the life of this Administration, nor even perhaps in our lifetime on this planet. But let us begin.

In your hands, my fellow citizens, more than mine, will rest the final success or failure of our course. Since this country was founded, each generation of Americans has been summoned to give testimony to its national loyalty. The graves of young Americans who answered the call to service surround the globe.

Now the trumpet summons us again—not as a call to bear arms, though arms we need—not as a call to battle, though embattled we are—but a call to hear the burden of a long twilight struggle year in and year out, "rejoicing in hope, patient in tribulation"—a struggle against the common enemies of man: tyranny, poverty, disease and war itself.

Can we forge against these enemies a grand and global alliance, north and south, east and west, that can assure a more fruitful life for all mankind? Will you join in that historic effort?

In the long history of the world, only a few generations have been granted the role of defending freedom in its hour of maximum danger. I do not shrink from this responsibility—I welcome it. I do not believe that any of us would exchange places with any other people or any other generation. The energy, the faith, the devotion which we bring to this endeavor will light our country and all who serve it—and the glow from that fire can truly light the world.

And so, my fellow Americans: ask not what your country can do for you—ask what you can do for your country.

My fellow citizens of the world: ask not what America will do for you, but what together we can do for the freedom of man.

Finally, whether you are citizens of America or citizens of the world, ask of us here the same high standards of strength and sacrifice which we ask of you. With a good conscience our only sure reward, with history the final judge of our deeds, let us go forth to lead the land we love, asking His blessing and His help, but knowing that here on earth God's work must truly be our own.

LYNDON BAINES JOHNSON   (*1965–1969*)
Inaugural Address, January 20, 1965
Capitol Steps, Washington, D.C.

My fellow countrymen:

On this occasion, the oath I have taken before you and before God is not mine alone, but ours together. We are one nation and one people. Our fate as a nation and our future as a people rest not upon one citizen but upon all citizens.

That is the majesty and the meaning of this moment.

For every generation, there is a destiny. For some, history decides. For this generation, the choice must be our own.

Even now, a rocket moves toward Mars. It reminds us that the world will not be the same for our children, or even for ourselves in a short span of years. The next man to stand here will look out on a scene that is different from our own, because ours is a time of change—rapid and fantastic change—baring the secrets of nature—multiplying the nations—placing in uncertain hands new weapons for mastery and destruction—shaking old values and uprooting old ways.

Our destiny in the midst of change will rest on the unchanged character of our people and on their faith.

They came here—the exile and the stranger, brave but frightened—to find a place where a man could be his own man. They made a covenant with this land. Conceived in justice, written in liberty, bound in union, it was meant one day to inspire the hopes of all mankind, and it binds us still. If we keep its terms we shall flourish.

First, justice was the promise that all who made the journey would share in the fruits of the land.

In a land of great wealth, families must not live in hopeless poverty.

In a land rich in harvest, children just must not go hungry.

In a land of healing miracles, neighbors must not suffer and die untended.

In a great land of learning and scholars, young people must be taught to read and write.

For the more than thirty years that I have served this nation, I have believed that this injustice to our people, this waste of our resources, was our real enemy. For thirty years or more, with the resources I have had, I have vigilantly fought against it. I have learned and I know that it will not surrender easily.

But change has given us new weapons. Before this generation of Americans is finished, this enemy will not only retreat—it will be conquered.

Justice requires us to remember: when any citizen denies his fellow, saying: His color is not mine or his beliefs are strange and different, in that moment he betrays America, though his forebears created this nation.

Liberty was the second article of our convenant. It was self-government, it was our Bill of Rights. But it was more. America would be a place where each man could be proud to be himself: stretching his talents, rejoicing in his work, important in the life of his neighbors and his nation.

This has become more difficult in a world where change and growth seem to tower beyond the control and even the judgment of men. We must work to provide the knowledge and the surroundings which can enlarge the possibilities of every citizen.

The American covenant called on us to help show the way for the liberation of man, and that is our goal. Thus, if as a nation, there is much outside our control, as a people no stranger is outside our hope.

Change has brought new meaning to that old mission. We can never again stand aside prideful in isolation. Terrific dangers and troubles that we once called "foreign" now constantly live among us. If American lives must end, and American treasure be spilled, in countries that we barely know, then that is the price that change has demanded of conviction and of our enduring covenant.

Think of our world as it looks from that rocket that is heading toward Mars. It is like a child's globe, hanging in space, the continent stuck to its side like colored maps. We are all fellow passengers on a dot of earth. And each of us, in the span of time, has really only a moment among his companions.

How incredible it is that in this fragile existence we should hate and destroy one another. There are possibilities enough for all who will abandon mastery over others to pursue mastery over nature. There is world enough for all to seek their happiness in their own way.

Our nation's course is abundantly clear. We aspire to nothing that belongs to others. We seek no dominion over our fellow man, but man's dominion over tyranny and misery.

But more is required. Men want to be a part of a common enterprise—a cause greater than themselves. And each of us must find a way to advance the purpose of the nation, thus finding new purpose for ourselves. Without this, we will simply become a nation of stangers.

The third article is union. To those who were small and few against the wilderness, the success of liberty demanded the strength of the union. Two centuries of change have made this true again.

No longer need capitalist and worker, farmer and clerk, city and countryside, struggle to divide our bounty. By working shoulder to shoulder together we can increase the bounty of all.

We have discovered that every child who learns, and every man who finds work, and every sick body that is made whole—like a candle added to an altar—brightens the hope of all the faithful.

So let us reject any among us who seek to reopen old wounds and rekindle old hatreds. They stand in the way of a seeking nation.

Let us now join reason to faith and action to experience, to transform our unity of interest into a unity of purpose. For the hour and the day and the time are here to achieve progress without strife, to achieve change without hatred; not without difference of opinion but without the deep and abiding divisions which scar the union for generations.

Under this covenant of justice, liberty, and union, we have become a nation; prosperous, great, and mighty. And we have kept our freedom. But we have no promise from God that our greatness will endure.

We have been allowed by Him to seek greatness with the sweat of our hands and the strength of our spirit.

I do not believe that the Great Society is the ordered, changeless, and sterile battalion of the ants.

It is the excitement of becoming—always becoming, trying, probing, falling, resting, and trying again—but always trying and always gaining.

In each generation—with toil and tears—we have had to earn our heritage again.

If we fail now, then we will have forgotten in abundance what we learned in hardship; that democracy rests on faith, that freedom asks more than it gives, and that the judgment of God is harshest on those who are most favored.

If we succeed, it will not be because of what we have, but it will be because of what we are; not because of what we own, but rather because of what we believe.

For we are a nation of believers. Underneath the clamor of building and the rush of our day's pursuits, we are believers in justice and liberty and union. And in our own Union we believe that every man must someday be free. And we believe in ourselves.

That is the mistake that our enemies have always made. In my lifetime—in depression and in war—they have awaited our defeat. Each time, from the secret places of the American heart, came forth the faith that they could not see or that they could not even imagine, and it brought us victory. And it will again.

For this is what America is all about. It is the uncrossed desert and the unclimbed ridge. It is the star that is not reached and the harvest that is sleeping in the unplowed ground.

Is our world gone? We say farewell. Is a new world coming? We welcome it—and we will bend it to the hopes of man.

To these trusted public servants and to my family, and those close friends of mine who have followed me down a long winding road, and to all the people of this Union and the world—I will repeat today what I said on that sorrowful day in November last year: I will lead and I will do the best I can.

But you, you must look within your own hearts to the old promises and to the old dreams. They will lead you best of all.

For myself, I ask only in the words of an ancient leader: "Give me now wisdom and knowledge that I may go out and come in before this people: for who can judge this, thy people, that is so great?"

RICHARD MILHOUS NIXON *(1969–1974)*
Inaugural Address, January 20, 1969
Capitol Steps, Washington, D.C.

Senator Dirksen, Mr. Chief Justice, Mr. Vice-President, President Johnson, Vice-President Humphrey, My Fellow Americans—and my fellow citizens of the world community:

I ask you to share with me today the majesty of this moment. In the orderly transfer of power, we celebrate the unity that keeps us free.

Each moment in history is a fleeting time, precious and unique. But some stand out as moments of beginning, in which courses are set that shape decades or centuries.

This can be such a moment.

Forces now are converging that make possible, for the first time, the hope that many of man's deepest aspirations can at last be realized. The spiraling pace of change allows us to contemplate, within our own lifetime, advances that once would have taken centuries.

In throwing wide horizons of space, we have discovered new horizons on earth.

For the first time, because the people of the world want peace, and the leaders of the world are afraid of war, the times are on the side of peace.

Eight years from now America will celebrate its 200th Anniversary as a nation. Within the lifetime of most people now living, mankind will celebrate that great new year which comes only once in a thousand years—the beginning of the Third Millennium.

What kind of a nation we will be, what kind of a world we will live in, whether we shape the future in the image of our hopes, is ours to determine by our actions and our choices.

The greatest honor history can bestow is the title of peacemaker. This honor now beckons America—the chance to help lead the world at last out of the valley of turmoil and onto that high ground of peace that man has dreamed of since the dawn of civilization.

If we succeed, generations to come will say of us now living that we mastered our moment, that we helped make the world safe for mankind.

This is our summons to greatness.

I believe that American people are ready to answer this call.

The second third of this century has been a time of proud achievement. We have made enormous strides in science, industry, and agriculture. We have shared our wealth more broadly than ever. We have learned at last to manage a modern economy to assure its continued growth.

We have given freedom new reach. We have begun to make its promise real for black as well as for white.

We see the hope of tomorrow in the youth of today. I know America's youth. I believe in them. We can be proud that they are better educated, more committed, more passionately driven by conscience than any generation in our history.

No people has ever been so close to the achievement of a just and abundant society, or so possessed of the will to achieve it. And because our strengths are so great, we can afford to appraise our weaknesses with candor and to approach them with hope.

Standing in this same place a third of a century ago, Franklin Delano Roosevelt addressed a nation ravaged by depression and gripped in fear. He could say in surveying the nation's troubles: "The concern, thank God, is only material things."

Our crisis today is in reverse.

We have found ourselves rich in goods, but ragged in spirit; reaching with magnificent precision for the moon, but falling into raucous discord here on earth.

We are caught in war, wanting peace. We are torn by division, wanting unity. We see around us empty lives, wanting fulfillment. We see tasks that need doing, waiting for hands to do them.

To a crisis of the spirit, we need an answer of the spirit.

And to find that answer, we need only look within ourselves.

When we listen to "the better angels of our nature," we find that they celebrate the simple things, the basic things—such as goodness decency, love, kindness.

Greatness comes in simple trappings.

The simple things are the ones most needed today if we are to surmount what divides us, and cement what unites us.

To lower our voices would be a simple thing.

In these difficult years, America has suffered from a fever of words; from inflated rhetoric that promises more than it can deliver; from angry rhetoric that fans discontents into hatreds; from bombastic rhetoric that postures instead of persuading.

We cannot learn from one another until we stop shouting at one another—until we speak quietly enough so that our words can be heard as well as our voices.

For its part, government will listen. We will strive to listen in new ways—to the voices of quiet anguish, the voices that speak without words, the voices of the heart—to the injured voices, the anxious voices, the voices that have despaired of being heard.

Those who have been left out, we will try to bring in.

Those left behind, we will help to catch up.

For all our people, we will set as our goal the decent order that makes progress possible and our lives secure.

As we reach toward our hopes, our task is to build on what has gone before—not turning away from the old, but turning toward the new.

In this past third of a century, government has passed more laws, spent more money, initiated more programs, than in all our previous history.

In pursuing our goals of full employment, better housing, excellence in education; in rebuilding our cities and improving our rural areas; in protecting our environment and enhancing the quality of life; in all these and more, we will and must press urgently forward.

We shall plan now for the day when our wealth can be transferred from the destruction of war abroad to the urgent needs of our people at home.

The American dream does not come to those who fall asleep.

But we are approaching the limits of what government alone can do.

Our greatest need now is to reach beyond government, to enlist the legions of the concerned and the committed.

What has to be done, has to be done by government and people together or it will not be done at all. The lesson of past agony is that without the people we can do nothing; with the people we can do everything.

To match the magnitude of our tasks, we need the energies of our people—enlisted not only in grand enterprises, but more importantly in those small, splendid efforts that make headlines in the neighborhood newspaper instead of the national journal.

With these, we can build a great cathedral of the spirit—each of us raising it one stone at a time, as he reaches out to his neighbor, helping, caring, doing.

I do not offer a life of uninspiring ease. I do not call for a life of grim sacrifice. I ask you to join in a high adventure—one as rich as humanity itself, and exciting as the times we live in.

The essence of freedom is that each of us share in the shaping of his own destiny.

Until he has been part of a cause larger than himself, no man is truly whole.

The way to fulfillment is in the use of our talents. We achieve nobility in the spirit that inspires that use.

As we measure what can be done, we shall promise only what we know we can produce, but as we chart our goals, we shall be lifted by our dreams.

No man can be fully free while his neighbor is not. To go forward at all is to go forward together.

This means black and white together, as one nation, not two. The laws have caught up with our conscience. What remains is to give life to what is in the law: to insure at last that as all are born equal in dignity before God, all are born equal in dignity before man.

As we learn to go forward together at home, let us also seek to go forward together with all mankind.

Let us take as our goal: where peace is unknown, make it welcome; where peace is fragile, make it strong; where peace is temporary, make it permanent.

After a period of confrontation, we are entering an era of negotiation.

Let all nations know that during this Administration our lines of communication will be open.

We seek an open world—open to ideas, open to the exchange of goods and people, a world in which no people, great or small, will live in angry isolation.

We cannot expect to make everyone our friend, but we can try to make no one our enemy.

Those who would be our adversaries, we invite to a peaceful competition—not in conquering territory or extending dominion, but in enriching the life of man.

As we explore the reaches of space, let us go to the new worlds together—not as new worlds to be conquered, but as a new adventure to be shared.

With those who are willing to join, let us cooperate to reduce the burden of arms, to strengthen the structure of peace, to lift up the poor and the hungry.

But to all who would be tempted by weakness, let us leave no doubt that we will be as strong as we need to be for as long as we need to be.

Over the past 20 years, since I first came to this Capital as a freshman Congressman, I have visited most of the nations of the world. I have come to know the leaders of the world, and the great forces, the hatreds, the fears that divide the world.

I know that peace does not come through wishing for it—that there is no substitute for days and even years of patient and prolonged diplomacy.

I also know the people of the world.

I have seen the hunger of a homeless child, the pain of a man wounded in battle, the grief of a mother who has lost her son. I know these have no ideology, no race.

I know America. I know the heart of America is good.

I speak from my own heart, and the heart of my country, the deep concern we have for those who suffer, and those who sorrow.

I have taken an oath today in the presence of God and my countrymen to uphold and defend the Constitution of the United States. To that oath I now add this sacred commitment: I shall consecrate my office, my energies, and all the wisdom I can summon to the cause of peace among nations.

Let this message be heard by strong and weak alike:

The peace we seek—the peace we seek to win—is not victory over any other people, but the peace that comes "with healing in its wings"; with compassion for those who have suffered; with understanding for those who have opposed us; with the opportunity for all the peoples of this earth to choose their own destiny.

Only a few short weeks ago we shared the glory of man's first sight of the world as God sees it, as a single sphere reflecting light in the darkness.

As the Apollo Astronauts flew over the moon's gray surface on Christmas Eve, they spoke to us of the beauty of earth—and in that voice so clear across the lunar distance, we heard them invoke God's blessing on its goodness.

In that moment, their view from the moon moved poet Archibald MacLeish to write: "To see the earth as it truly is, small and blue and beautiful in that eternal silence where it floats, is to see ourselves as riders on the Earth together, brothers in that bright loveliness in the eternal cold—brothers who know now they are truly brothers."

In that moment of surpassing technological triumph, men turned their thoughts toward home and humanity—seeing in that far perspective that man's destiny on earth is not divisible, telling us that however far we reach into the cosmos, our destiny lies not in the stars but on earth itself, in our own hands, in our own hearts.

We have endured a long night of the American spirit. But as our eyes catch the dimness of the first rays of dawn, let us not curse the remaining dark. Let us gather the light.

Our destiny offers not the cup of despair, but the chalice of opportunity. So let us seize it not in fear, but in gladness—and, "riders on the Earth together," let us go forward, firm in our faith, steadfast in our purpose, cautious of the dangers; but sustained by our confidence in the will of God and the promise of man.

GERALD R. FORD
Transcript of Address by New President
August 7, 1974

Mr. Chief Justice, my dear friends, my fellow Americans:

The oath that I have taken is the same oath that was taken by George Washington and by every President under the Constitution.

But I assume the Presidency under extraordinary circumstances never before experienced by Americans. This is an hour of history that troubles our minds and hurts our hearts.

Therefore, I feel it is my first duty to make an unprecedented compact with my countrymen. Not an inaugural address, not a fireside chat, not a campaign speech, just a little straight talk among friends. And I intend it to be the first of many.

I am acutely aware that you have not elected me as your President by your ballots. So I ask you to confirm me as your President with your prayers. And I hope that such prayers will also be the first of many.

If you have not chosen me by secret ballot, neither have I gained office by any secret promises. I have not campaigned either for the Presidency or the Vice Presidency. I have not subscribed to any partisan platform. I am indebted to no man and only to one woman, my dear wife.

As I begin this very difficult job, I have not sought this enormous responsibility, but I will not shirk it. Those who nominated and confirmed me as Vice-President were my friends and are my friends. They were of both parties, elected by all the people and acting under the Constitution in their name.

It is only fitting then that I should pledge to them and to you that I will be the President of all the people.

Thomas Jefferson said the people are the only sure reliance for the preservation of our liberty. And down the years, Abraham Lincoln renewed this American article of faith asking is there any better way for equal hopes in the world.

I intend on next Monday to request of the Speaker of the House of Representatives and the President pro tempore of the Senate the privilege of appearing before the Congress to share with my former colleagues and with you, the American people, my views on the priority business of the nation and to solicit your views and their views.

And may I say to the Speaker and the others; if I could meet with you right after this—these remarks I would appreciate it.

Even though this is late in an election year, there is no way we can go forward except together and no way anybody can win except by serving the people's urgent needs.

We cannot stand still or slip backward. We must go forward now together.

To the peoples and the governments of all friendly nations and I hope that could encompass the whole world, I pledge an uninterrupted and sincere search for peace. America will remain strong and united.

But its strength will remain dedicated to the safety and sanity of the entire family of man as well as to our own precious freedom.

I believe that truth is the glue that holds government together, not only our Government but civilization itself. That bond, though stained, is unbroken at home and abroad.

In all my public and private acts as your President, I expect to follow my instincts of openness and candor with full confidence that honesty is always the best policy in the end.

My fellow Americans, our long national nightmare is over. Our Constitution works. Our great republic is a government of laws and not of men. Here, the people rule.

But there is a higher power, by whatever name we honor him, who ordains not only righteousness but love, not only justice but mercy.

As we bind up the internal wounds of Watergate, more apinful and more poisonous than those of foreign wars, let us restore the Golden Rule to our political process. And let brotherly love purge our hearts of suspicion and of hate.

In the beginning, I asked you to pray for me. Before closing, I ask again your prayers for Richard Nixon and for his family. May our former President who brought peace to millions find it for himself.

May God bless and comfort his wonderful wife and daughters whose love and loyalty will forever be a shining legacy to all who bear the lonely burdens of the White House.

I can only guess at those burdens although I witnessed at close hand the tragedies that befell three Presidents and the lesser trials of others.

With all the strength and all the good sense I have gained from life, with all the confidence of my family, my friends and dedicated staff impart to me and with the goodwill of countless Americans I have encountered in recent visits to 40 states, I now solemnly reaffirm my promise I made to you last December 6 to uphold Constitution, to do what is right as God gives me to see the right and to do the very best I can for America.

God helping me, I will not let you down.

Thank you.

Governor ELLA GRASSO
Inaugural Message to the
Connecticut General Assembly
January 8, 1975

Mr. President, Mr. Speaker, my fellow State Officers, Members of the General Assembly, Reverend Clergy, Honored Members of the Judiciary, My Family and Honored Guests:

It is good to be back home with you in this House.

Twenty-two years ago almost to the day, as a newly elected representative from my hometown of Windsor Locks, I took for the first time the oath which you have taken today.

The special meaning of that moment for me then—and for you today—is easier to share than to explain.

I am honored to share such a moment with you.

Many influences in our lives, and many aspirations of our hearts and minds, have combined to bring us here together.

We know that we share with the rest of the country an economic crisis with roots in international developments over which we have no control.

We and the country await the development of a clear national policy for meeting and controlling that economic crisis.

Certainly the people of Connecticut stand ready to contribute their full measure of sacrifice—where sacrifice is called for—in achieving the goal of victory over recession and inflation—provided the burden of sacrifice is equitably shared.

Meantime, here at home, the state of our State is disarray. The financial condition of state government today is unsound. A balanced budget and an operating surplus do not exist.

The situation is serious. The long range prospects are not encouraging.

But our course is clear.

We must turn around the condition of our State, giving new direction to policies that affect the lives of our people.

In so doing, we will be honest and forthright.

In the Budget Message next month, I will be forced to discuss a gap between revenues and expenditures now measured at some $200 million—which may get worse if the national economic slide continues.

The discussion will be painful. Expenditure cuts are always difficult to accept.

But we will present to the people of Connecticut all the facts in our possession so that they too can understand and participate in the hard decisions ahead.

In the handling of our State's affairs, we must exercise the strictest restraints to balance the budget in this fiscal year. Planning for the new fiscal year will require heroic effort to keep the budget in balance.

This is our goal as we work for lean, efficient, and humane state government capable of handling its assigned tasks effectively.

At the same time our professional corps of skilled civil servants will be treated with the respect they deserve. The merit system will be restored and strengthened.

From top to bottom, we will have a state government in which career employees will be proud to serve.

When state agencies need reorganizing, constructive change will come. The need to overhaul the departments of public works and welfare is imperative. Every agency will be evaluated in terms of performance as we endeavor to assure that every tax dollar spent meets the test of maximum effective use. I am pleased that an interim Volunteer Transition Staff, composed of experts in many fields, will assist in this program evaluation.

Revenue estimates will be as accurate as the tools of modern fiscal forecasting permit.

By measuring more accurately the cost of efficient and effective programs, we will be able to develop a budget structure that is geared to produce those revenues necessary to meet the cost—and no more than the cost—of these essential programs.

I repeat to you my commitment that will be accomplished without recourse to a state personal income tax.

Ours will be an open government.

The Governor's office and all state agencies will be open to all citizens to discuss their problems, answer their inquiries, and act on their complaints.

The Governor's area offices in Fairfield County and eastern Connecticut will serve as extensions of the Capitol office. The Governor and agency heads will go to the people throughout the State. The "right-to-know" law will be rewritten and strengthened to ensure that the processes of local and state government will be totally open to public view and constructive public criticism.

I have made full public disclosure of my income and assets and will require the same of all top level appointees. I invite my fellow State Officers and the Members of the General Assembly to join me in this action.

In state government, leasing policy will be reformed. Meanwhile, I will support the request of the Legislature's Special Subcommittee on State Leases that no leasing commitments will be made until new legislation is adopted to reform the state leasing procedures.

When serious budgetary and tax decisions are to be made, they will be made after public hearings, not only in Hartford, but also across the State. Then the taxpayers of Connecticut will have a voice in decisions affecting their lives, their pocketbooks, and their welfare.

We will create a partnership of state and local government. Partisan political considerations will play no part in the granting of state assistance. There will be a Coordinator of Municipal Affairs right in the Governor's office to help local officials cut through red tape and to speed requests for help, guidance and information to the correct place in state government. In turn, the agencies will become responsive to the needs of local governments.

Despite the limited financial resources of our State and the need to tighten our belts, we must not forget the reason government exists: To provide necessary human services to the people.

Even in these difficult times—especially in these difficult times—we must provide help for the elderly, for children, the handicapped, and the ill, and fulfill our responsibilities to the Veterans of our nation's service.

Recognizing the problems of local communities in providing for education, we will work to develop the means to better meet our children's needs. Vocational and higher education programs will prepare young people for the years ahead.

We will strengthen the Department on Aging, creating a cabinet-level post for its commissioner. We will shepherd the orderly transfer of all youth services into a single, responsive agency.

Most important, we must insure that the services we provide people—help people.

In my administration, citizens will be able to turn with confidence to the Department of Consumer Protection knowing it is an agency where their problems will be solved, not shelved.

The Department of Environmental Protection will work more cooperatively with local communities, providing technical expertise and a willing hand in solving, not creating problems.

In short, the agencies will again be responsive to the concerns of local officials and the problems of individual citizens.

We will work with—and for—all our people. We will afford equal opportunity for all our citizens, as we affirm the rights of every individual. Working together with this General Assembly, I hope to see action to make the regulation of utilities more responsive to the public, to hold down ever-escalating utility bills and to bring back public confidence in utility regulation.

With your help, we will create a Utility Control Authority to replace the Public Utilities Commission.

I want to see utility regulation that takes into consideration energy planning, energy conservation, the demands of the environment and the pressing need for protecting the public. An independent consumer advocate under legislative auspices, competent commissioners and sufficient expert staff would deal effectively with large utility companies.

We will consider creation of a public bonding authority to help utilities finance expensive construction at lower cost to the public.

Transportation is another top priority for our State.

At long last we will create a state transportation plan so that we can claim our fair share of federal funds. We will forge a single, unified transportation network that will balance automobiles, buses and trains in a way to provide maximum benefit, preserve our valued landscape and protect our environment.

Over the next crucial months, with the help of the Legislature, we will develop a plan where funds from several sources, including some new revenue from pension funds, will be used to help banks in our State finance home mortgages. We must use our resources to open up the housing market, provide homes for families, create jobs and offer real help to the ailing Connecticut home building industry.

While our State and the country suffer today from a combination of inflation and recession we cannot and will not sit and "wait it out." The times call for planning and they call for action.

The Commerce Department, new though it is, needs to be re-vitalized. Its top priority will be to find the ways and means to retain and strengthen Connecticut companies already providing jobs and services to our State.

We will improve the corporate climate with tax incentives for expansion and research, help ailing and marginal industries, and forge an aggressive out-of-State campaign to attract new industry and seek out for our own those major "growth industries" that can make our economy more stable.

We will bring the State's Council of Economic Advisors close to the Governor's office, give it more specific duties, and make it a more vital, contributing force in forecasting and advising the Governor about our economy.

And we will go to Washington, as well—to secure the federal aid to which the State is entitled. I have named Lt. Governor Bob Killian to give personal direction and leadership to federal/state relations and administrative operations.

With this staunch commitment, I believe we can bring to Connecticut more federal dollars that will provide our people with more and better services.

Just as the machinery of the legislative and executive branches must become more responsive and responsible, it is imperative that our courts, which administer justice, perform this sacred task with even-handedness and efficiency. It is our responsibility in conjunction with the Judiciary to assure this objective.

Justice delayed is justice denied.

As Governor, I will be called on to select new judges. To assure that their selection reflects the highest level of qualification and competence, I will establish an ad hoc committee to review my recommendations for judicial appointments, and I will ask advice and guidance from the Judiciary Committee of the Bar Association in evaluating my recommendations.

Last July, when I accepted my Party's nomination for Governor, I said that "the business of Connecticut can be conducted openly, compassionately and efficiently—with prudence and economy. It can; it must; and so it will." Today, as I stand before you, my conviction is stronger still.

Working in close partnership with the General Assembly, we will realize our goals.

I intend to maintain to the best of my ability the most open and cooperative relationship with the Legislature in our State's history.

I intend to seek your counsel on a continuing basis.

We will evaluate programs you develop as well as programs I suggest so that we may, in our combined judgment, most effectively meet the needs of our people. We will ensure that both the legislative and executive branches of state government consider, particularly in these difficult times, the financial impact of all state legislation on local government and the taxpayer.

In this spirit of cooperation, I have invited the heads of state agencies, leaders of the General Assembly and the men and women who do the State's work to meet with me tomorrow in the Hall of the House. We will review government spending during the remainder of this fiscal year and the next state budget. We will share ideas on how to meet the economic challenges that face us—how to hold down the costs of government, yet provide the services required. The goals we have set for this administration—the goals I summon you to help us reach—must be developed within the tortured limitations of a depleted treasury and limited financial resources. We must provide government that is efficient, that is compassionate, that is humane.

But I remind you that in no state in the nation is there a greater reservoir of skill and talent and imagination. And no state in the nation has a prouder tradition of public service by leaders of every sector of our economy and our society.

I look to you and to our community leaders as indispensable members of the new Connecticut team.

I know that there will be a swift and positive response, for we all have a common stake in the health and growth of Connecticut and a common loyalty to the special qualities which make up the Connecticut way of life.

In the raging troubles of our world and time, Connecticut's role may seem small indeed.

But we will fulfill that role mindful of the lives that are touched by every program, aware of our heritage and our responsibilities to the people and to the communities of which we are a part. More than once in human history, a frail and tiny ship has opened a pathway to a new world.

And the Connecticut tradition is rich in examples of men and women who refused to cower before what seemed an encircling doom.

I remind you of Abraham Davenport who addressed this very General Assembly one day in the year 1780 when an eclipse of the sun was believed to signal the end of the world. "The day of judgment," he said, "is coming, or it is not. If it is not, there is no occasion for alarm. If it is, I wish to be found in the line of my duty. I move, therefore, that candles be brought."

Those candles burn today, their flame sustained by Him who brought us here.

By their light, let us set about our duty, recalling the words that
Harry Truman spoke on this same day, January 8, 1947:

America was not built on fear.
America was built on courage,
   on imagination and the unbeatable
   determination to do the job at hand.

With God's help we will do our job and do it well.

Glossary

Abu Dhabi   One of the territories of the United Arab Emirates.

Adirondacks   A mountainous region, circular in outline, in northeastern New York State, discovered by Samuel de Champlain in 1609. The term *Adirondack* literally means "tree eater," a label given to a local Indian tribe who made soup from tree bark during food shortages. There are more than five million acres of forest preserved and this region is one of America's outstanding tourist attractions.

Alinsky, Saul   Community organizer and social reformer. Principal work done in the 1950s and 1960s.

Anokye, Okomfo   (seventeenth century) Founding priest and philosopher of the Ashanti nation of Ghana. Reputed to have worked miracles and commanded the descent from heaven of the Golden Stool.

Aristotle   (384–322 B.C.) Greek philosopher who studied under Plato in Athens; tutored Alexander the Great (c. 342–335); later taught in Athens. His lectures on rhetoric have been preserved in the single greatest theoretical work ever written called *The Rhetoric*.

baobab   The large tree that produces seeds covered with silky hairs and fruit called "sour gourd" or "monkey bread;" found in nearly all of tropical Africa.

bar mitzvah   A Jewish synagogue ceremony for a boy at the completion of his thirteenth year, regarded as having reached the age of religious duty and responsibility.

barrios   Usually refers to urban communities with large concentrations of Mexican-Americans. In some cases, the term may apply to only lower socioeconomic Spanish-speaking neighborhoods.

Bathurst   Bathurst is the seaport capital city of Gambia, an independent state in West Africa. Gambia derives its name from the large river in West Africa.

Beecher, Henry Ward   (1813–1887) Famous American preacher who spoke out against slavery and for women's right to vote. He was pastor of the Plymouth Congregational Church in Brooklyn, N.Y., for the last forty years of his life.

Bitzer, Lloyd   Communicationist, University of Wisconsin. A leading rhetorical theorist whose concept of the rhetorical situation has had a profound impact on communication theory.

Bond, Julian   Georgia state legislator and original member of the Student Nonviolent Coordinating Committee.

Burke, Kenneth (1897–) One of the foremost contemporary writers of philosophy, literary, and rhetorical criticism. Many consider Burke to be as essential to an understanding of rhetoric as Aristotle.

Byzantine Of or relating to the ancient Eastern or Greek Empire of the Byzantium from A.D. 395 to 1453; the Greek language employed by the later Byzantine writers or medieval Greeks.

Cascades Mountain range in the northwest United States.

Castaneda, Carlos Anthropologist. Author of several important works, including *The Teachings of Don Juan* and *Tales of Power.*

Chavez, Cesar Civil rights leader, labor organizer, and principal American migrant worker rights campaigner during the 1960s and 1970s.

Chicano Used positively for a person of Mexican-American heritage.

Chomsky, Noam Linguistician, Massachusetts Institute of Technology. Considered by some to be the most original thinker in contemporary linguistic theory. Main work emphasizes transformational analysis and rules of grammar.

Churchill, Winston (1874–1965) British statesman and author. As Britain's Prime Minister, he was influential in international affairs and was one of the most famous speakers.

Cicero, Marcus Tullius (106–43 B.C.) Roman orator, statesman, and philosopher; *De Oratore* is perhaps his most famous work; placed heavy emphasis on delivery for successful oratory; the *Orator* and *Brutus* are his most important critical works; his fundamental belief was that the truly great orator was the orator who could move his listeners to action; Rome's foremost theoretician and practitioner of the art of rhetoric.

Clay, Henry (1777–1852) American lawyer and statesman; U.S. senator, member of the House of Representatives; received nickname of "Great Pacificator" because of his position on the Missouri Compromise of 1820; but perhaps received greatest recognition as a statesman for a series of resolutions known as "Compromise of 1850," where he sought to avoid civil war.

Cooke, Benjamin Communicationist. Professor at Howard University, Washington, D.C. Chief research has been Afro-American nonverbal behavior.

Corax Rhetorician of fifth century B.C. Regarded as a founder of Greek teaching of rhetoric; devised speech to meet the practical demands of Greek citizens who were required to speak publicly to obtain the return of their stolen property; usually given credit for the development of the first system of rhetoric in Greece.

cultural pluralism Term used to indicate viability and acceptance of several cultures operating in the same society.

Darrow, Clarence Seward (1857–1938) Famous American lawyer who was defense counsel in several widely publicized trials, including those of Nathan Leopold and Richard Loeb charged with killing Bobby Franks (1924), John Thomas Scopes of Dayton, Tenn., charged with violating state law forbidding teaching of evolution in publicly supported schools (famous so-called "Monkey Trial" of 1925), and blacks in the Scottsboro case of 1932.

demagogue, demagoguery A speaker who tries to influence people by concentrating on their fears, prejudices, and passions; unprincipled politician or mob leader or agitator.

Demosthenes (385–322 B.C.) Athenian orator and statesman; regarded as greatest of the Greek orators. Became a professional speech writer; perhaps his most famous speech was "On the Crown," a defense of his political career.

denouement The final unraveling of a plot; that part of the play or story in which the mystery is cleared up, the outcome.

Dewey, John (1859–1962) American philosopher and educator; believed the philosophy of pragmatism as formulated by William James. Wrote books on *How We Think* (1909), *Democracy and Education* (1916), and *Logic: The Theory of Inquiry* (1938), among others. Sometimes called the father of "reflective thinking."

Douglass, Frederick (1817–1895) Foremost abolitionist voice of the nineteenth century. Douglass occupied various posts in the United States government after the Civil War, including Minister Resident and Consul General to the Republic of Haiti.

DuBois, William Edward Burghardt (1868–1963) American black educator, editor, and writer; received both his B.A. and Ph.D. from Harvard (Harvard's first black Ph.D.); editor of *The Crisis* (1910–1932); author of *The Souls of Black Folk* (1903) and others.

dyad Any two-member communication interaction; for example, friend and friend, parent and child, doctor and patient, husband and wife, and so on.

Edwards, Jonathan (1703–1758) American congregational preacher and theologian who became successor of his grandfather, Solomon Stoddard, in Northampton, Mass.: led a revival (1734–1735) known as the Great Revival; often used technique of fear to persuade members of his congregation.

egalitarian One who advocates or believes in the principle of equal rights for all.

ethos Along with pathos (emotion) and logos (logic), ethos (character) make up the rhetorical proofs; ethos is made of goodwill, good sense, and good character, and of these, according to Aristotle, good character is the most important; sometimes used synonymously with "source credibility."

eulogies Usually spoken (sometimes written) laudation of a person's life or character; often given during funeral ceremonies as a form of honor.

European Renaissance A new birth, resurrection, or revival, but particularly the revival of letters and art that marks the transition from medieval to modern European history, beginning in Italy in the fourteenth century and gradually spreading throughout Western Europe.

exigencies State of being urgent, a pressing need or demand, a case requiring immediate attention, assistance, or remedy; a critical period or condition; a pressing necessity.

forensic An argumentative thesis, an oral argument, a debate, often dealing with legal issues, the courts of justice, public discussion.

Fortran Early computer language.

Franklin, Benjamin (1706–1790) American statesman, scientist, and philosopher. Published *The Pennsylvania Gazette* newspaper (1730–1748), wrote *Poor Richard's Almanac* (1732–1757) under the assumed name of Richard Saunders. Began experiments with electricity (1746) and tried famous kite experiment (1752). Helped draft Declaration of Independence and one of its signers; signed a memorial to Congress asking for the abolition of slavery (1790).

genealogy A record of individual or family descent from some ancestor; especially a list, in order, of ancestors and their descendants.

genre A collection or grouping of speeches that are similar; for example, Presidential Inaugural Addresses and Fourth of July speeches.

Gonzales, Corky Mexican-American civil rights leader in Colorado.

Gregory, Dick Black social satirist.

Hamilton, Charles Political scientist, Columbia University. Urban politics is his major research area.

Harding, Vincent Founder of Institute of the Black World, Atlanta.

Harms, L. S. Communicationist, University of Hawaii. Several books on communication, including *Human Communication: The New Fundamentals.*

Hayne, Robert Young (1791–1839) American politician, lawyer, and U.S. senator, and governor of South Carolina (1832–1834), who was noted for his brilliant debate with Daniel Webster on principles of the Constitution; authority of the federal government and state rights.

homeostatic, homeostasis Term borrowed from biology. Usually refers to a state of balance.

humanistic Refers to an attitude centering on human interests and ideals.

invention Refers to the property of conceiving messages. In classical rhetorical theory was frequently applied to the development of argument from personal sources, message sources, and audience sources.

James, William (1842–1910) American psychologist and philosopher; known as one of the founders of pragmatism; considered *attention* to be the primary avenue of human behavior.

Johnson, Kenneth Director, Institute of Race Relations, University of California, Berkeley. Major work on black language and education.

Jordan, Barbara U.S. congresswoman (D-Texas).

Kennedy, Edward U.S. senator (D-Massachusetts).

Kennedy, John Fitzgerald (1917–1963) Thirty-fifth President of the United States (1961–1963); member of the U.S. House of Representatives (1947–1953); senator (1953–1960); assassinated at Dallas, Texas, November 22, 1963.

Kochman, Thomas Anthropologist-communicationist, University of Illinois-Chicago Circle. Major work has been on nature of language in urban settings, interethnic interactions, and black vernacular styles.

King, Martin Luther, Jr. (1929–1968) Theologian, civil rights leader, author. Books include *Stride Toward Freedom* and *Why We Can't Wait.*

Kunstler, William Civil rights lawyer. Gained fame as a defender of the Chicago Seven, Black Panthers, and Attica brothers.

Malcolm X (1925–1965) Black revolutionary. Minister of Islam. Major publication *The Autobiography of Malcolm X.*

Napoleonic Wars, Napoleon Bonaparte   (1769–1821) A French emperor from 1804–1815; general, conqueror, and legislator. Was defeated by the British at Waterloo; called the "Little Corporal." He displayed genius for military strategy.

Newmark, Eileen   (1949–   ) Cross-cultural communicationist. Trainer for international programs and cross-cultural consultant. Writings include work on perception theory and simulations.

Ortega y Gasset, José   Born in Madrid, Spain in 1883 he was one of the leading intellectuals of the Spanish Republican government. After establishment of the Republic, Ortega became a member of Parliament. He also held the chair of metaphysics at the University of Madrid.

Osei Tutu   King of Ashanti in the eary seventeenth century.

Perelman, Chaim   Belgian rhetorician. Major work is *The New Rhetoric*.

Plato   (427–347 B.C.) Original name was Aristocles (surnamed Plato because of broad shoulders). Greek philosopher; disciple of Socrates; teacher of Aristotle. Founded a school in Athens called The Academy, which became in essence the first university known in history. Famous works include *Republic* (search for justice in construction of an ideal state) and *Phaedrus* (attacking the prevailing conception of rhetoric) among others.

Powell, Adam Clayton   Former U.S. congressman (D-New York).

Quintilian, Marcus Fabius   (c. A.D. 35–c. 100). Roman rhetorician who taught oratory in Rome about 68 A.D. Wrote a series of twelve books called *Institutio Oratoria* (*The Training of an Orator*) containing principles of rhetoric, a practical exposition of Roman education and description of methods used in the best Roman schools. It is one of the most valuable contributions of ancient times to educational theory.

Ramus, Peter   (1515–1572) French philosopher and mathematician, best known as a critic of Aristotelianism.

rhetoric, rhetorical   Generally, the systematic study of oratory or persuasion.

Roosevelt, Franklin Delano   (1882–1945) Thirty-second President of the United States (1933–1945); the only president to serve three terms. In the election campaign of 1932 he outlined a program associated with his name, the "New Deal," which promised aid to farmers, public electricity, and other new deals. In his first inaugural address he conveyed confidence that America could overcome the economic depression with the memorable statement, "The only thing we have to fear is fear itself."

Thoreau, Henry David   (1817–1862) American writer famous for his retirement writings at Walden Pond at Concord, Massachusetts (1845–1847) where he devoted himself to a study of nature—published *Walden* (*Life in the Woods*) 1854.

Tisias   Sicilian student of Corax who developed the earliest known theoretical book on public persuasion in the ancient world of the fifth century B.C.

Wallace, Karl   Communicationist. Former professor at universities of Illinois and Massachusetts. A major theorist for over twenty-five years. Among his works is *A History of Speech Education in America*.

Washington, Booker Taliaferro   (1856–1915) Black educator; born a slave in Franklin County, Virginia. After youthful hardships, he gained an education at Hampton Institute (1872–1875) and was chosen in 1881 to establish and head a school at Tuskegee, Alabama.

Webster, Daniel (1782–1852) U. S. statesman, orator, senator, and lawyer. Argued effectively for national unity. In 1820 he delivered the bicentennial speech at Plymouth, Massachusetts and critics compared him with Demosthenes or Edmund Burke because of his impressive delivery. In 1862, in Faneuil Hall, Boston, he gave the dual eulogies of John Adams and Thomas Jefferson, who had both died on the Fourth of July. He believed that slavery was an evil for both black and white. Although his influence was great, Webster once said, "I have done absolutely nothing. At 30 Alexander had conquered the world; and I am 40."

Wellington, Arthur Wellesley (1769–1852) British soldier and statesman; defeated Napoleon in the famous Battle of Waterloo in 1815.

Whitfield, George (1714–1770) Educated in Oxford, England. Great revivalistic preacher; extensive influence on the religious awakening in 18th Century Britain and America.

Winans, James Communicationist. A major essay, "The Literary Criticism of Oratory," dominated the critical theories of public address for more than thirty years after its publication in 1925.

Index